COMMUNALISM AND INDIAN PRINCELY STATES

Travancore, Baroda and Hyderabad in the 1930s

Communalism and Indian Princely States

Travancore, Baroda and Hyderabad in the 1930s

DICK KOOIMAN

MANOHAR
2002

First published 2002

ISBN 81-7304-421-X

Published by
Ajay Kumar Jain for
Manohar Publishers & Distributors
4753/23 Ansari Road, Daryaganj
New Delhi 110 002

Typeset by
Kohli Print
Delhi 110 051

Printed at
Print Perfect
Delhi 110 064

Contents

Tables

Illustrations

Acknowledgements

WITH PLEASURE and gratitude I acknowledge the institutions, libraries, friends and colleagues whose support and advice lightened my task in completing this book, which was part of a larger research programme on Global Culture and Local Identity, formulated and carried out by the Department of Cultural Anthropology of the Vrije Universiteit, Amsterdam. The research seminars organized by this department as well as those by the Centre for Asian Studies Amsterdam (CASA) offered an appropriate platform for discussion of preliminary findings with colleagues. I thank, in particular, Professor Peter Kloos, for many years Director of the Research Programme, whose ideas on globalization inspired me in the writing of the fourth chapter. The staff of the Social Science Library of the Vrije Universiteit offered most efficient assistance.

Funds for travel and research abroad granted by the Department of Cultural Anthropology of the Vrije Universiteit and the Netherlands Organization for Scientific Research (NWO), The Hague enabled me to study a large number of primary sources in the Oriental and India Office Collections (OIOC) of the British Library and the School of Oriental and African Studies (SOAS) in London. The librarians and archivists of these institutions greatly facilitated my work. Mrs Patricia Kattenhorn (OIOC) lent help in tracing old photographs and kindly explained why her department held more photos from the 1920s than the 1930s. Dr Kenneth H. Robbins (Virginia, USA) generously offered me the use of his private collection of photographs and pictures on Indian princely states, but technical problems stood in the way. I am gratful to the British Library, Oriental and Indian Office Collections, London, for kind permission to reproduce the 4 photographes in this volume.

In Trivandrum I worked in the State Legislative Library and the Central Archives (West Fort) but was disappointed to find the Travancore Residency records in the Kerala State Archives in great disarray due to their transfer to a new building at Nalanda quarter (1991). I thank Professor S. Uma Devi and Dr K.K. Kusuman, University of Kerala, and Dr Michael Tharakan, Centre of Development

Studies, Trivandrum for their critical questions and encouragement. The assistance of Dr P.S.M. Moideen, the present Director of the Kerala State Archives is also acknowledged.

In Baroda Professor Gita Bajpai, Head of the History Department of the Maharaja Sayajirao University, served as my local guide. I thank Mrs Maharajh, Head Librarian, for permission to work in the University (Hansa Mehta) Library, and the Government of Gujarat Department of Archives for permission to study the records of the Huzur Political Office in Baroda.

Professor P. Venkatramaiah and Dr Kanakalatha Mukund offered me hospitality and opportunities to discuss my research with colleagues at the Centre for Economic and Social Studies (CESS) in Hyderabad. Professor T.R. Sharma, Dean of the School of Social Sciences, invited me to the Central University, Hyderabad, and Dr Lal Rosem, Commissioner of the Andhra Pradesh State Archives (APSA), allowed me to consult records in his archives. I had stimulating discussions with Dr V.K. Bava, former Director APSA.

I am obliged to Professor Ian Copland, Department of History, Monash University, for his valuable studies on Indian states and for his constructive comments on the organization of this study. Mrs Phyl Chandler, of Filton College, Bristol, improved my English and Mrs Nan Kasanpawiro, our departmental secretary, solved problems with the word processor. Drs Hans de Visser (Department of Cartography, University of Amsterdam) designed the maps and Mr Ger Ruys gave me the benefit of his graphical expertise. Finally, I thank my wife Tineke, and our daughters Margreet and Watzelien, for making life easier when the writing became harder.

Abbreviations

APSA	Andhra Pradesh State Archives
AISML	All-India States Muslim League
AISPC	All-India States People's Conference
AS	Arya Samaj
BPM	Baroda Praja Mandal
CWC	Congress Working Committee
EIC	East India Company
HFMK	History of the Freedom Movement in Kerala
HM	Hindu Mahasabha
HPO	Huzur Political Office (Baroda)
HSPC	Hyderabad State Political Conference
HSC	Hyderabad State Congress
ICR	Indian Constitutional Reforms (Report on)
ICS	Indian Civil Service
INC	Indian National Congress
ISC	Indian States Committee 1929 Indian Statutory Commission 1930
JPC	Joint Political Conference (Travancore)
LMS	London Missionary Society
OIOC	Oriental and India Office Collections
PICR	Proposals for Indian Constitutional Reform
RAB	Report on the Administration of Baroda
RAHP	Report on the Administration of Hyderabad City Police
RAND	Report on the Administration of H.E.H. the Nizam's Dominions
RAT	Report on the Administration of Travancore
RRC	Report of the Reforms Committee (Hyderabad)
RTC	Round Table Conference

SFHS	The Struggle for Freedom in Hyderabad State
SMAP	Sri Mulam Assembly Proceedings
TEDEC	Travancore Economic Depression Enquiry Committee
TERC	Travancore Education Reforms Committee
TPPP	Travancore: The Present Political Problem
TPSRC	Travancore Public Service Recruitment Committee
TSC	Travancore State Congress
WWI	World War I

Introduction

PRINCELY INDIA

THE PROBLEM of communalism looms large over present-day India. Mutual rivalry and frequent violent outbursts between members of different religious communities are a threat to the sovereignty and integrity of the Indian state and society. No attempt to come to grips with this urgent social problem can serve its purpose, if it fails to take note of the particular historical circumstances that shaped its emergence, and this book is a contribution to the understanding of the communal problem.

Whereas communalism is often attributed to British colonial policies of divide and rule, in this book the emergence of communalism will be studied in those areas of the subcontinent where British influence was less intrusive: the Indian states. Hence, apart from exploring the historical background to inter-religious relations, this book is also a study of indirectly-ruled princely India, with strong emphasis on the last decades before Independence. The main questions are the growth of communalism in the Indian princely states and the impact of government measures like electoral arrangements and federal schemes on religious identity perceptions.

Most studies on the last decades of the British Raj in India tend to concentrate on the national movement and communalism in British India and ignore the large number of people and the vast areas ruled by the semi-independent, so-called native princes in Indian India. This historiographical neglect of the Indian princely states may be attributed to their lack of economic importance to the Empire, the inadequacy and inaccessibility of the historical sources, and the complications inherent in a freedom movement directed against an Indian administration.

The history of British India is much better known. This 'brightest jewel in the crown of the British empire' was polished in the course of a military conquest that lasted from 1757 to 1857. After obtaining the revenue rights over Bengal (1757–65) the East India Company extended its influence to the south and around 1800 the last resistance of the main southern power, Mysore, was broken. In a kind of circular movement the Company then pushed on along the western coast up to the north, annexing large regions like Maharashtra (1818), Sind (1844) and Punjab (1849). The circle was more or less closed by the annexation of some central-Indian states in 1856. The violent outburst of the Mutiny in 1857, largely provoked by this aggressive expansion policy, brought the military conquests to a standstill.

Annexation was not the only policy adopted by the Company. Especially at the time of Governor-General Lord Wellesley (1798–1805), it concluded treaties of subsidiary alliance with a large number of Indian princes, offering them military protection in return for the cession of territory or the payment of a tribute for the upkeep of the necessary forces. Wellesley brought many states under subsidiary alliances, among them Hyderabad, Travancore and Baroda. Their rulers had to give up control over their external and military affairs, but were granted a semi-independent existence on the fringe of the emerging British Indian empire. They were allowed to maintain their own administrations, pass their own laws and to levy their own taxes on the vital condition that they agreed to rule in accordance with the advice that the British Government might occasionally think it necessary to offer. That advice was given by a British Resident or Agent, who came to assume a position of considerable importance at the respective courts.

The aim of these alliances, of course, was to pacify India in a quick and cheap way.[1] However, the status of subordinate ally did not guarantee a prince undisturbed rule, and several states that entered into a treaty relationship with the British were subsequently brought under direct rule. Also, not all treaties were subsidiary and the majority of states had no treaties at all. They had to content themselves with the exchange of agreements of a less comprehensive character or *sanads*, i.e. unilateral grants recognizing rights and privileges as from an acknowledged superior authority.[2]

For the colonial government the Indian princes were useful allies. Neutralized by treaties, they speeded up military conquest by not halting the British siege-train; left in power, they facilitated administration that otherwise might have become a heavy burden on the Company. The subsidiary alliances had the additional strategic advantage of

[1] Jeffrey 1978: 18.

[2] Relations with the Indian States, secret note by the Political Department, India Office, 26.7.1943, R/1/5/63; see also Robert E. Holland, The Indian States (draft in typescript), 1925, Vol. I: Chapter II, R/1/5/58 and Menon 1995: 5.

having created a vast body of influential princes deeply interested in the continuance of the British dominion. As Sir John Malcom, a trusted colleague of Wellesley, avowed in 1825, 'the . . . security of our vast oriental possessions is involved in the preservation of native principalities which are dependent on us for protection . . . their co-existence with our rule is of itself a source of political strength'.[3]

The truth of this became evident in 1857 when the vast majority of reigning princes remained loyal to their British overlords. Lord Canning referred with gratitude to the valuable support received from the princely states which served as 'breakwaters in the storm which would have swept over us in one great wave'.[4] To reward loyalty, adoption *sanads* were issued guaranteeing the princes of the larger states that their rule should be perpetuated according to their own laws of succession. In 1861 a special order of knighthood was instituted, known as the Star of India, and Sayajirao III, Maharaja of Baroda till 1939, became one of its honoured recipients. Hyderabad had also sided with the British and later, during World War I, it chose for the Allied Forces against Turkey which earned its ruler, the Nizam, the title of 'His Exalted Highness' apart from the traditional appellation of 'Faithful Ally of the British Government'.[5]

After 1857 Queen Victoria declared in a famous proclamation that her government desired no extension of its territorial possessions in India and would respect the rights, dignity and honour of the native princes as its own.[6] Annexation had come to an end, but also interference by the British Indian Government in the internal affairs of the states was increasingly losing importance as an instrument of policy. Though the paramount power never formally relinquished its right to intervention, recourse to this measure was taken in exceptional cases, as in Baroda in 1875 when Malharrao Gaekwad was deposed on the grounds of 'notorious misconduct, gross mismanagement of the state and incapacity to carry the suggested reforms into effect'.[7] A new young ruler was installed, Sayajirao III (1875–1939), and he received

[3] Quoted in Menon 1995: 7.

[4] Quoted in Handa 1968: 22. Here Canning must have thought of Sir William Sleeman who already in 1853 considered the states to be potential 'breakwaters' in case of turmoil, see Houben 1987: 108.

[5] Both titles were conferred on the Nizam in January 1918. For more details see Memoranda on the Indian States 1930, Calcutta 1930: 76. (Personal Communication, Ian Copland)

[6] Full text in Sever 1985: 232–4.

[7] Quoted in Handa 1968: 29.

the able assistance of Sir T. Madhava Rao, a staunch supporter of the British Raj who earlier had been a very successful Dewan in Travancore. In spite of these incidents, annexation and direct intervention became things of the past. Under the Viceroyalty of Lord Curzon (1899–1905) the old imperial policy flared up for a while, but this proved to be a temporary return to a largely bygone practice.[8]

One of the few states where the threat of intervention was never definitely struck from the political agenda was Hyderabad, which in the 1920s was forced to employ civil servants from the Government of India's Political Department. The reasons for that, described in subsequent chapters, lay in what the British considered to be 'the idiosyncracies of successive generations of Nizams'.[9]

About two-fifths of Indian territory and one-fourth of the entire Indian population thus remained under indirect rule in states headed by Indian rulers. Their geographical spread was such that from the mountains of the north to Kanyakumari in the south (Travancore) one might travel almost entirely through territory of the Indian princes without touching British India. There were more than 550 of these states, the majority small and insignificant like the hundreds of 'village-states' in Kathiawad, but some were large kingdoms with their own currency, postal system, railway network and airline. Hyderabad, which proudly styled itself the Premier State of India, was nearly equal in size to Great Britain and comprised about 1/15th of the Indian empire in area and about 1/20th of its total population.

Map 1 shows that the princely states were located inland (Kashmir, Rajputana, Hyderabad, Mysore) rather than in coastal areas. In that sense, Travancore with its coastal location and sea ports was rather exceptional. Moreover, their territories were not known for the cultivation of valuable crops or for mineral products. Early in the nineteenth century the rich cotton fields of Gujarat were carefully carved out of the remaining state of Baroda. In the south, Travancore with its great variety of spices and plantation products was allowed a protracted semi-autonomous existence, but Malabar with its large pepper-producing areas was placed under direct rule.

Thus there were two different political systems. The territories of British India were governed by the Crown according to the statutes of

[8] Ashton 1982: 33 ff.

[9] Ashton 1982: 83. Also Tasker (Member of the Nizam's Executive Council), 1937, L/P&S/13/1200.

Parliament and enactments of the Indian legislature, but princely India remained under the sovereignty of the Crown and the personal, often autocratic rule of its own rulers. This was 'surely the oddest political set-up that the world has ever seen', to quote Francis Wylie[10] who in 1940 became Political Adviser to the Viceroy.

The Governor-General-in-Council, the Political Department and the Residents and Agents appointed by it, held the motley collection of princely states together. The Council had no Political Member, but the Viceroy was in charge of all affairs related to the Indian states. As the Viceroy was usually too much absorbed by his many official obligations to give the states all due attention, in actual practice it was the Secretary to the Political Department (after 1937 called Political Adviser) who exercised the functions of the Crown in its relations with Indian states. He had at his disposal the Indian Political Service, recruited from the Indian Civil Service and the Indian army, the main officers being Residents and Political Agents. As far as these Residents and Agents were concerned, their powers and duties were never clearly defined and depended to a large extent on the discretion of the British officer on the spot and the measure of sovereignty enjoyed by the state concerned.[11]

The concept of paramountcy was to remain extremely vague. The Indian States Committee was of the opinion that the concept did not allow for a precise definition and simply concluded that paramountcy had to define itself according to the shifting necessities of time and circumstances.[12] Yet, one idea that ran like a common link through all possible interpretations was that in all circumstances British authority must be treated as paramount and supreme irrespective of past treaties and the stipulations therein.[13] Under this interpretation the states had to remain both subordinated and isolated, as no state, big or small, could justifiably claim to negotiate with the paramount power on a footing of equality. That was the hard lesson the Nizam of Hyderabad had to learn (Chapter 2). Besides, no communication or correspondence with another state was permitted except with the previous sanction of the Viceroy. The colonial power remained in full control of foreign policy, defence and inter-state relations and never abandoned its right of interference in state affairs. Especially for that latter reason,

[10] Wylie 1970: 519. Also Butler 1931: 45.
[11] Datt 1936: 179–81.
[12] ISC 1929: 31.
[13] Handa 1968: 31–2.

the majority of the leading princes, even though loyal to the Crown, never acquiesced in the British interpretation of paramountcy. From their point of view, they had been forced to surrender their external and military affairs due to temporary weakness, but were still entirely free in all matters affecting their internal administration.

The more than 550 states showed a great diversity in geography, history and the measure of sovereign powers retained by their rulers.[14] Their remarkable variety was so great that it is impossible to attempt a general discussion of all of them. The number of gun salutes that was allowed to a state was in strict accordance with a prestigious hierarchy. In the 1930s, only five states, including Baroda and Hyderabad, enjoyed the privilege of twenty-one gun salutes, whereas Travancore could receive only nineteen. The 24 states receiving salutes of seventeen guns or more accounted for more than 70 per cent of the population of all states together.

NATIONALISM AND THE STATES

I discuss below the history of the Indian states with special emphasis on the last decades before Independence. This is a turbulent and widely-studied period of nationalism in British India and the eve of its final victory. In British-ruled India, ruled as it was by a foreign hand, the aims of the national movement were clear enough. But what did nationalism mean to the people of the states, governed by local princes and surrounded by a largely Indian bureaucracy?

In 1939 Rushbrook Williams, a champion of the princely order, expressed the widely held view that in the states there being no 'alien rule', there was no cause to react against it, and that the interests of the rulers and the ruled were identical. Even at that time, rather more people left British India to live in the states than the other way around. Rushbrook Williams acknowledged the existence of discontent because of the apparent shortcomings of the states' governments, but attributed it, as Lord Dufferin had done with the Congress in British India, to that vocal but unrepresentative section of the local intelligentsia which did not happen to be absorbed in the state service.[15] Without sharing this cavalier dismissal of all grievances, one may agree that for many people in the subcontinent it was problems like tenancy

[14] Holland, The Indian States, 1925, Vol. II: Chapter VII, R/1/5/59.
[15] *The Times* 7.1.1939.

rights and caste and social inequality that informed political activity far more than any notion of an anti-imperialist struggle.

British colonial officers, who were largely responsible for the creation of the two Indias, tended to see them as almost different worlds. William Barton, who after a distinguished career in the political service became Resident in Hyderabad, wrote in 1934 that the achievements of the Indian political genius were to be found at their best in the states.[16] That idea of an ancient but vital political tradition, cultivated also by the British, made many Indians consider the states not only as symbols of past glory, but also harbingers of future independence, islands of freedom washed by the waves of imperialism. Early nationalists looked to the progressive among the Indian princes for leadership in the national awakening and the Gaekwad of Baroda for one seems not to have been completely insensitive to the flattery of the nationalists he patronized. Up to the 1920s the Indian National Congress (INC) passed resolutions in support of princes whose power was threatened. On their part, several Indian rulers favoured the INC not only with their royal attendance but also with handsome donations, at least in the early years.

In due course, however, at least in the major states, political movements emerged that reflected the wish of local elites to have some share in their own administration. As the Indian rulers were seen as the fountainhead of all power, these movements took a critical stand vis-a-vis the princely governments which were increasingly thought to be non-representative and authoritarian, if not feudal, remnants of a bygone age. These movements may be called nationalist in the sense that they aimed at constitutional reform including a shift in the centre of allegiance from the ruler to the people. One of the main themes in the following chapters is an analysis of the rise of these movements and the extent to which they sought to mobilize support by appealing to shared cultural symbols, foremost of which were religion and language.

The demand for constitutional reforms in the states entered into fragile alliances with an all-India nationalism that held British presence responsible for all forms of social and political oppression. The crucial question is how these alliances took shape and whether nationalism as a fight for freedom and responsible government grew out of local circumstances or was imported from neighbouring British

[16] Barton 1934: 4.

India. Speaking about political developments in Hyderabad, Ramesan[17] emphasizes the internal forces with local people 'yearning to fall in line with British India', and Louise Ouwerkerk, who served Travancore state in the 1930s as a professor at Women's College, argues that the demand for constitutional advance 'needed no stimulus from outside'.[18] Jeffrey, on the other hand, is definitely of the opinion that nationalism spread the other way around, from British India to the states,[19] whilst William Barton, voicing the view of many in the Political Department, considered the INC a group of power-hungry politicians who came to the states to serve their own selfish ends. British policy may also have played an important part in bringing political activists from British India and the states together. According to Copland,[20] it was the government of India's decision to give military support to a few smaller states against popular turmoil that transformed the struggle for responsible government in the states into a larger struggle against imperialism. But that was only in 1939.

Most nationalist historians assume the impact of imperialism to have been so pervasive as to make it impossible to consider the Indian states as anything but imperial vassals and their rulers as puppets in the hands of the British. Such an interpretation makes it more acceptable to speak of nationalism as a common underlying force manifesting itself both in the British provinces and the territories under Indian princes. It found a perceptive expression in Kripalani's speech at the Meerut Congress (1946) where he attributed the Indian states problem, like the communal problem, to a lack of all-India feeling. The power of the princes, in the words of Kripalani, was buttressed by the foreigner who misused it for his imperial purposes, in consequence of which the princes had to adjust their conscience to the dictates of the Political Department.[21]

In 1947 India and Pakistan became independent. The violence that erupted between Hindus and Muslims at Partition is only too well-known. 1947 was the year of not only separation but also unification and integration: the many large and small states that lay spread over the subcontinent merged into the newly established India or

[17] Ramesan IV 1966: v.

[18] Ouwerkerk 1994: 186.

[19] Jeffrey 1978: 12–13.

[20] Copland 1985: 133–4.

[21] Speech Kripalani, 54th session INC at Meerut, in *The Hyderabad Bulletin*, 23.11.1946, Lothian Collection Nr. 6.

Pakistan. The parochialism of the smaller states was shattered and gave way to participation in broader political and socio-economic frameworks.

THE COMMUNAL PROBLEM

Merger into the Republic of India—which the large majority of states chose to join—involved an enormous enlargement of scale in matters of government administration, political mobilization and socio-economic organization, all of which presuppose a concomitant rise of an all-India consciousness. '[T]he real integration had to take place in the minds of the people', V.P. Menon, one of the architects of the integration of the Indian states, very properly observed.[22] Integration on a subcontinental scale, however, could give rise to a number of counter-forces. People who felt lost as constitutionally-defined citizens in the wide world of a secular-democratic republic, might cling to their more familiar, close-to-home identities of religion, caste region and culture. For the post-1947 period we may ask what kind of problems the divergent political traditions of directly and indirectly ruled areas represented for attempts to build an integrated nation-state.[23]

One of the most dramatic problems independent India had to face was the problem of religious identity and conflict. At Independence India became a secular state and the Rudolphs have pointed out that the founding myth of secularism was grounded in the traumatic experiences of Partition in 1947. The lesson of Partition that informed that myth was that 'religious politics kills'.[24] Pakistan went through the same experience but seems to have drawn a different lesson, whereas India may have taken that lesson to heart but not for long. Before 1980 the main challenge to the Indian central government came from linguistic movements and rural class struggle, but soon the communal question, as manifested in frequent conflicts between groups designated by their religious affiliation, became a more dominant problem. In this book, we will give central place to that problem of communal conflict. However, we will occupy ourselves with what happened in

[22] Menon 1995: 490.

[23] Hurd (1975) and Wood (1984) have done some pioneering work in this field by studying British versus princely legacies in styles of leadership and economic reform, but much work remains. See also Copland 1995.

[24] Rudolph and Rudolph 1987: 38; 1988: 77–8.

the period before the establishment of the Indian republic rather than with what happened immediately after. Was communalism a legacy of the colonial period, constructed by an alien government out to divide and rule a large but subjected population or did it have its roots in Indian soil?

Problems of communalism and social identity receive ever-growing attention from social scientists. A few comments about this concept may not be out of place. As Fredrik Barth[25] wrote about thirty years ago, communities define themselves by drawing a boundary line demarcating one particular community from another. These boundaries are largely symbolic and stress one or more cultural attributes shared by those who together make up that community.[26] However, these culturally-defined shared characteristics represent competing criteria and do not define one single group. Since people rarely, if ever, belong to a community which will claim to represent or exhaust all the layers of their complex selfhood, they can be mobilized along different, mutually exclusive, lines of communal identity.[27]

The inevitable result of this argument must be that a community is never a socially homogeneous unit. Nevertheless, the distinctive characteristic of the phenomenon called communalism is the belief that a group of people, because they have one ascriptive identity in common (religion or language), also share common interests in all other fields (political, economic). By placing all emphasis on that shared cultural attribute, an earnest attempt is made to overcome disturbing internal diversity by postulating a higher but largely 'imagined unity'.[28] Depending on the selection of attributes, imagined unity may be ascribed to a nation (Anderson 1983), or to a religious, caste or linguistic community. Under British Indian colonialism, the religious definition

[25] Barth 1969: 14 ff.

[26] Cohen 1989: 14.

[27] Alavi and Harris 1989: 223; Shah 1994: 1133; Sudipta Kaviraj quoted in Chakrabarty 1994: 149.

[28] Here I follow the definition of communalism as given in the work by Bipan Chandra (1984; 1988: 398 ff.). More recent research by Ghyanshyam Shah confirms the validity and usefulness of this definition. In a survey held by him in Surat during the summer of 1993 about 525 people were asked about communal divisions and related issues. Except for a small minority of 3 per cent, informants subscribed to the view that members of the same 'qaum' (caste or religious community) have common socio-economic interests, even though (maybe characteristically!) most of them were vague as to what these common interests actually meant (Shah 1994: 1136–7).

of community became so dominant that in common discourse communalism has become more or less synonymous with communalism of the religious variety.

The mobilization of people on a religious basis may be aimed at the improvement of their welfare. Mathew (1989) has studied religious communities in Travancore and Kerala and concludes that their policies were primarily aimed at strengthening their position in education and political representation. That type of communalism, he suggests, may ultimately contribute to a peaceful evolution of a pluralistic secular society. But more often than not, the mobilization of religious groups slides into cultural dominance, exclusivism, and even violence; that violence may vary from the representational, in a denial of identity, to physical aggression and acts of bloodshed. It needs to be emphasized that the problem of communalism, as defined above, is not something peculiar to India. Elsewhere, similar social phenomena are studied under different terms like ethnicity, tribalism or pillarization. In fact Chakrabarty has suggested we study Hindu-Muslim or upper-lower caste conflicts under the term racism, a form of intolerance practised not only by white people but also by Indians among themselves.[29]

Searching for explanations of the emergence of communalism, some historians argue for the importance at the grassroots level of popular passions and sentiments that are supposed to flow more or less naturally into modern communalism. Pandey has shown how colonialist writers constructed a kind of standard narrative of communal riots, which conceptualized communalism as a phenomenon expressive of the fundamental irrationality of Indian society. He rightly objects that this essentialist interpretation does not care to explain in what particular historical contexts these primordial sentiments were translated into political action.[30] However, Pandey's suggestion that the imagined religious communities of British administration left their social imprint in the form of sectarian conflict seems to deprive Indian people of their independent political agency and responsibility. As several historians have shown, the lofty appeals to communal symbols and cultural traditions often mask elite ambitions to status and power that arise from mutual competition or a sense of deprivation. Pursuing that line, Brass (1991) and others regard communalism first and foremost as a creation of narrow political interests which try to

[29] Chakrabarty 1994: 144–5.
[30] Pandey 1992: 24–32.

identify their own socio-economic aspirations as those of the entire community. An exclusive emphasis on material interests, however, may too easily lead to a dismissal of religion as a mere ideological smoke-screen, whereas, as Van der Veer has reminded us, religious belief and practice are major constituents of people's social identities.[31] While acknowledging the importance of popular culture and religious values, the approach adopted in this book will be to discuss communalism primarily as an instrument of elite politics and gravitate to the role of leaders, political parties and social movements. That approach has much to do with the kind of archival sources available and the perspective thence derived.

Contemporary sources indicate that the harmful impact of communalism in its different guises was more pronounced in British India than in the Indian states. In the latter there was serious militancy from time to time, but Hindu-Muslim riots were not so frequent and much less serious as in the directly administered provinces. The Maharaja of Bikaner could justifiably claim in his 1932 New Year address, 'As in this State, so in the States generally, the communal question does not really exist.'[32] On the eve of Independence, Indian princes seized upon this relative peace to argue in favour of a continuation of their rule. Nevertheless, in the 1930s the INC had to move very carefully to prevent itself from getting entangled in the strong undercurrents of communalism that became manifest political movements in the states. That brings us back to the question raised before. Was communalism something specific to British India and, as some argue in the case of nationalism, carried over to the Indian states? In that way, the Meo movement in Alwar state has long been viewed as caused by the external instigations of *mullahs* from beyond the border.[33] Or was it primarily, if not ex-clusively, rooted in the large number of internal social divisions that characterize Indian society at large?

SEPARATE ELECTORATES

The princely states were only indirectly controlled by representatives of British paramount power. A theory, current among British political officers, was that these states were less prone to communalism, because they were theocracies in which expressions of religious

[31] Van der Veer 1994: ix.

[32] Quoted in Copland 1998: 1.

[33] Mayaram 1997: 93 ff.

unorthodoxy were forbidden and one religious group dominated the darbar.[34] This theory fails to convince. The states generally were no theocracies, as we will see later on, and other religious communities could share in official patronage and be co-opted into administrative positions. In a recent paper Copland has refined this argument. As no separation had taken place between state polity and religious establishment, subjects were used to acquiesce in an institutionalized subordination which allowed their community to exist though not on equal terms.[35] Though this unsecular mode of governance may have restrained communal conflict, it could easily work the other way round. As Governor-General Lansdowne wrote in 1893, the condition of inferiority imposed on members of one community by those of another was always liable to result in a fight for power in which differences in religious outlook and cultural symbolism might assume a prominent part.[36]

Sen has argued that with the gradual introduction of divisive systems of elections and confrontational systems of government based on simple majority rule, communal conflicts became progressively frequent in the Indian states as well.[37] In 1930 the Indian Statutory Commission did not explain Hindu-Muslim conflict away with the usual reference to 'religious practices which are only too likely to provide mutual ill-feeling', but pointed to a deeper cause: so long as people had no part in the conduct of their own government, there was little for members of one community to fear from the predominance of the other.[38] That consideration made a devolution of power a hazardous affair and could be used by Indian rulers to reject any scheme of responsible government. However, even though political change stimulated communal struggles for power, the history of a state like Travancore seems to suggest that communal tensions were running high even before there was any question of political reform. Therefore, we also have to take into consideration the particular religious complexion of a state, the rate of literacy and the level of political mobilization that was achieved as a function of these factors.

The policy of the British Indian government to provide religious communities with separate electorates has often been cited as a power-

[34] Copland 1988: 811 ff.

[35] Copland 1998: 7 ff.

[36] See Lansdowne's dispatch of 1893 quoted in Copland 1998: 25.

[37] Sen 1993: 627, 631.

[38] ISC I 1930: 29, quotation p. 26.

ful explanatory factor in the emergence of communalism. From the end of the nineteenth century the British provinces saw the gradual introduction of representative political institutions. Of vital importance, of course, was the way in which access to these new institutions came to be organized. For that purpose, separate electorates were introduced in British India, along with cautious steps towards direct election. In case of separate electorates, voters belonging to one community were placed in a separate constituency to elect their own representative. This was first granted to Muslims (1909) and later extended to the Sikhs, Indian Christians and Anglo-Indians (1919).

These separate electorates have come in for wide-spread criticism, especially in nationalist quarters and handbooks of history. The distribution of political privilege along lines of religion is alleged to have divided people in mutually exclusive, often hostile—if not openly combative—groups, culminating in the creation of imagined religious communities, confronting each other instead of their common oppressor.[39] Official colonial discourse however firmly denied the accusation of a deliberate divide and rule, contending that the government's real problem was how to rule a divided India[40] and most authors agree that communalism had strong roots in Indian society itself with its many social divisions and cleavages; 'we divide and you rule', an Indian delegate said at the 1931 Round Table Conference.[41] Nevertheless, separate electorates remain subject to strong suspicion.

At this point the intriguing question arises, which turn the development of communal relations in British India might have taken, if the British presence had made itself less intrusively felt in matters of legislation and election. That kind of question is not often posed by the professional historian who is expected to study events as they took place and not ask what might have happened if a certain factor were eliminated. Fortunately however, the Indian situation offers us an unparalleled field of comparison with the co-existence of British India

[39] Chandra 1988: 142, 408–9; Sarkar 1983: 20–1, 59; S. Gopal in Frontline 29.1.1993, p. 108. Stavrianos' handbook on Third World History, which has been in use at my university for several years, states very definitely that separate electorates 'ultimately resulted in the costly and tragic division of the peninsula into two sovereign states' (Stavrianos 1981: 238).

[40] Quoted in Robinson 1974: 164.

[41] Mansergh in Philips and Wrainwright 1970: 50. Chakrabarty (1994: 149) has acknowledged that the British in earmarking seats in legislative assemblies for different communities according to ideas of proportionality may have been prompted by considerations of distributive justice.

and the Indian states. Since the states continued a semi-autonomous existence till 1947, they were largely left free to make their own electoral arrangements, if they wanted to make any at all. Forms of communal reservation in representative institutions were indeed introduced, but only to a limited extent, and the hotly disputed separate electorates of British India seem never to have entered their territories. The question may be asked why the Indian states remained free of the allegedly divisive potential of separate electorates and whether this had anything to do with the slower emergence of communal animosities.

Looking for a share in the government, nationalists in the British Indian provinces had to face the dominating presence of foreigners in the administration of their own country. Even though qualified Indians were since the nineteenth century discreetly admitted to the lower ranks, European officers held the key positions. No serious observer will accuse the nationalists of communalism or racism in their fight to enter the bastion of government and eventually to supersede it. But how was that in the Indian states? Many states were known to have employed quite a number of outsiders, however defined, in running their bureaucracy. The demand for participation and later responsible government placed Indians against Indians. In this emerging confrontation an appeal to communal identities, as observed above, could be instrumental in harnessing elite demands, but it also suggests that the threat of more virulent forms of communalism was always present. Seen from that perspective, it seems hardly believable that Indian states were less prone to the communal evil.

THE PROCESS OF GLOBALIZATION

Another line that will be followed in this study is to place the emergence of communalism in the Indian states within the framework of the globalization discussion. For that purpose I will make use of the three-tier structure of analysis as developed by Kloos (1995, 1996). Central in his discussion is the national state which emerged in the last centuries, and has since then become dominant over almost the whole globe, but now seems largely to have outlived its potential as a socio-political and cultural unit. That state is rapidly losing its sovereignty in the face of the growing importance of supra-national institutions and structures interfering in many of its internal affairs. This emergence of a world-wide socio-political system is called globalization. At the same time, national integrity is challenged from below by groups within the state or astride its boundaries, clamouring for political autonomy and cultural identity denied them by the illusion of national homogeneity and sovereignty. The process of identity construction at the lower level is called localization.

The paradox is that in a world that in many ways is becoming more and more unified, local, often ethnic, identities are becoming more and more important too, culturally as well as politically.[42] Assuming that there is a complex and necessary relationship between the two processes, Kloos (1996) formulates a double hypothesis, first that the very process of globalization calls forth movements that lead to the creation of local sub-state identities and secondly that movements in search of local identities, in their turn, make use of global forces to attain their ends. In this study I will try to apply this frame of analysis to a study of the integration of the states into a larger Indian Union in the first part of the twentieth century.

In the course of that period, the Indian princely states became increasingly involved in a desperate fight for political survival. The British government wished to bring the states into political federation with the directly administered provinces. These plans, embodied in the 1935 Government of India Act, implied the transfer of important powers from the states to a new federal structure. Meanwhile the nationalist movement, operating at an All-India level, was also working for a scheme of political unification, and left the states even less hope of a continued separate existence. At the same time, the larger states were attacked from below by local movements that demanded more freedom to express identities based on a shared cultural heritage of religion and language. Facing the prospect of merger into a larger socio-political unit, these ethnic or communal movements were looking for wider solidarities, establishing links with kindred groups across state boundaries. In Hyderabad, for instance, these tendencies both from above and below became more and more acute, coming to a head at the end of the 1930s. True, the Indian princely states were no nation states, being neither fully sovereign nor the embodiment of their peoples' will. Taking due note of these important differences, I still think there is sufficient ground for studying socio-political

[42] More than twenty years ago Isaacs described these centrifugal tendencies in the era of globalization as a 'massive retribalization' of the world, see Harold R. Isaacs in Nathan Glazer and Daniel P. Moynihan (eds), *Ethnicity: Theory and Experience*, Cambridge: Harvard University Press, 1975: 29, quoted in Ahmed 1996: 3050.

developments in the larger Indian states in terms of a globalization-localization process at the level of a subcontinent.

Political integration and administrative participation mean that numbers became important. We may ask whether communalism was encouraged not so much by electoral arrangements and the threat of federation but by deeper considerations of numbers, that had acquired a new and hitherto unknown significance. In the modern state that came with the British, techniques of government were closely related to techniques of enumeration and measurement. Everything was counted and most dramatically so in the census. 'Measurement is central to our modern ideas about fairness and justice and how we administer them', Chakrabarty observes. The lesson to be drawn from the census and other similar reports was that communities could be enumerated and in numbers lay one's political clout. In consequence, 'Counting Hindus, Muslims, Sikhs, and Untouchables became a critical political exercise particularly in the twentieth century as the British began to include Indian representatives in the legislative bodies in very measured doses'.[43]

A similar though tardier numerical exercise was started in the Indian states and in the following chapters we will look for the effects it may have had on communal relations.

THE STRUCTURE OF THE BOOK

Probing into the past experiences of all Indian states is an impossible task in view of their sheer number and diversity. This study is confined to three major states, Travancore, Baroda, and Hyderabad, all of them having treaty relations with the paramount power. The choice for these was determined by a mix of historiographic considerations and chance occurrence.

There are not many books on the Indian states and hardly any on the problem of communalism in their territories. Not long after Independence V.P. Menon wrote his *Integration of the Indian States* (1956), which reflects the views of the Indian government—as might be expected from a secretary to Sardar Vallabhbhai Patel, the first Indian minister of the States Department—and concentrates on the period immediately before and after 1947. Several years later Urmila Phadnis published a study on the major developments that led *Towards the*

[43] Chakrabarty 1994: 147–50.

Integration of Indian States 1919–47 (1968). Though more sensitive to the long-term perspective, she is not particularly concerned with communal questions and pays only scant attention to popular movements at the grassroots level. Another important work appeared ten years later, *The Princes of India in the Twilight of Empire, 1914–39* (1978), by Barbara Ramusack. This deals mainly with that small number of princes who ventured beyond the confines of their states to the broader orbit of All-India politics. That did not include the rulers of Travancore and Hyderabad who for different reasons chose to keep aloof from politics outside their borders. Moreover, Ramusack, in spite of her title, is virtually silent on the eventful years between 1935 and 1939. More recently, Ian Copland, with his impressive record of publications on Indian states, completed his *The Princes of India in the Endgame of Empire, 1917–47* (1997). His focus is on high-level political problems related to integration especially in northern India.

There are a few studies of the history of individual states on the eve of Independence, like Chiriyankandath (1985) and Daniel (1985) on Travancore and Yazdani (1985), Pernau-Reifeld (1992) and Bawa (1992) on Hyderabad and Vidal (1997) on the state of Sirohi in Rajasthan. Copland (1988, 1998) and Mayaram (1997) belong to the very few who did research on communal relations in the princely states. The number of these historical studies has remained rather limited. Amidst these studies the present volume seeks its place, by addressing the problem of emergent communalism in Travancore, Baroda and Hyderabad in the 1930s and from a comparative perspective, which has not been attempted to date.

There were some other reasons for the choice of these three states. With Travancore state I felt rather familiar because of earlier research on the impact of missionary efforts on the social position of the lower Hindu castes. The often strained relationships among religious communities made me wonder what made conditions in Travancore so different from other states. In British India, there were few riots between Hindus or Muslims on the one hand and small communities like Christians, Jews, Parsis and Jains on the other (although most of the latter were economically better off than the former) but in Travancore, even though violent conflict was rare, there was serious tension especially between Hindus and Christians. This exceptional situation invited me to make a comparative analysis between Travancore and British India, especially in the field of communal identity formation.

A comparative study of British India and just one princely state, however, would offer too narrow a base for making any substantial statement. Therefore, I decided to include Baroda. Baroda is of a similar size as Travancore but lies in a different part of India and is not reputed to be ridden by religious animosities and conflicts. Nonetheless, what Travancore and Baroda have in common is that both states were ruled by a Hindu-dominated government. In reply to comments received on an earlier study of communalism in Travancore and Baroda (Kooiman 1995), I felt the need to include a state ruled by Muslims. Hyderabad was an obvious choice in view of its political importance and historical sources. Even though that state had no Muslim majority population, Hyderabad enshrined the memories of eight centuries of Muslim dominance and its ruling elite claimed to head a state that represented the last remnant of the Mughal empire.

I open the discussion with a short history of Travancore, Baroda and Hyderabad. That history will focus on the social relations within these states, educational achievements and levels of economic development, as all these aspects may have a bearing on the emergence of communal identity feeling. As we have defined communalism as a shared identity expressed in religio-cultural symbols but largely meant for secular ends, the question of power and its division among the major claimants becomes of crucial importance. Therefore, the next chapter gives a review of the constitutional developments that took place in British India and the three states. In introducing legislative bodies, elections and responsible ministers British India clearly took the lead, but some states were not slow in following.

In Chapter 3 inquiries are made into a possible connection between the introduction of separate electorates and the emergence of communalism. That will be done by making a comparison between British India and the states of Travancore and Baroda. Whereas British India saw several stages of constitutional reform including electoral safeguards for purposes of communal representation, the paramount power refrained from imposing similar reforms on princely India, as these reforms were thought not to be equally suitable for the different conditions in Indian states.[44]

In Chapter 4 the formation of communal identities will be analysed as part of a larger process of political integration that had, in

[44] Statement by Secretary of State for India in the House of Commons (1919) quoted in letter from Government of India, Foreign and Political Department, dated 10.7.1919, R/2(883/136).

the 1930s, slowly but unmistakably begun to take place. Situating that part of the discussion especially within the recent history of Hyderabad, the three-tier political framework as developed by some globalization theorists will be used to discuss All-India policies, the state government and the movements working at the local level. As the third and the fourth chapters virtually represent two different case studies, the main conclusions that can be drawn from them will be given at the end of each of these chapters.

A NOTE ON THE SOURCES

The sources used for this study originate to a large extent from those departments of the colonial government that were in charge of the affairs of the states. They were produced within an administrative structure that got its final shape after 1857.

In 1858 power over the Indian territories was transferred to the British Crown. Henceforth Indian policies were determined by a Secretary of State for India in London who was a member of the Cabinet of Ministers and responsible to the British Parliament. Under his supervision the administration in India was carried on by the Governor-General or Viceroy, assisted by an Executive Council and provincial governors, while the management of local administration was vested in a relatively small number of district officers.

Within the India Office in London, established in 1858, the supervision of the British Indian government's relations with the Indian princely states and with neighbouring countries was entrusted to the Political and Secret Department. The Department's Political Secretary, though directly responsible to the Secretary of State, was the man in charge. His service produced the 'L/P&S series' which form a major source for this study. The series contains valuable collections on subjects as the Chamber of Princes, political reforms and the affairs of individual states.

In India it was first the Foreign Department that was responsible both for foreign affairs and relations with the princely states. By the beginning of the twentieth century, when the burden of work became too much for a solitary departmental secretary, a Political Department was created (1914) within the Foreign and Political Department to take charge of relations with the states. Only under the 1935 Government of India Act did the Political Department become a separate and independent office and it was the Viceroy who was entrusted with all relations with the Indian states, thus accentuating the princes' personal loyalty to the Crown. In 1937 he received the additional title of Crown Representative in India and the Political Secretary became his Political Adviser.

The files produced by the Political Department in India and its political officers are our main (English-language) source on Indian princely states. Called the Crown Representative Records, they contain in their R/1 series the files of the department's headquarters that moved with the climate from Delhi to Shimla, while the R/2 series contain the files of records kept locally by Residents and Agents in the states. In 1947 these were selectively transferred to the United Kingdom. The Crown Representative Records include the fortnightly reports that Residents and Political Agents submitted to the Political Department, and, together with other papers, were forwarded to the India Office in London.[45]

All these files, produced in India and London, are preserved as part of the Oriental and India Office Collections (OIOC) of the British Library. Hyderabad, Baroda and Travancore belonged to the select number of larger states that were supervised by a Resident (smaller states being grouped together under a Political Agent). Hyderabad and, from 1876, Baroda stood in direct communication with the Political Department of the Government of India. From 1923 Travancore, earlier under the supervision of the Government of Madras, also corresponded directly with the Political Department. The Resident of Travancore was henceforth called Agent to the Governor-General for the Madras states (Travancore, Cochin and Pudukkottai), but in 1937 he regained the title of Resident. For clarity's sake, in this text we shall refer to him as the 'Resident'.

In view of their importance and direct correspondence with government, the three states are well represented in the departmental records. The quality of these records, of course, was to a large extent dependent on the individual Residents, who held a twofold responsibility: they were servants of the Government of India and at the same time had to watch over the interests of their accredited states. This

[45] A few years ago the Crown Representative Records have been re-ordered under a new system of classification. As I had collected some data at an earlier date, sometimes I will refer to the old system R/2/(889/236) instead of R/1/1/3066.

ambiguous position required great qualities of character and flexibility, but the selection and training of potential candidates left much to be desired. Nepotism counted heavily in a candidate's favour, and even in the 1930s, relations or friends in high places were almost essential to ensure appointment to the few top positions as Resident. Opportunities for promotion or prestigious assignments were limited and the great concern for rank and correct form, usually associated with princely India, placed a heavy burden on relations inside the Political Service. The continuous call to select 'the best pick of men', especially when negotiations on federation started in earnest, is an indication that all was not well with recruitment.

The attitude of the princes to the Political Department was marked by a similar ambiguity. For their political protection and survival the princes had to rely on the officers of the department, who generally had a soft corner for Indian royalty. At the same time, they took a strong dislike to Residents who, serving as the eyes and ears of government, showed too active an interest in their affairs. In 1943 Sir Arthur Lothian, Resident in Hyderabad, wrote that no Resident who did his duty and refused to wink at what happened, could remain on good terms with His Exalted Highness, the Nizam.[46] Hyderabad, which saw the appointment of several strong-willed and reformist Residents to its capital in the twentieth century, was the scene of some interesting trials-of-strength between prince and Resident. Yet, there were also more easy-going officers, who merely tried to keep their princes good-humoured. They could pass on questions for information from the Political Department to their respective state governments and return the answers as their own without any check or comment.[47] This prompted the Political Department in London to express the need for better and more detailed reports. In 1938 it urged Residents and Agents to do much more touring and generally to be

[46] Lothian, letter to Sir Henry Craik, Political Adviser, 23.5.1943, in Lothian Collection Nr. 6.

[47] For instance, the Dewan's report on the 1939 disturbances in Baroda (Confidential File No. 134, HPO Baroda) was copied almost verbatim in the Resident's Fortnightly Report for the second half of January 1939 (R/1/1/3394). Another interesting case was recorded by Louise Ouwerkerk. She personally witnessed the excitement in Travancore at the formation of the Travancore State Congress in 1938, but later read in the OIOC that the Resident had 'nothing to report' for that fortnight (Ouwerkerk 1994: 187).

more attentive to what was happening in their states. But the Department acknowledged as its main problem the scarcity of good men.[48]

The great reliance on official sources does not mean that Indian points of view will be neglected in this study. Fortunately, the Political Department files and Crown Representative Records contain a lot of correspondence with Indian state authorities, including the ruler and his Prime Minister or Dewan, documents about political movements in the states, and Indian newspapers published in the states and outside. Moreover, Travancore and Hyderabad both have their source publications on the local Freedom Movement, that can be supplemented by the memoirs and reminiscences of several political leaders.

[48] Minute Paper, Political Department, 1938, L/P&S/13/887. The critical comments on the Political Service presented here are largely based on the writings of former Residents and Political Secretaries like Barton (1934: 276–9), Butler (ISC 1929) and Lothian (Correspondence in Lothian Collection Nr. 6). See also Ramusack 1978: 239–40.

1

The Princely States of Travancore, Baroda, and Hyderabad

ORIGINS

SITUATED ON the south-western tip of the Indian peninsula between the mountains of the Western Ghats and the Arabian Sea, stretching from Cochin in the north to Cape Kanyakumari in the south, Travancore had emerged as a major eighteenth-century power in the south.[1] Attacked from the north by the kings of Mysore its ruler was forced, by the treaties of 1795 and 1805, to enter into a military alliance with the East India Company (EIC) and recognize the British as paramount. Travancore had to pay a substantial annual subsidy in exchange for continued military protection, and the EIC assumed the role of Commercial Agent controlling the important trade in pepper and other spices. Although these treaties were said to be binding 'as long as the sun and moon shall endure', Travancore hardly escaped annexation in the 1850s. Alarmed by repeated complaints of maladministration and a declining state of revenue, the Madras government warned the Raja that prompt remedial measures were needed to save Travancore from being placed under the direct management of the Company. The state monopoly on the pepper trade, earlier a major consideration for non-annexation, was also put forward as a serious drawback stifling the eagerly awaited economic progress. The timely outbreak of the Mutiny, however, proved a blessing in disguise and assured Travancore's semi-independent survival.

The formation of Baroda state may be called a pure accident of history, much more so than Travancore. The founders of the Gaekwad monarchy, who came from the area around Poona, were Maratha military adventurers who started to build their influence in this region in the first half of the eighteenth century. They defeated the local repre-

[1] De Lannoy 1997.

sentatives of the Mughals, but did not succeed in establishing unchallenged independence from the Peshwa, who ruled over the Maratha federated kingdom. In the middle of the eighteenth century the Peshwa and the Gaekwad[2] decided to divide the region among themselves without consideration of administrative convenience and solely on the ground of their revenue yielding capacity.

When the EIC joined battle with the Peshwa, Gaekwad entered into treaties with the same Company (1805 and 1817) and managed to retain his scattered possessions. After Maratha power was finally eliminated in this region, lands in Gujarat formerly claimed by the Peshwa were further divided between the Company and the Gaekwad, the British keeping the great trading cities of Ahmedabad and Surat and their surrounding districts. A subsidiary force was placed in what now was to become Baroda state and instead of an annual subsidy for its maintenance, the most valuable revenue districts were ceded to the British—which further increased the scattered nature of Baroda state.[3] On the map Baroda looks like a jigsaw puzzle consisting of five major territorial divisions of flat and fertile land and a large number of smaller pieces thrown arbitrarily across British-ruled Gujarat and Kathiawad.

Flung across the centre of the Indian subcontinent, almost separating north India from its southern extremity, lay the old state of Hyderabad. It was carved out of the crumbling Mughal Empire by Mir Qamaruddin Khan, a distinguished general of Aurangzeb.[4] Appointed Subahdar or Viceroy of the Deccan in 1713 with the title of *Nizam-ul-mulk*, he had little difficulty in centralizing the administration of this region under his personal control. By the middle of the eighteenth century Hyderabad, like Travancore and Baroda, was established as an independent power. After Mir Qamaruddin's death the successors of the Asaf Jah family assumed *Nizam* as their hereditary title. Yet Mughal authority continued to be the source of symbolic legitimacy for Hyderabad even after the last vestiges of this empire had been swept away.[5]

In the second half of the eighteenth century the French and the British were contesting power in the Deccan. The French had succeeded in gaining a commanding influence at court, but later on

[2] Although the Maharaja of Baroda is often referred to as the Gaekwad, Gaekwad is actually a surname and not a title or designation.

[3] RAB 1944–5: 3; Hardiman 1978: 107–8.

[4] Menon 1995: 314.

[5] Barton 1934: 43; Leonard 1971: 570.

Hyderabad was increasingly drawn into the British sphere of influence. In 1766 the EIC and the Nizam concluded one of the first treaties[6] under which an Indian ruler was forced to accept military assistance from the Company in exchange for a huge annual subsidy. Later, when payment of that subsidy fell heavily into arrears, it was replaced, as in the case of Baroda, by the transfer of vast tracts of territory, the most important of which was the rich cotton-growing province of Berar (1853). A Resident was sent to Hyderabad, instructed, in the words of a later Governor-General, 'to keep a watchful eye upon His Highness's conduct' but at the same time to establish 'a confidential and friendly communication between the two governments'.[7] As subsidiary allies the two governments together fought the Marathas whose persistent and effective encroachments on Hyderabad territory forced the Nizam to move his capital from Aurangabad to the more central Hyderabad. The military threat of the Marathas made Hyderabad and Baroda fly for survival into British arms, as the menace of Mysore had done in the case of Travancore. But whereas the Marathas and Mysore were finally defeated and their kingdoms annexed, Hyderabad was able to survive this turbulent period and, like Travancore and Baroda, maintain a semi-autonomous existence under British paramountcy.[8]

It is generally assumed that the Indian states declined rapidly under the effects of the subsidiary alliances. The care and solicitude with which they were henceforth fostered, so the argument runs, led to an ossification of what earlier was a dynamic political system. In the past a bad or weak ruler could be removed by a war or a quiet palace revolution, but now British protection held him in his place whatever he did, as long as mismanagement went not that far as to affect the annual subsidy or the safety of the empire. This military guarantee against external aggression as well as internal revolution deprived many rulers of all interest in good government and placed a premium on their indolence. In consequence, Indian states are said to have shown less social progress than British India.[9]

However, this theory did not entirely satisfy contemporary opinion. No less an authority than Lord Elphinstone wrote in the 1830s that no Indian prince had put himself under protection of the Company until his government 'was in such a state of decay as to be incapable

[6] This treaty and later ones are described in more detail by Yazdani 1976.

[7] Quoted in Raza Ali Khan 1990: 182.

[8] *Gazetteer of Hyderabad* 1909: 15 ff.

[9] Thompson 1944: 22–3; Jeffrey 1978: 6 ff.

of subsisting by any other means'.[10] Much later, the Indian States Committee discreetly reminded the rulers that their states were either rescued or created by the British.[11] Whereas the redoutable Maratha and Mysore powers were eliminated, the treaty states were politically weak, from the beginning. They advanced side by side with the EIC, but the mutual relationship developed to be far from equal.

We should also not forget that for many colonial officials the concept of a backward and stagnant princely India was too attractive a proposition to be easily dismissed. The oriental lethargy in which the states appeared to survive by reason of the half-contemptuous toleration of the colonial government served as a comfortable contrast to what the British saw as great developments in their own territories, providing legitimacy to them. The concept was further compounded by officers of the Political Department who often felt much sympathy for princely India which they considered to be the real India.[12] The wish to preserve this 'real India' may have played a part in the reluctance to meet the rulers' requests to have European instead of Indian ceremonial, which was seen as servile and humiliating.[13] William Barton went out of his way to emphasize the different character of the states: there the village as an economic and social unit was still intact, industrialization had not stretched out its tentacles, and no civil disobedience ruffled the surface of public life. Through pageantry, ceremonial and frequent durbars there was a close identity between ruler with subjects. Democracy, according to Barton, was not popular among either the rulers or their people. (Neither was it popular among men like Barton, who, as political officers, were largely responsible for the perpetuation of the princely order.)

Pernau-Reifeld has pointed out that, Indian rulers eagerly cultivated the orientalist notion that people in the states were better off than those under British rule.[14] Barton, however, was not ready to acknowledge that a loosening of paramountcy control would further increase people's happiness. Life in an Indian state might seem idyllic, he said, but misgovernment always remained possible and then 'the reluctant hand of paramountcy' inevitably stretched out. Also, mismanagement could never be ruled out and Barton reminded his readers that in the

[10] Quoted in Yazdani 1976: 1.

[11] ISC 1929: 24.

[12] ISC 1929: 12; Rushbrook Williams 1930: 4; Thompson 1944: 27; Butler 1931.

[13] Grievances of Indian Princes, note by R. Glancy, 1931, L/P&S/13/789.

[14] Pernau-Reifeld 1992: 373.

past states had often been 'nursed back from bankruptcy to opulence by British Officers'.[15]

In the following sections we will try to ascertain to what extent general statements about social retardation or a paradise lost apply to the states of Travancore, Baroda and Hyderabad.

RELIGIOUS COMPOSITION

The population of each state had its own religious complexion. Travancore, with its rich diversity of numerous castes and religious sects, offers most interesting material for a comparative analysis. In 1931 its population numbered 50,90,000 people, packed together in an area of only 7,625 square miles. Baroda state was almost of the same size covering an area of 8,135 square miles but had a much smaller population of 24,43,000 people. That population was less diverse and predominantly Hindu. Hyderabad with its 82,698 square miles was much larger than both Travancore and Baroda but less densely populated: in 1931 its total population amounted to 1,44,36,000 people (see Table 1).

In analysing the composition of the states' populations we will make use of the decennial census reports and other official publications. Under the conditions prevailing in India, the 1931 Travancore census observed, 'the most satisfactory method of dividing the people into groups for social, political and economic purposes seems to be the one based on religion combined with race or caste'.[16]

The identification of caste and religion with specific political and economic interests as suggested by the census touches the heart of the communal problem. Apart from that, modern government methods of counting and classification have affected the formation of new subjective identities, as historians have convincingly demonstrated. Anderson (1991) and Chakrabarty (1994) have pointed out that what was strikingly new about the modern census was not so much the construction of categories as their quantification. The following chapters will bear testimony to the political importance of enumeration, as numbers could serve to support claims to political and economic benefits.

According to the 1931 Travancore census Hindus, including tribal people, made up 61.6 per cent of the population. Internally, however,

[15] Barton 1934: 69, 279.

[16] Census of Travancore 1932 I: 329.

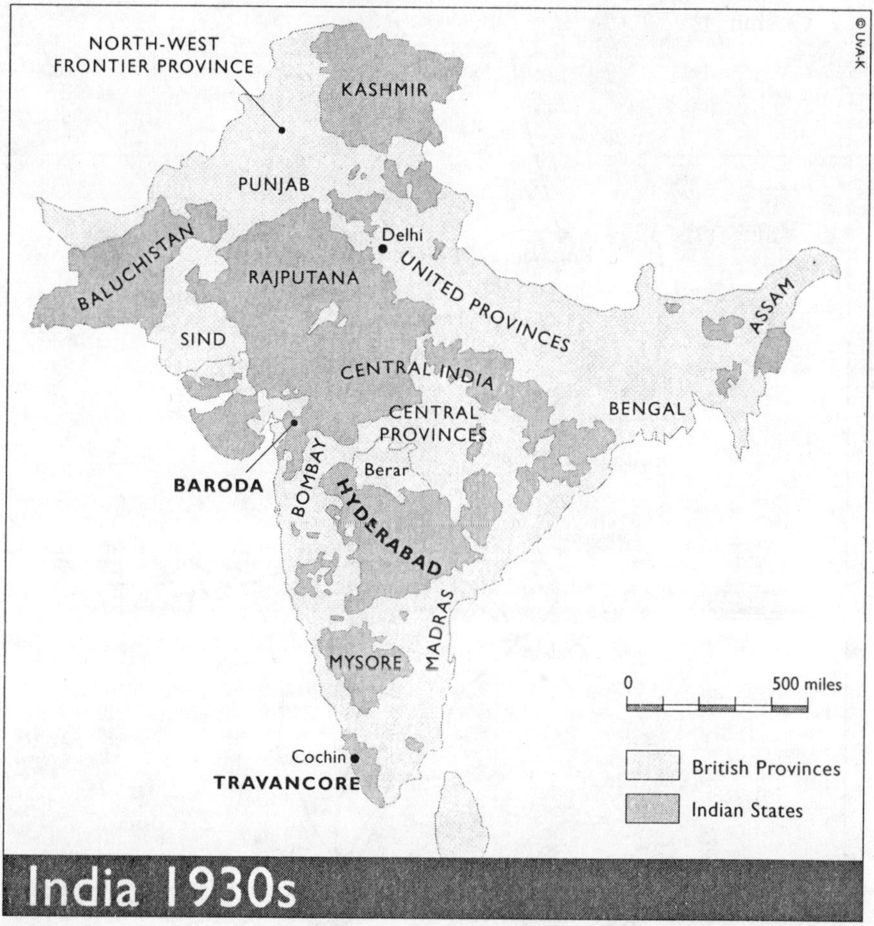

Map 1: India in the 1930s

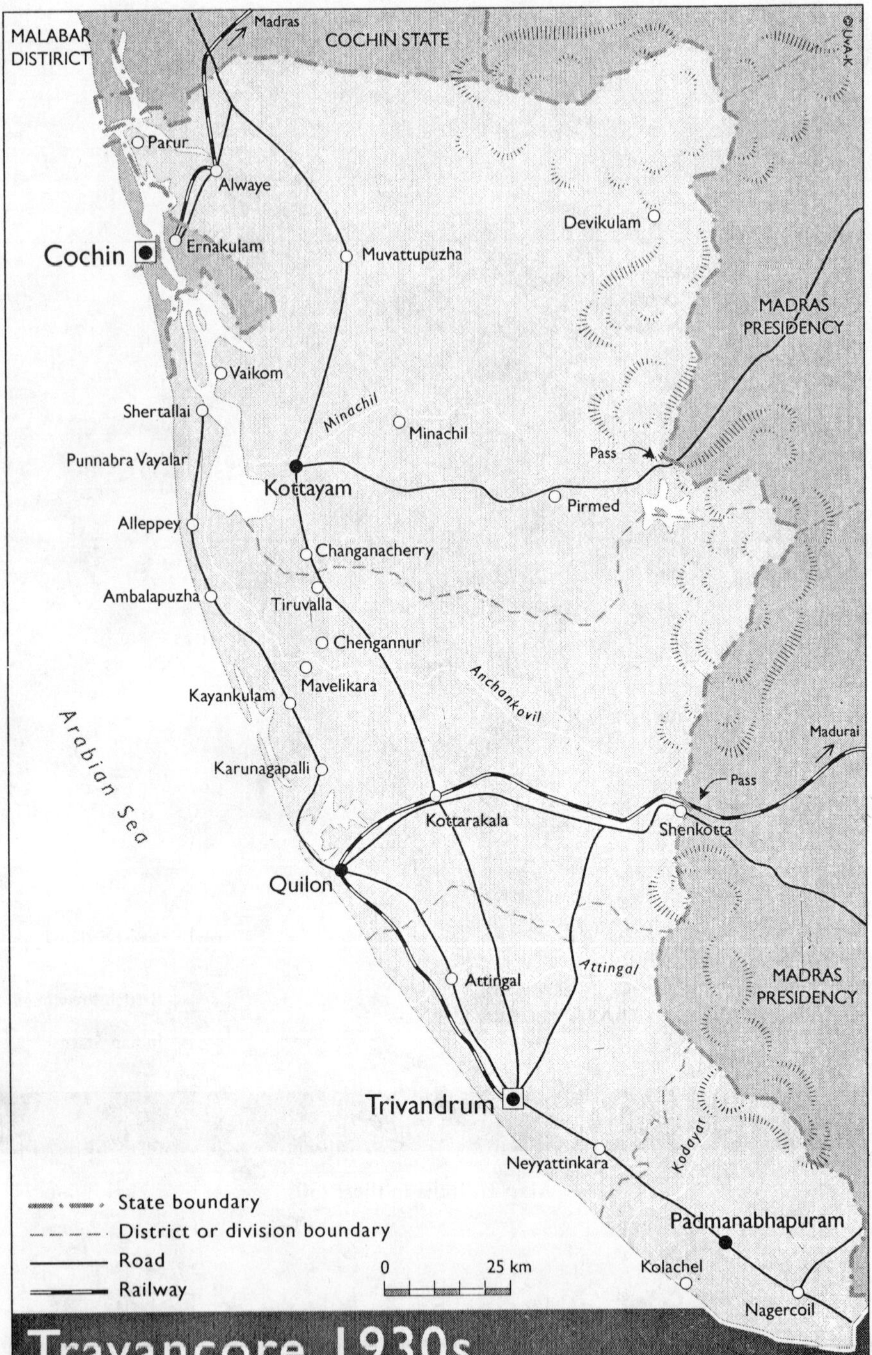

Map 2: Travancore in the 1930s

the Hindus were sharply divided. The report returned nearly 500 different castes, 77 of which received separate treatment. In terms of socio-economic position there was a small number of rather exclusive Brahmins enjoying extensive landed property, with, at the other end of the social hierarchy large communities of untouchable agricultural labourers (Pulayas, Pariahs) who were largely excluded from public life by a rigorous application of the concept of distance pollution. Nayars and Ezhavas were the largest intermediate Hindu groups making up respectively 17 and 22 per cent of the population. Both groups were primarily engaged in agriculture, but Nayars formed the dominant caste of warrior-aristocrats and were firmly entrenched in the administrative services.

The *vaishya varna* was absent in Travancore but its place was taken by Muslims and Christians who engaged in small business and trade. Muslims numbered only 6.9 per cent of the population, but the Christian share amounted to no less than 31.5 per cent. This exceptionally high percentage was due first of all to the presence of numerous Syrians who trace their origins in India to the arrival of St. Thomas the Apostle. The arrival of later Christian missionaries created several splits in this Syrian community. Some of them switched their allegiance from the old patriarchs in western Asia to the Pope in Rome and formed the Syrian Catholic church. Others, influenced by Protestant reformers, reorganized themselves as the independent Mar Thoma church, whilst a third major group, the orthodox Jacobites, managed to ward off both Catholic and Protestant interference and adhered to their old traditions.

Another reason for the high number of Christians along this coast is to be found in the work of a large number of missionary societies leading to the establishment of new churches for Latin Catholics, Anglicans, Independents and several others. The Syrians were equal in rank to the Nayars but most of the new converts, Catholic and Protestant, came from the lower rungs of Hindu society. Although enjoying a much higher status than these converts, many Syrians assumed leading positions in the newly established churches.[17]

Like Travancore, Baroda had a small Muslim minority numbering

[17] There was a wide gulf separating Latin Catholics (22 per cent of the Travancore Christian population) from the more respectable Syrian Catholics (28 per cent). More detailed information on the various Christian groups in Travancore (Kerala) in Kooiman 1993.

7.5 per cent in 1931. Hindus represented the large majority of the population, amounting to 88 per cent, and the main difference with Travancore was the negligible proportion (0.3 per cent) of Christians. (The rulers of Baroda did not allow Christian missions to enter their territories and missionaries had to operate from border areas.) Other religious minorities were also numerically insignificant, Jains numbering 2 per cent and Parsis 0.3 per cent of the population.

Of these religious communities Muslims and Jains were the most urban, larger towns containing double the proportion of Muslims and Jains in the general population. Baroda city was also exceptional in its linguistic composition: whereas in Baroda state only 1.5 per cent of the people spoke Marathi as its first language, in the larger towns and district headquarters the corresponding percentage was much higher, in Baroda city no less than 22 per cent. This concentration of a Marathi-speaking minority in a few administrative centres reflects the history of the state which was built in the course of the eighteenth century by a conquering war-band from the Deccan. Maharashtrian Brahmins, following in the wake of Gaekwad's conquests, had dominated the top levels of the bureaucracy.

Among the Hindus in Baroda, Brahmins numbered about 5 per cent of the population with some larger concentrations in temple centres in Kathiawad. Banias (4 per cent) had become the representative custodians of commercial interests, whereas the consolidation of agrarian interests had taken place under the Patidars (20 per cent). There were large artisan and labouring groups, and the untouchables or Depressed Classes made up 8 per cent of the population.[18]

Travancore, with its large percentage of Christians and low-caste Hindus, was considered to be a Hindu state. In the middle of the eighteenth century, Prince Martanda Varma had dedicated his kingdom to the Sri Padmanabha temple in Trivandrum. This religious grant of the whole state made Travancore, at least in theory, a divinely sanctioned Hindu polity with the king as the earthly trustee of his tutelary deity, Sri Padmanabha. Hyderabad, on the other hand, was Muslim in the sense that it was ruled by a Muslim royal dynasty surrounded by a select circle of powerful Muslim nobles. Many of these nobles traced their ancestry to pre-Mughal kingdoms, others had come as followers of the first Nizams. Resident Barton reported that till far into the twentieth century some of them had their own police,

[18] Census of Baroda 1932 I: 374–5, 397, 411.

troops, law courts and even private bands.[19] Together they constituted Hyderabad state which many Muslims, both in Hyderabad and outside, considered to be the last heir of the former Mughal Empire. Until recently local inhabitants used the word 'Mughlai' to differentiate between state and British jurisdiction and by the late 1930s the ideology of a Muslim state still motivated many high-ranking officials.[20] When after World War I Sir Ali Amin was asked by the Nizam to become his Prime Minister, he accepted, saying that to serve the king of Hyderabad was the same as to serve Islam.[21] The novelist E.M. Forster also sensed a Muslim atmosphere when in 1921, coming from Dewas state, he wrote about having 'passed abruptly from Hinduism to Islam', adding that to him the change came as a relief.[22]

Nevertheless, Hyderabad's Muslims were no more than 10.6 per cent of the population, only slightly more than those of Travancore and Baroda. As they were to a large extent associated with administration, Muslims were over-represented in the urban population (32 per cent). The capital Hyderabad numbered, in fact, 41 per cent of Muslims, while within the old walled city, the centre of power, they formed a clear majority.[23] Most of the Muslim aristocracy also lived in Hyderabad in preference to their estates in the districts. The urban elite, with its court traditions, stood far above the poor Muslims, but did not exclude all Hindus. The number of Hindus in Hyderabad was even higher than that in Hindu-dominated Travancore state: in 1931 its percentage was 84.4 per cent (Table 1).

The Christian minority in Hyderabad was very small. Christian missions had started early in the nineteenth century and both Protestants and Roman Catholics carried on medical, educational and evangelistic work. From 1881 to 1931 the percentage of Christians increased more than tenfold. This phenomenal rise, especially in the 1921–31 period, was mainly due to Anglican and Methodist missionaries in Telengana, who gained numerous converts from the Malas and Madigas. Even so, in 1931 the Christian part of the population was no more than 1 per cent.

[19] Barton 1934: 202.

[20] Lothian 1951: 77; Leonard 1978a: 91.

[21] Quoted in Ramesan IV 1966: 4.

[22] Forster 1983: 98.

[23] Census of Hyderabad 1933 I: 232, 245; Naidu 1990: 30 ff.

TABLE 1: POPULATION: TRAVANCORE, BARODA, AND HYDERABAD, 1931

	Travancore	*Baroda*	*Hyderabad*
Total number	50,95,978	24,43,007	144,36,148
Sex ratio (females per 1,000 males)	987	942	959
Density (population per square mile)	668	299	175
Hindu (percentage)	61.6	88	84.4
Muslim (percentage)	6.9	7.5	10.6
Christian (percentage)	31.5	0.3	1.1
Other (including tribals)	—	4.2	3.9

SOURCE: Census of 1931 for Travancore, Baroda and Hyderabad. In Travancore the tribal population was included in the Hindu body.

In Travancore, with its large number of Christians, the situation was absolutely different. For those Travancoreans who were concerned about the communal balance the report on the 1931 census disclosed an alarming result. The Christian share of the population showed a steady increase, from 23.6 per cent in 1901 to 31.5 per cent in 1931 (the Indian average being 1.8 per cent). As the established Syrian churches were not prone to accept converts from the untouchable castes, the growth of Christianity is attributed to missionary activity and a high fertility rate. The number of Hindus, on the other hand, showed a sharp decline. In spite of the gradual incorporation of hill tribes into Hinduism, the Hindu percentage had dropped from 69.9 per cent in 1901 to 61.6 per cent in 1931, far below the Indian average of 68.2 per cent.

In Hyderabad also the number of Hindus was on the decline, from 90.3 per cent in 1881 to 84.4 per cent in 1931. Here, the decline seems largely to have been a definition problem. Whereas a steady stream of so-called 'animists' was flowing into the main river of Hinduism, animism was redefined in such a way as to embrace ever more groups at every census, with the result that from 1881 to 1931 their number had grown from 0.2 to 3.8 per cent.[24] Among the Hindu part of the population these census figures do not seem to have aroused sensibilities similar to those in Travancore. The 1931 Baroda census also created no feelings of uneasiness. Here, the proportion of Hindus was growing since the 1901 census, largely by the incorporation of tribals, whereas that of the Christians had slightly declined.

[24] Census of Hyderabad 1933 I: 234, 243.

EDUCATIONAL LEVELS

Travancore was famous for its enlightened educational policies. Before 1900 the government had started the distribution of educational grants-in-aid to private agencies willing to manage schools that were open to all communities including the lowest castes. This policy enabled missionary societies to dominate the Travancore educational system, especially at the primary level. In 1933 the state enumerated 3,072 vernacular primary schools, the large majority of them privately-managed and in receipt of government grants-in-aid. The same applied to the vernacular middle schools, which in 1933 numbered 285 institutions. The majority of the English educational institutions were also privately managed but did not stand in need of grants, as they were running at a profit. At the top of the educational pyramid stood seven English colleges, all of them affiliated to the University of Madras, and in the 1930s Travancore proudly launched its own university.[25] The large government effort is reflected in the distribution of state expenditure: more than a fifth of state revenue was spent on education alone and in 1930–1 the percentage was actually 23.6.[26]

The number of schools in Travancore was high and so was the rate of literacy. It increased from 10 per cent in 1891 and 28.9 per cent in 1931 to 55 per cent in 1941, four times the Indian average and on a par with a contemporary European state of comparable size like Portugal. This level of literacy stimulated a flourishing local press[27] and active political participation. The benefit of education, however, was very unevenly spread among the population: in 1931, 40.8 per cent of the men were literate as against 16.8 per cent of the women, 29 per cent of the Christians as against 12 per cent of the Muslims. Among the Brahmins nearly 50 per cent could read and write in the vernacular as against only a low percentage of the Pulayas.[28]

[25] TERC 1933: 88, 153, passim.

[26] RAT 1930–1: 16-17, 191 ff.; Census Travancore 1932 I: 56.

[27] According to Handa (1968: 65, 126) there was not a single independent paper appearing from any of the states, no liberty of the press and no freedom of expression. This statement is certainly not true for Travancore where in the 1930s over a hundred dailies and weeklies were printed and circulated, even though they were always in danger of having their licences cancelled and their presses attached. As Ouwerkerk (1994: 65) observes, Travancore was a nation of newspaper readers (and hearers) who early developed the art of agitation through the press. See also Kumar n.d.: 56–7.

[28] Census of Travancore 1931 and 1941. In these percentages the population below five years of age is excluded. See also Chiriyankandath 1985: 9.

Baroda too could show a proud record of educational achievement. Its government assumed direct responsibility for the establishment and management of a large school system, especially after the formation of a Vernacular Education Department in 1875. One of its most spectacular innovations was the introduction of compulsory free education, first as an experimental measure in Amreli district, and then rapidly extended and by 1906 made applicable to the whole state both for boys and girls between the ages of seven and twelve.[29] In 1946 there were 2,563 government primary schools, with 6,746 teachers, and 41 government secondary schools with 477 teachers.

In the nineteenth century local talent had to turn to British India for academic education as was the case with Govindbhai Desai, the first among the Patidars of Gujarat to take a B.A. LL.B. examination in the 1880s (Elphinstone College Bombay) and for forty years a loyal servant of the state. But in the twentieth century, the state had four colleges affiliated to Bombay University, and technical education was provided at the Central Technical Institute and several technical schools in the districts. Special schools and educational facilities were made available for students from poor and backward classes who might otherwise lag behind.[30]

Teaching may have been poor, and compulsory education impossible to enforce, especially for children who had to assist in earning the family income. Nevertheless, government efforts did show encouraging results. In 1891 the rate of literacy in Baroda state was 8 per cent as opposed to 10 per cent in directly administered British Gujarat. But by 1931 there was a complete reverse: literacy in Baroda state was 20.9 per cent, as opposed to 13 per cent in British Gujarat and 11 per cent in the Bombay and Madras Presidencies.

As in Travancore, literacy was unevenly spread: in 1931 the number of Hindus able to read and write was 19.8 per cent, slightly below the state average, whereas Parsis had 79.6, Jains 57.7, Christians 39.2 and Muslims 25.4 per cent literacy. The female literacy rate of 7.9 per cent was also much lower than the male 33.1 per cent.[31] In

[29] The *Gazetteer of the Baroda State* (II 1923: 311 ff.) contains an interesting description of the many practical problems involved in the introduction of compulsory education in an agrarian society accustomed for ages to use its children in the fields, and the administration by local authorities of a penalty system for offenders under the Act. See also Pandya 1915 and Desai 1926.

[30] RAB 1944–5: 14 ff., 28, 180.

[31] Census of Baroda 1932 I: 315, 334 ff.; Hardiman 1978: 118.

1946 the *Baroda Administration Report* boasted of the advanced state of literacy among the younger women (12 per cent) as a result of compulsory education, but Baroda still lagged far behind Travancore in female education, especially in English. Between 1876 and 1933 educational expenditure in Baroda state rose from one to 17 per cent of total state expenditure, dropping to 12 per cent in 1945.[32]

Compared with Travancore and Baroda, Hyderabad was decidedly backward. The state formally assumed responsibility for education in 1854, but this task was entrusted to the revenue authorities, and did not receive due attention. Even after the establishment of an Education Department (1860), the actual management remained in the hands of revenue officials. After 1900 schools were gradually transferred to local boards and in 1909 the Education Department came under a Director of Public Instruction whose proposals were submitted to the Prime Minister through an Assistant Minister for Education.

In 1931 Hyderabad had about 4,300 educational institutions with 2,91,000 students, apart from a number of private schools, many of them managed by Hindus and receiving government aid.[33] In 1938–9 the official administration report placed the total number of schools of all types and grades at 5,224 and that of scholars at 3,84,696. Whereas in 1883 Hyderabad had only 148 primary schools, in 1938-9 their total number had increased to 4,842 and the number of pupils enrolled in them to 2,97,932. At that time, there were 203 high schools.[34] Technical institutes were founded: an industrial school in 1889 in Aurangabad, and a small engineering school in 1896 in Hyderabad city. Several post-primary industrial and commercial schools were later opened.

As far as higher education is concerned, Hyderabad had a few Arts Colleges, all purely state institutions and some affiliated to Madras University. Yet the field of higher education was dominated by two institutions, Osmania University and Nizam College. The pride of Hyderabad's educational achievements undoubtedly was the founding

[32] Hardiman 1978: 117; RAB 1944–5: 58.

[33] According to the 1931 census, Hyderabad had 4,256 public schools with 2,91,930 students and 1,082 private schools with 41,384 students (Census of Hyderabad I 1933: 28). If we exclude the private schools this information more or less tallies with the Reforms Committee's Report mentioning 4,336 educational institutions and 2,90,192 pupils in 1930-1 (RRC 1938: 7 ff.). See also Leonard 1978a: 83. Quite different figures are given by Bawa 1992: 135.

[34] RAND 1941: xxvi.

of Osmania University in 1917–18, strongly promoted by Nizam Mir Osman Ali Khan and his Éducational Secretary Sir Akbar Hydari. This institution, with total control over its curriculum, was fully independent of the British Indian educational system. It was also the first university to use an Indian language (Urdu) as its medium of instruction. Nevertheless, English was increasingly regarded as the key to the modern world. Already in 1886–7 Nizam College, an amalgamation of several local English-medium schools, was affiliated to Madras University. Whereas Osmania had a larger student body, Nizam College continued to attract the best students in the state. Even so, the government preferred to recruit most of its administrative officials not locally but from Aligarh in north India.[35]

Quantitative data on educational expenditure are confusing and contradictory. According to the *Gazetteer of Hyderabad*, average state expenditure on education as a percentage of the total budget for the ten years ending 1900 was 1.75 per cent. Pernau-Reifeld states that in 1931 it had risen to 10 per cent, but Copland, quoting secondary sources, maintains that in 1938–9 Hyderabad spent less than 16 per cent of its budget on education, health and development together, as against 25 per cent in Bombay and 30 per cent in Madras.[36] A more general statement was made by the Financial Secretary to the Nizam's government who noted that the annual expenditure on education had increased from about half a crore rupees in 1920 to one and a half crores in 1945.[37] With all their shortcomings these figures clearly indicate that Hyderabad spent much less on education than the other two princely states.

Schools in Hyderabad state were open to children of all castes, but few tribal persons or persons of the lower classes availed of the opportunities. Muslims, though only a minority of the population, dominated the classrooms. In 1901 the percentage of Muslims in primary and secondary schools and colleges was 42, 45 and 83 per cent respectively, a result which at that time the *Gazetteer of Hyderabad*

[35] Yazdani 1985: 83 ff.; Bawa 1992: 138–40.

[36] *Gazetteer of Hyderabad* 1909: 86; Pernau-Reifeld 1992: 394; Copland 1988: 787. In 1938–9 total expenditure on education only was Rs 84,28,399 excluding collegiate education (RAND 1941: xxvi).

[37] Note on the Industrial, Commercial and Financial Developments in the Hyderabad State by Nawab Mir Nawaz Jung, Financial Secretary, H.E.H. the Nizam's Government, in *Hyderabad Political Notebook*, Vol. II (1919–45), n.d.: 136, Lothian Collection Nr. 63.

TABLE 2: LITERACY RATES TRAVANCORE, BARODA, AND HYDERABAD, 1931

	Travancore	*Baroda*	*Hyderabad*
General	28.9	20.9	5.0
–Male (in English)	40.8 (3.1)	33.1 (2.8)	8.5 (1)
–Female (in English)	16.8 (0.7)	7.9 (0.2)	1.2 (0.1)
Hindus	26.8	19.8	4.0
–Brahmins	49.0	80.0	40.3
–Depressed	3 (Pulaya)	2.1 (Tribal)	0.7 (Adi Hindu)
Muslims	12.0	25.4	12.4
Christians	29.0	39.2	17.1

SOURCE: Census 1931 for Travancore, Baroda and Hyderabad. Children below five years of age excluded.

could in all frankness attribute 'to the position held by Muhammadans in a State of which the ruler belongs to their religion'.[38] Proportionate to their numbers Hindus may have been more successful in examinations, but the quite exceptional situation obtained that in quantitative terms the Muslim minority was much better educated than the Hindus (Table 2).

In 1931 no more than 5 per cent of the population in Hyderabad state was literate. That means that the rate of literacy in 1931 was not only far below that of Travancore and Baroda, but also less than half the percentage in the neighbouring British provinces. Nevertheless, the 1931 Hyderabad census reported that over the last decade the government had paid greater attention to education than at any time before, resulting in an increase in literacy from 1.3 (1901) and 3.3 per cent (1921) to 5 per cent (1931).[39]

The higher the Hindu caste, the higher the level of literacy: Vellalas enjoyed a rate of 59.2 per cent and Brahmins 40.3 per cent, but Dhers and Madigas did not reach even one per cent, whereas Muslims with 12.4 per cent were well above the average. The Christian literacy rate came down from 44 per cent in 1901 and 25 in 1921 to 17 per cent in 1931, because of a large influx of illiterate converts. The education of girls had not kept pace with that of boys, and in 1931 female literacy

[38] *Gazetteer of Hyderabad* 1909: 74 ff., quotation pp. 77–8.

[39] Literacy figures in the *Gazetteer of Hyderabad* 1909: 78 differ from the later Census, because of changes in definition and classification: after 1911 the category 'Learning' was abolished and children below 5 years of age were excluded (see Census of Hyderabad 1933 I: 194 ff.).

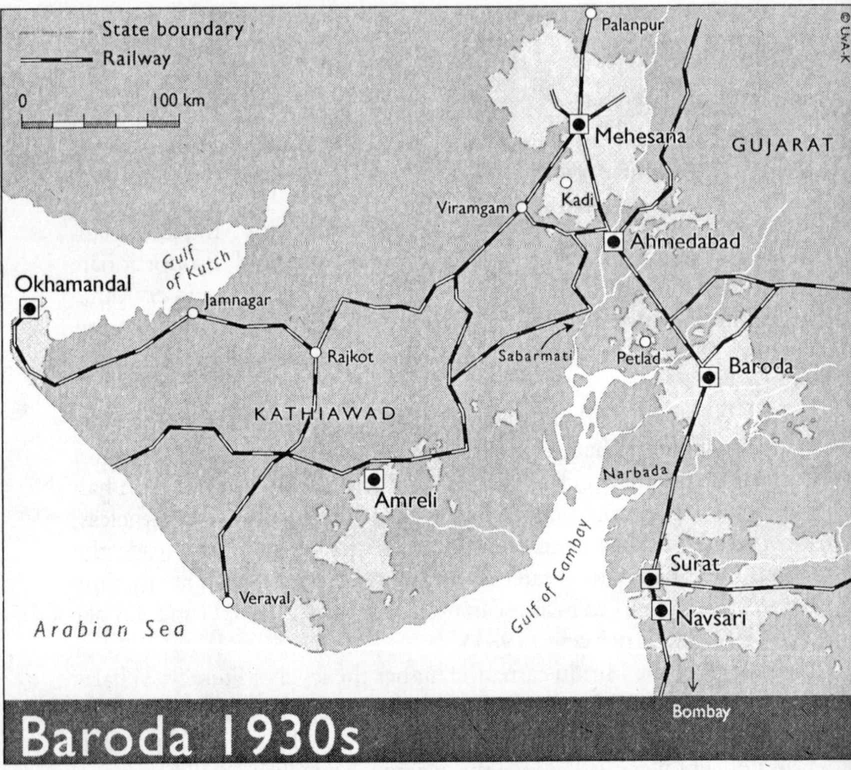

Map 3: Baroda in the 1930s

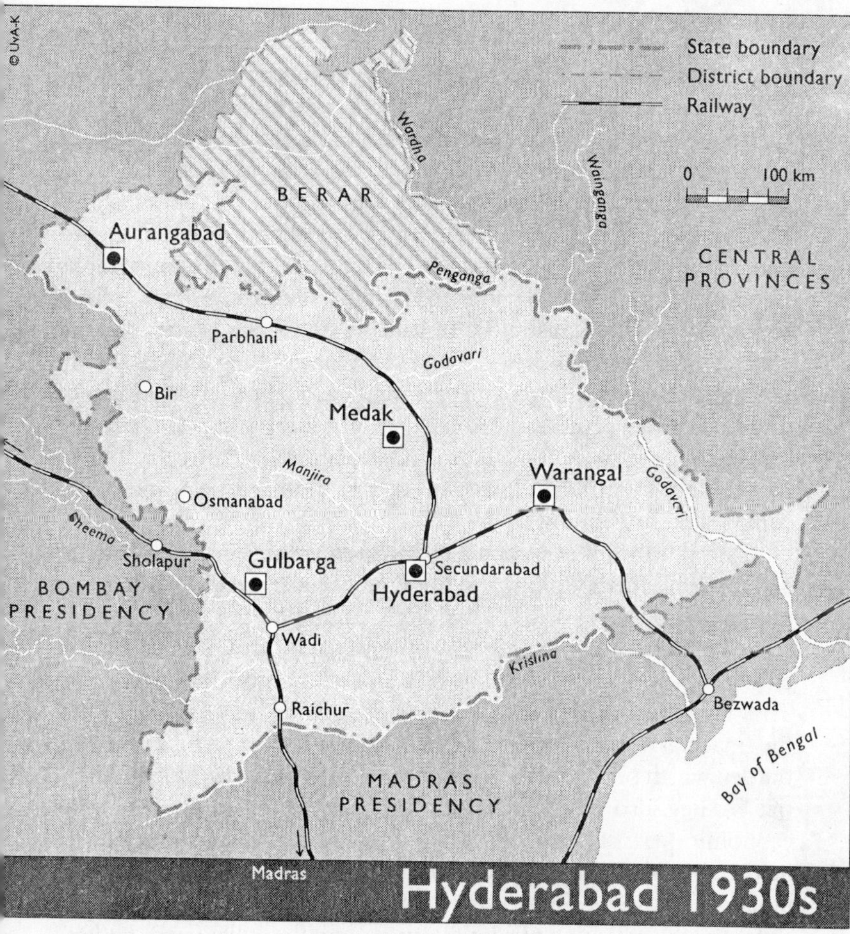

Map 4: Hyderabad in the 1930s

was only 1.2 per cent as against 8.5 per cent for males. Literacy in English was very low, 0.6 per cent in 1931 , mainly among Vellalas and Christians.

ECONOMIC DEVELOPMENT

John Hurd raising the question of the economic consequences of indirect rule in India, argued that, apart from ecological, social and economic factors, wide disparities in economic development were also caused by a political dualism. '[W]ith two political systems existing side-by-side, economic consequences were inevitable.'[40] To substantiate his point, he compared directly and indirectly ruled areas that were geographically contiguous and shared similar factors like topography, water supply and cultural patterns, leaving only economic and political factors as possible causes. So Travancore and Cochin, for instance, were matched by the British district of Malabar. Using indices like the percentages of male employment, immigration, literacy and the level of urbanization, Hurd came to the conclusion that, despite the lack of statistical significance for literacy and urbanization, 'the great majority of princely states had lower levels of economic development than comparable British districts.'[41]

In a critique Simmons and Satyanarayana rejected most of Hurd's assumptions, methodology and findings. Some of their arguments are relevant to our discussion. First of all, Simmons and Satyanarayana made the point that the economy of imperial India was an indivisible entity and not simply the sum of two dichotomous political units. They immediately weakened that point by adding (in a footnote!) that the financial tribute imposed on many states proved to be a crippling burden which put a serious constraint upon their development potential.[42] They also questioned the utility of generalizing about the economic performance of British India and the Indian states, as neither British India nor the states were in any sense homogeneous units. In my view, Hurd was perfectly aware of this and therefore shifted to the matching of contiguous areas with similar factor endowments. Of much more importance is Simmons and Satyanarayana's warning that a precise measurement of regional economic disparities in pre-Independence India is highly problematic because of the weak

[40] Hurd 1975a: 172.

[41] Ibid., 175.

[42] Simmons and Satyanarayana 1979: 185.

statistical base. In our study of Travancore, Baroda and Hyderabad we also have to cope with that lack of reliable and comparable statistical data. Unable to make definite statements about the economic conditions in these states, we shall have to content ourselves with indicating a general outline.

Hurd also published an article on the influence of British policy on the industrial development in the princely states in which he asserts that states generally offered attractive prospects to industrial ventures. In most states there was no labour legislation restricting the freedom of capital, and trade unions were generally not permitted. Apart from that, many state governments offered generous concessions like free land and tax relief to attract industrial investment. In spite of all these inducements, there was little expansion of industry before 1931, measured in terms of the percentage of workers employed in large-scale industry in the Indian states.

From an early date the Government of India had claimed the right of supervision of all dealings between state governments and outside capitalists. But actual policy was one of almost total non-interference in the states' commercial affairs. The government needed to be informed, but did not prevent the states from using their advantages. Hurd could find no instance in which the Government of India refused sanctions for industrial projects. Nevertheless, his conclusion is that British policy bears a large part of the responsibility for the plight of the states. Lacking resources, the states could not guarantee repayment of loans. By withholding its backing to loans, the non-interference policy had the same effect as an active policy of constraint would have had.[43] Lacking sufficient resources and denied British guarantees most state darbars were unable to compete for funds, and industry could not avoid falling economically behind comparable areas of British India.[44]

Richter on his part is of the opinion that the oft-mentioned differences in economic development between princely and British India have frequently been overstated, and that many of these economic

[43] In 1923 the Government of India laid down Resolution No. 1130–445 to say that those rulers who were members of the Chamber of Princes in their own right, should ensure that in granting prospecting licences and mining leases more than 50 per cent of the capital was subscribed by state-cum-British interests 'to safeguard interests of Empire and Rulers concerned'. Under the Registration of Capital Goods Scheme the import of plants had to be registered with the Commerce Department, New Delhi, before an export licence was granted (L/P&S/13/1223).

[44] Hurd 1975b.

differences are not fully attributable to princely rule.[45] He may be right. Economically the former princely territories still lag behind the former British provinces and, as Copland has observed, Rajasthan and Madhya Pradesh, the princely heartland before 1947, are among the poorest parts of India.[46] Yet, the British East India Company was not eager to annexe territories that were not in any material sense attractive and rewarding. Direct rule remained limited to economically viable and potentially profitable areas and, therefore, differences in levels of development were present at the outset. Let us take a closer look at each of the three states.

In both Travancore and Baroda landowning peasant cultivators were the most important class in rural society. In 1865 the Travancore Dewan, Sir T. Madhava Rao, had granted full ownership rights to the numerous cultivators of government lands. The same law allowed unrestricted transfer of landed property, and later land reforms ensured the tenants of private landlords of legal protection and permanent occupancy rights. On his transfer to Baroda Madhava Rao introduced a similar reform there by ruling that sharecroppers were to be recognized as legal owners of the land subject only to due payment of land revenue. Patidars were among those who most benefited from these new revenue settlements, both in Baroda and in the British districts of Gujarat.[47]

In Hyderabad too, agriculture was the main basis of the revenue system but this state had remained more feudal in character. In the 1930s more than half of the land was *khalsa* or public domain with ryots holding directly from the state. The remainder, about 42 per cent of land, scattered all over the state, was privately administered by several classes of feudal lords and office-holders. Most important among them, of course, was the Nizam himself whose crownlands or *Sarf-i-Khas*, located close to Hyderabad City, occupied about 15 per cent of the state's territory. The other 27 per cent of private lands were the exclusive property of hereditary tax-free jagirdars, the largest of which belonged to Nawab Salar Jung and the Paigah nobles.[48] In the extant

[45] Richter 1978: 333.

[46] Copland 1996: 151.

[47] Rutten 1991: 74–5.

[48] Nawab Salar Jung belonged to a prominent noble family that provided the state with some of its most able Chief Ministers. The Paigah nobles were no less important. Defence of the state was their hereditary function and the large jagirs granted to them were meant for the maintenance of their troops. See also the Nizam's Government's *Report of the Royal Commission on Jagir Administration* (1947).

sources figures of the percentage distribution of land in Hyderabad fluctuate, especially after the 1920s. This is probably due to the last Nizam's policy of placing large estates on the death of their owner under the Court of Wards procedure pending a final settlement on succession—which often resulted in outright confiscation.[49]

Economic developments in the three states took quite a different course, especially so in Travancore. After 1857 and under strong pressure from European capitalist interests, the commercial development of agriculture in Travancore was strongly encouraged by the government. The government, led by Madhava Rao, began to abolish a number of state monopolies. In 1860, the monopoly of pepper was abolished, followed in 1863 by that of tobacco. The removal of all inland duties in 1836 was now extended to a wider field: in 1865 Travancore joined the British Indian system of free trade, adopting British Indian tariffs and removing most of the duties on trade between Travancore and other parts of British India. Similar legislation, gently pushed by the Government of India, was passed in most of the other states but generally much later. The opening of postal services in Travancore together with the introduction of the telegraph (1861) facilitated Travancore's communications with the outside world. Railways, however, were slow in coming: the first railway line from Quilon to Tirunelvelly (Madras Presidency) was only opened in 1904.[50] Travancore's openings were to the sea.

From the second half of the nineteenth century the economy of Travancore became gradually integrated with the international commodity market. The basis for this integration was laid by the large-scale investment of private foreign capital in plantations (coffee, tea and rubber) and agro-processing industries (coir and coconut oil). It was European coastal firms, with generous support from the government,[51] that dominated these sectors, exercizing almost complete control over the principal spheres of commercial and financial activity, from production and exchange to shipping and insurance. According to Mahadevan, the Travancore economy was 'an essentially export-oriented agro-based industrial complex characterized by the overall predominance of foreign capital'.[52] Even as late as 1940–1 this

[49] Leonard 1978a: 73; Gazetteer Hyderabad 1909: 52–6; RAND 1941: i.

[50] Kumar n.d.: 26.

[51] Baak 1995: 51 ff.

[52] Mahadevan 1991: 167.

export-oriented complex employed over 84 per cent of the total workforce in organized industries. The emphasis on the production of exportable cash crops grew to such an extent that already in the nineteenth century the state had become dependent on imports of essential foodstuffs.[53]

By the 1920s this commercialization of the economy had given rise to a nascent entrepreneurial class, mainly from the Syrian Christian and Ezhava communities. Syrians started investing in plantations, but later their capital diversified from plantations into commercial banking. There was, however, no large-scale investment in modern industry and the 1931 census mentions the existence of 159 factories employing altogether about 19,000 persons. The coir industry is usually associated with the rise of Ezhava entrepreneurs. Yet, even though Indian participation was increasing, also from outside Travancore, European coastal firms clearly dominated this sector. The subordination and external orientation of the Travancore economy was not particularly favourable to the growth of an entrepreneurial class which remained relatively weak and unable to take advantage of the opportunities for modern industrial investment.[54]

Most probably, the lack of industrial investment in Travancore was caused by the fact that local merchants and capitalists did not feel encouraged by official attitudes. Isaac and Tharakan (1986) argue that Syrian Christians, who had both potential and capacity to assume entrepreneurial roles, were prevented from investing in modern industry by what they felt to be a discriminatory policy on the part of the state. Bagchi (1972) has argued the same for industrialists in British India who refrained from taking financial risk under a colonial government. In the case of Travancore, Mahadevan (1991) has tried to downplay state reluctance as an explanatory factor by emphasizing geographical isolation and rational choice. Nevertheless, the state government was too important a factor to be completely left out of account.

The situation in Travancore was rather exceptional. In contrast to that, conditions in Baroda and Hyderabad, were not significantly different from British India in terms of economic structure. In 1887 all transit duties in Baroda were abolished and in 1909 all import and export duties went the same way with the exception of the Maharaja's possessions in Kathiawad. In 1901 the local currency (*Babashahi*)

[53] Kumar n.d.: 29–30.

[54] Mahadevan 1991: 169.

was withdrawn and substituted by British Indian silver coinage as the currency of the state and a few years later the Bank of Baroda was inaugurated.[55] By these and other measures Baroda was drawn more closely into the network of commodity production in British India and this provided the more developed sections of local merchant capital with the opportunity of active participation in a wider market.

The Baroda government, especially in the person of Maharaja Sayajirao III (1875–1939), became a zealous patron of industrial development. It established state enterprises, a sugar factory and a textile mill (1884–5), as an object lesson to local capitalists, to be handed over into private hands as soon as possible. As it was difficult to mobilize the necessary capital, the Maharaja's government conducted an industrial survey, exploring and demonstrating the economic potential of the state (1893–6). An Industrial Fund was started to encourage enterprising subjects by financial support, followed by the establishment of a Department of Trade and Industries (1915) to advise traders, manufacturers and artisans about industrial development. Last but not least, significant tax concessions were granted, and water, land, and raw materials belonging to the state were offered at favourable rates.[56] Local enterprise found also an obliging patron in R.C. Dutt who was appointed Revenue Minister (1902) and later Dewan. Dutt was a well-known critic of the colonial economy, who argued that the financial drain from India was responsible for the continuing poverty of India.[57]

The Maharaja's government thus played a very distinctive role in the industrialization process. In 1942 Shah concluded that industrial development as it stood at that time was mainly the result of state efforts.[58] Nevertheless, in a critical revision of this rather general praise of Sayajirao's industrial leadership, Tripathi (1987) has shown that no enterprise could hope to prosper in the state, unless it subserved not only the interest of the government but also the financial interest of the ruler himself. Further, almost until the early 1940s the local industry

[55] Political General Correspondence, Confidential File No. 34 3C, HPO Baroda. Tripathi and Mehta (1990: 121) argue that at the beginning of the twentieth century the authorities in British India still treated Baroda as a foreign country for customs purposes.

[56] Streefkerk 1985: 48–9, 111–14 and 1997: M-4. According to Sergeant (1928: 241 ff.) these departments were established in 1909.

[57] Tripathi and Mehta 1990: 119.

[58] Shah 1942: 140.

was rather narrowly based with textile mills accounting for the bulk of the labour force as well as invested capital. This local textile industry, numbering 16 mills in 1937, was almost exclusively controlled by a few leading firms of the Gujarat Bania and Patidar castes, like the Mafatlals. Their entry into industry was also facilitated by the state's favourable location on the main railway lines linking Bombay, Ahmedabad and Delhi, and Baroda's initiative, as the first state in India, to build its own network of railways, including the construction of wooden coaches and a repair shop.[59]

In the same way, the Hyderabad government took an active interest in the promotion of local industries. In 1918 it established a Commerce and Industries Department to provide large-scale entrepreneurs and cottage industries with scientific assistance and advice, and technical and industrial training. Financial support to the corporate sector began with state aid to the Shahbad Cement Company of the Tatas, set up in 1925. As part of its industrial policy, government set aside a crore of rupees to be invested in large industries and government securities, the profits accruing therefrom to be utilised for loans for the development of cottage and small-scale industries. This Industrial Trust Fund, established in 1929, took pioneering initiatives and provided technological and institutional support to a wide range of industries.[60] No tax was levied on local industries and the state took care of a favourable legal framework.[61]

In 1874 the first railway line between Secunderabad and Wadi was opened. Defying all opposition from the Government of India, the state was able to connect the cotton-producing districts of Marathwada and the coal fields in Telengana to trading centres in the state and beyond.[62] These internal connections were of vital importance, as local textile mills were thus enabled to obtain their energy from the state's own coalfields. In the beginning of the twentieth century both railway and coal mining companies were taken over by the state. The railways became the first completely state-owned undertaking[63] (the Nizam's State Railway 1930) and were later to launch a road transport service and civil aviation as well.

[59] Erdman 1971: 6 ff; Hardiman 1978: 116–17, 120 ff; Mahadevan 1991: 165, 187.

[60] Census of Hyderabad I 1933: 25–7.

[61] Subbarao 1991: 214.

[62] Ray 1988: 148 ff.

[63] Subbarao (1991: 211) calls Hyderabad the first princely government to set up a state railway, a claim similar to that raised by Hardiman (1978: 129) for Baroda.

Thus, like Baroda but unlike Travancore, Hyderabad offered a great deal of protection and support to indigenous industry. Furthermore, the state possessed important assets in the supply of good quality cotton, coal and oil seeds. In spite of that, Hyderabad's industrial basis remained weak. It is not easy to get a clear outline of the state's industrial performance before World War II, as there are many official reports on agricultural indebtedness, tenancy, and jagir administration, but not on industry, commerce and trade.[64] Census and Administration Reports made regular announcements of the opening of new mills, not only in textiles but also in cement, tobacco, ceramic, sugar and oil seed crushing; in 1935–6 the Hyderabad Iron and Steel Works were started with financial help from the Industrial Trust Fund.[65] Yet, no overall picture of industrial progress emerges from this scattered evidence and—to take just one indicator—the value of manufactured products as a proportion of the total value of exports remained small: from 1919 to 1939 it increased from 2 to 7 per cent only.[66]

Another most striking feature was the relatively restricted role of external capital, Indian and British alike. Partly, this can be explained by legal and social restrictions on non-*mulki* (outside) investment and the preference given to local capital. We will revert to the *mulki* versus non-*mulki* controversy in later chapters. The Government of India also proved reluctant to further outside investment in the state. When in 1939 Mir Laiq Ali, a prominent industrialist and Hyderabad's last Prime Minister, tried to enlist technical support for his prospected construction company from a French firm, the Government of India raised several objections till the plans were overtaken by the outbreak of war.[67]

The local sources of industrial finance on which Hyderabadi entrepreneurs had to fall back were not so much commercial banks as traditional money markets. The Hyderabad State Bank was established only in 1942. As Subbarao (1991) has pointed out, the amorphous group of Hyderabadis that ventured in industrial enterprise 'consisted of traditional landed gentry, traders, moneylenders and contractors'. Their own share of investment was not particularly significant, nor were they known for technical or organizational expertise. But most of these industrialists were landed gentry with vital connections with

[64] Reddy 1987: 5.

[65] Census of Hyderabad I 1933: 25; RAND 1941: xv, xvi.

[66] Subbarao 1991: 213.

[67] See File Hyderabad: Trade Questions, L/P&S/13/1223.

the civil service apparatus. Subbarao observes that these indigenous entrepreneurs remained largely dependent on the administration. They could not free themselves from the constraints of the feudal social order and when the state finally collapsed, most of the local capitalists were not able to survive.[68]

Barton, a British Resident with reformist zeal, held a different opinion on the role of the state, especially the Nizam. In 1925 he complained of the ruler's almost pathological propensity to collect *nazars*. According to the Nizam, *nazars* were donations offered voluntarily by his people out of love and esteem for his person, but the Resident rejected them as forced contributions and even outright extortion. *Nazar* was a drain on capital resources, with the ruler amassing a large amount of wealth. The accumulation of crores of rupees as dead capital, Barton argued, hindered economic progress to an appreciable degree and should instead be invested in railways, irrigation and roads, for which there was great scope. The lesser property owners, nobles and *jagirdars* proved reluctant to come forward as potential investors, as they were unable to break away from their narrow short-term perspective. According to Barton, they were obsessed with the terror of their children being reduced to beggary on their deaths by confiscation or manipulation by the Nizam, who placed large estates on the death of their owner under his own charge.[69] Yazdani, however in a defence of the last Nizam, holds the view that confiscation was not in the interest of the ruler, but in that of the estates themselves, and only benefited the local subjects.[70]

COMPARATIVE OBSERVATIONS

In view of the glaring absence of reliable and systematic data on industrial development, it is virtually impossible to make detailed comparisons between the states of Travancore, Baroda and Hyderabad. From scattered sources we may collect information on the type of mills, the distribution of the labourforce and the total amount of capital invested in joint stock companies. But these data are not always fully comparable, as they apply to different years and are constructed on the basis of

[68] Subbarao 1991: 236, quotation p. 218; Bawa 1992: 209.

[69] Memorandum from W. Barton, Resident Hyderabad, 11.12.1925, R/1/1/1465. See also Bawa 1992: 214.

[70] Yazdani 1985: 67.

TABLE 3: JOINT STOCK COMPANIES IN BOMBAY, MADRAS, TRAVANCORE, BARODA, AND HYDERABAD

	Number of Companies		*Paid-up Capital (Rs 1,000)*		*Average Capital of Company*	
	1931–2	*1941–2*	*1931-2*	*1941–2*	*1931–2*	*1941–2*
Bombay	1,05 1	1,801	9,88,495	11,97,606	9,41,000	6,65,000
Madras	839	1,515	1,48,510	1,97,632	1,77,000	1,30,000
Travancore	653	368	17,605	30,306	27,000	82,000
Baroda	44	78	16,184	26,041	3,68,000	3,34,000
Hyderabad	41	81	17,675	26,202	4,31,000	3,23,000

SOURCE: Department of Commercial Intelligence and Statistics, India 1935: iii and 1943: iii.

divergent definitions. Therefore, to give at least some idea of the level of industrial development, I present two tables based on lists produced by the Department of Commercial Intelligence and Statistics of the Government of India. Table 3 shows the number of joint stock companies in the three states and two neighbouring British provinces, Bombay and Madras, for the years 1931–2 and 1941–2.

Travancore had a large number of joint stock companies in 1931, much larger than the other two states together and not far behind of Madras. These joint stock companies were mainly in banking and insurance (529) and trading and manufacturing (66). It is remarkable also, that according to this source Travancore numbered 13 companies in printing and publishing, as against only one in Baroda and none in Hyderabad. In 1941 the number of companies in Travancore had dropped whereas the avarage amount of capital per unit increased, indicating a greater concentration of capital, a trend that set Travancore apart from the rest of India. In 1931 Travancore had 37 tea and other plantation companies (coffee, rubber), as against none in Baroda and Hyderabad.

Table 4 shows the number of large industrial establishments in the three states and the number of persons employed in 1931.

Data for Travancore have been given along with Cochin under the heading Madras states and the number of labourers does not include night shifts. As can be seen, Baroda and Hyderabad are well represented under the category textiles and cotton gins and presses.

TABLE 4: NUMBER OF LARGE INDUSTRIAL ESTABLISHMENTS AND LABOUR EMPLOYED (1931)

	Travancore & Cochin		*Baroda*		*Hyderabad*	
	Establishment	*Labour*	*Establishment*	*Labour*	*Establishment*	*Labour*
Textiles	1	700	17	10,873	12	6,548
Engineering	5	663	5	620	16	4,012
Mineral & Metals	2	62	—	—	4	121
Food, Drink, Tobacco	26	845	1	91	35	2,165
Chemicals, Dyes	19	1,812	9	1,760	8	495
Paper, Printing	3	163	5	276	2	506
Wood, Stones, Glass	42	3,741	6	1,031	7	1,001
Skins, Hides	—	—	—	—	8	574
Gins, Presses	—	—	117	8,214	201	14,880
Miscellaneous	32	12,416	—	—	8	222
Grand Total	130	20,402	160	22,865	303	31,143

SOURCE: Department of Commercial Intelligence and Statistics, India 1934: iv–xi.

Travancore and Cochin on the other hand show 26 rice mills under the category Food and Drink and 40 Bricks and Tiles under Wood, Stone and Glass. As a percentage of the total population, the number of labourers employed in large industrial establishments was highest in Baroda (0.93) and lowest in Hyderabad (0.21). For Bombay and Madras the comparative percentages were 1.64 and 0.28.[71]

After World War II with its forced cessation of overseas imports and consequent boost in industrial demand there was a general economic upswing, also in the princely states. Attracted by favourable government policies and lower production costs, a good number of Indian business houses made significant investments in the states. In Travancore some Tamil business groups established new capital-intensive industries, especially fertilizers and chemicals, rayons and cements, which between them represented by far the largest share of investment in modern industry. On the eve of Independence Travancore had overtaken all other princely states in respect of total corporate paid-up

[71] These rather rough percentages have been computed from a combination of the Commercial Department List with population figures in the 1931 Census.

capital.[72] In Baroda the Tatas and Sarabhais invested in large chemical industries and the Birla group set up a factory for motors and rayon in the Okhamandal port area. After the War the number of factories under the Factory Act was 178, employing 43,300 workers, three-fourths of whom were employed by textile mills.[73] Hyderabad had its share of this post-War trend, but remained, in the words of its Prime Minister, 'relatively less industrialized than others'.[74] As it was the second largest producer of groundnuts, the chief raw material for vegetable oil, it was planning a huge manufacturing plant for its production. The Government of India, however, insisted on a centre-led plant allocation and feared that the state was overplaying its hand. Hyderabad complained of obstruction and discrimination by central authorities, and similar complaints about lack of cooperation could be heard from Baroda.[75]

To sum up, there were great differences between the states in communal composition, levels of education and economic progress. Travancore, with its large and influential Christian minority was a Hindu dominated state, whereas Hyderabad with its large Hindu majority was ruled by a Muslim dominated government. The impact of this peculiar religious complexion on the emergence of communalism in these states will be studied in Chapters 3 and 4. Travancore and Baroda were both far ahead of Hyderabad in terms of education, rates of literacy and, to a lesser extent, economic development. But whereas the Travancorean economy was more export-oriented and dominated by foreign capital, Baroda and Hyderabad were better integrated into the British Indian economy and offered a more suitable climate to local merchant groups for profitable investment.

It is often assumed that the Indian states, sealed off and upheld by British paramount power, remained stagnant in their development and showed less progress than the directly-ruled British territories. Such a

[72] The figures in the *Baroda Administration Report 1944–45* (1946: 27) differ from those mentioned by Mahadevan (1991: 163). Here I follow Mahadevan's data which are presented in such a way as to enable a comparative analysis of the level of investments in the major princely states.

[73] RAB 1944–5: 27, 143–7.

[74] Letter from Prime Minister Hyderabad to Resident, 20.8.1946, in Hyderabad Trade Questions, L/P&S/13/1223.

[75] Correspondence in Hyderabad Trade Questions, L/P&S/13/1223. See also speech by Homi Mehta at first meeting of Board for Industrial Advice, Baroda, January 1945, in *Baroda Affairs (1943–8)* L/P&S/13/1008.

statement certainly does not apply to Travancore or Baroda, or even to Hyderabad which, admittedly, were among the major and allegedly more modern of the states. Long before Independence and their integration into the Indian Republic these states had established their own universities, banks and railways. Also, the three of them had succeeded in a separation of the judiciary from the executive, and of state funds from their princes' private purse. In terms of educational policy and rates of literacy, Travancore and Baroda were not only far ahead of Hyderabad, but also of the neighbouring British districts. Baroda introduced compulsory schooling and special educational facilities for backward castes at a time the British Indian Government was not ready even to consider such measures. Where the British in their territories left the development of private industry to its own devices, the governments of Baroda and Hyderabad took an active part in the industrialization process in a way that closely resembled the policies of the Japanse Meji Government.[76] Even though the results of these efforts were not always impressive, the states were no flies in amber. What remains to be seen is their political development in comparison to the constitutional reforms introduced in British India.

[76] See the interesting comparative study by Tripathi (1997).

2

Constitutional Developments in British India and the Princely States Before the 1930s

SEPARATE ELECTORATES IN BRITISH INDIA

AFTER THE suppression of the Mutiny, the East India Company was dissolved and power over the Indian territories was transferred to the British Crown. Very soon, with the Indian Councils Act of 1861, a modest system of consultation was introduced in the directly ruled British provinces. This Act recognized local needs and welcomed local knowledge by including a few Indians of the government's own choosing as Legislative Council members. Therefore, since 1861 an Indian element took part in the making of laws. However, the councils were legislative committees of the government and not the germ of responsible institutions. Also, all non-official members were nominated.[1]

After 1861 there was a slow introduction of the principle of elected representation, first at the level of district boards and municipal councils. Although Lord Ripon in his resolution on local self-government (1882) envisaged these bodies primarily as instruments of political and popular education, he also considered that 'in course of time, as local knowledge and local interest are brought to bear more freely upon local administration, improved efficiency will in fact follow'.[2]

In these cautious steps provision was made for the inclusion of a small number of Indians with administrative experience or social standing. The franchise, based on property qualifications, was extremely limited and there was no special provision for the representation of particular communities.

[1] Non-official members are members not employed by the government in any of its administrative services.

[2] ISC I 1930: 299.

At the same time an emerging national movement set out to unite and represent all people irrespective of communal distinction. A first Indian National Congress (INC) was held in 1885 and soon the Muslims, as the major religious minority, found themselves in a very strategic position. Whereas the colonial government tried to keep them from joining the national movement, the INC in an effort to woo their support proved ready to offer them protection and safeguards. At its Poona session (1889) the Congress even went so far as to adopt a resolution asking for a reservation of seats for religious minorities in proportion to their share in the total population. The formulation of these particular demands had little to do with socio-religious rights but reflected the political aspirations of the Muslim upper and middle classes.[3]

The Indian Councils Act of 1892 did not yet provide for any constitutional safeguard of minority interests. In official circles there was a strong body of opinion in favour of some form of communal representation, but the small size of the provincial councils made implementation impracticable. The new councils had a majority of government officials, and membership was only by nomination. Yet there was indirect election in so far as most of the non-official members were nominated on the recommendation of municipalities, district boards, universities and chambers of commerce. The functions of the new councils were more than merely legislative, as they had also the powers to discuss the budget (but not vote on it) and address questions to the executive.[4]

Constitutional safeguards to minorities in British India were first elaborated in the Morley-Minto reforms of 1909. These safeguards gave statutory recognition to communal representation by providing for separate electorates for the Muslim minority. They have remained a topic of debate ever since.

Most Muslims were still inclined to support the government. Nonetheless, they felt increasingly concerned about the loss of their former pre-eminence. The Muslim elite, especially in the United Provinces, formed a powerful group represented in land ownership and government service. That strong position, however, was steadily weakening and the Muslim share in the highest government ranks declined from 64 per cent in 1857 to 35 per cent by 1913, though still more than

[3] Chandra 1981: 253 ff.
[4] ICR 1918: 147; ISC I 1930: 116.

double their population share in UP.[5] When the demand for popular elections and political representation grew, it sounded 'the tocsin of alarm in Muslim minds',[6] especially because a property qualification for the right to vote would always place them in a minority position. Therefore, in October 1906 a deputation of Muslim 'men of property and influence' led by the Aga Khan waited upon the Governor-General Lord Minto at Simla and asked him for reservation of seats to be chosen by separate Muslim electorates. It may be true that the deputation and even the address submitted to Lord Minto were co-produced by a few individual British officials,[7] but the demand clearly reflected the interests of the Muslim upper class who claimed to represent the views of all Indian Muslims.

Nationalist historiography has emphasized the government's evident willingness to comply. Lord Minto informed the deputation that he was in favour of accepting their claim to representation not only commensurate with their numerical strength, but also with their political importance and the value of their contribution to the empire. He even acknowledged the usefulness of separate electorates, as 'any electoral representation in India would be doomed to mischievous failure which aimed at granting a personal enfranchisement regardless of the beliefs and traditions of the communities composing the population of this continent'.[8] From the nationalist point of view this emphasis on religious identity as an important political consideration was a clear case of divide-and-rule.

Not only the Muslim deputation but also the British felt greatly satisfied with the Simla meeting. Lady Minto recorded in her diary that her husband had achieved a feat of statesmanship pulling back 62 million Muslims 'from joining the ranks of the seditious opposition'.[9] In line with this way of thinking, the colonial government welcomed the formation of the Muslim League a few months later as a 'native opposition to the Congress'. Seen in this light, later claims that Lord Morley, the Secretary of State for India, 'reluctantly . . . accepted' the Muslim claim for separate electorates sound far from convincing.[10]

[5] Engineer 1997: 2109.
[6] Spear 1978: 226.
[7] Chand 1972: 398; Sarkar 1983: 141.
[8] Quoted in Chand 1972: 366.
[9] Quoted in Chandra 1984: 267.
[10] ISC I 1930: 118. Sir Harcourt Butler, chairman of the Indian States Committee, echoed the same official sentiment when he wrote in 1931 that separate electorates

In his discussion of the 1909 reforms Francis Robinson does not believe that the argument of divide-and-rule has much to offer. He argues that there was a strong movement of pressure and agitation among the Muslims which the government simply could ill afford to ignore. Yet, although there was no deliberate attempt to foster communal hostility, Robinson also concludes that British policy makers did need to divide Indian society in order to govern. Inevitably, the effect of their rule was the exacerbation of internal divisions and the establishment of a separate Muslim identity in Indian politics by 1909.[11]

Under the Indian Councils Act (1909) the reformed provincial councils lost their official majorities, and their number of non-official members, most of whom henceforth were directly elected, was raised.[12] Muslims had from two to four members in each council, based on their separate electorates, but could also join in the election for the non-reserved seats which was mainly by groups of local authorities, large landholders, trade associations and universities. As far as powers were concerned, the opportunities of influencing policy by moving resolutions and asking supplementary questions were increased, but the councils remained advisory bodies and did not have any administrative control.

The Morley-Minto reforms came as a great shock to the INC, which at its annual meetings strongly repudiated the principle of separate electorates as injurious to the development of national unity. In spite of that, the Congress was so eager to enlist Muslim support for the anti-imperialist struggle that in 1916, in a dramatic reversal of policy, it decided on conceding the League's demand for separate electorates in all provinces in accordance with fixed proportions (the Lucknow Pact). This momentous decision, taken at a time when councils were still of minor importance, was, until it was formally cancelled in 1928, to create serious embarrassment for the Congress at future discussions of electoral reform.

The grant of a separate electorate for Muslims brought the idea of a

---

for Muslims were granted 'as a result of very powerful representation from that community which converted even Lord Morley against his will' (Butler 1931: 69). Lord Minto's objections seem largely to have been based on electoral-technical considerations ISC I 1930: 185).

[11] Robinson 1974: 163–4, 348–9.

[12] The Madras Legislative Council had a total of 46 members: 20 officials and 26 non-officials (21 elected and 5 nominated), and the Bombay Council also numbered 46 members: 18 officials and 28 non-officials (21 elected and 7 nominated).

similar privilege to the forefront in the minds of all minorities who feared submersion in a self-governing Indian state. Subsequently, during the discussion of the Morley-Minto reforms, the condition of the Depressed Classes was also propelled into the political arena, but as yet without result. From this date the term 'untouchable' was first used in print and gradually came to replace the term Depressed Classes.[13]

THE PRINCELY STATES AND THE UDAIPUR DECLARATION (1909)

One of the major aims of political reform in 1909 was the rallying of loyal elements as a counterpoise to the INC. The most effective counterpoise at that moment were the Muslims. But another useful ally were the rulers of the princely states, cultivated as the most trusted pillars of the imperial edifice in the face of nationalist danger. Therefore Lord Minto decided on a change from the established policy of close supervision of the princely states as exemplified in the reign of his predecessor Lord Curzon. He entered into a political partnership with the princes by stressing a policy of non-interference in their states. In this he was strongly supported by a new Political Secretary, Sir Harcourt Butler,[14] a famous champion of the so-called 'Oudh aristocratic policy' in British India. That policy aimed at co-operation with the great landed proprietors who were seen as the natural leaders of the peasantry whose influence could be used to underpin British rule.

In his famous declaration at Udaipur (1909), Minto praised loyal Rajputana for remaining free of the poison of sedition scattered elsewhere. He went on to say that he had always been 'opposed to anything like pressure on Durbars with a view to introducing British methods of administration'. Reforms should not be imposed from outside but should emanate from Durbars themselves and evolve in harmony with the traditions and diverse conditions of each state. Minto reminded political officers that they held a position of peculiar trust and urged that they would 'do wisely to accept the general system of administration to which the Chief and his people have been accustomed'.[15]

[13] Galanter 1984: 25–6.

[14] Strictly speaking, Butler at that time was the Foreign Secretary, as the Political Department was created only in 1914 (see Chapter 1: A Note on the Sources).

[15] Quoted in Sever II 1985: 375–7.

Political reform might not be part of that system of administration and accordingly, the new provincial councils were not allowed to move any resolution on matters affecting princely states.

A new Political Department Manual, prepared for the guidance of Residents and Political Agents, instructed these officers not to interfere in matters between the ruler and subject and not to inspect the administration of the states except at the wish of the rulers. In his introduction to the manual, Butler stated as a general principle that 'unless misrule reaches a pitch which violates the elementary laws of civilization, the Imperial Government will usually prefer to take no overt measures for enforcing reform'.[16]

As a matter of course, the decision where and when these laws of civilization were violated remained reserved to the paramount power. The general thrust of the manual, often quoted as the *mantra* of the young political officer in the post-Curzon era, was that the officer should remember that 'often the best work he did was what he left undone'.[17]

Travancore: Early Legislative Arrangements

A policy of laissez-faire was most welcome to the princely states with their divergent local traditions and particular stages of development. In Travancore, Baroda and Hyderabad, the ruler was considered the fountainhead of all power, authority and justice. Travancore may be said to have held a special place among them: it had been dedicated to Sri Padmanabha and its ruler was in fact the regent of the deity and his throne was surrounded by an aura of sanctity. In daily political practice the Maharaja ruled through a Dewan, who was the head of the administration and took full responsibility for all government actions. In a situation like that reforms could only come as a grant from the king to his people.

As far back as 1883, the student elite of Travancore had been writing articles in periodicals published outside the state criticizing their own government for employing outsiders in preference to sons of the soil. One of them openly raised the question whether the people of Travancore were 'doomed to remain forever hewers of wood and

[16] Extract from Manual of Instructions to Officers of the Political Department of the Government of India, 1924, L/P&S/13/887 File 14(2).

[17] Barton 1934: 277; Ashton 1982: 44.

drawers of water to a clique of foreign officers'. By 'foreign officers' were meant Tamil and Maharashtrian Brahmins who staffed the administrative services. The writer exhorted his countrymen that they could never expect to gain any political influence 'unless the power of the aristocracy of Raos is destroyed'.[18] This implied a fight both against the existing power structure and the strong Brahmin element in it, recruited from outside.

To assuage these feelings of dissatisfaction the Maharaja passed a regulation to provide for the establishment of a Legislative Council (1888) which made Travancore the first princely state to introduce such an institution. The council numbered no more than eight members, of whom at least two were non-officials, all of whom were nominated by the Maharaja.[19] This council was a deliberative body for the purpose of making laws and regulations and had no administrative functions. It was never the Maharaja's intention to surrender the rights he had, but only to constitute a parallel authority to inaugurate legislation.[20] Reflecting the existing balance of power, the council in its early years met in the office of the Dewan.[21]

The Travancore Council was inspired by the Indian Councils Act of 1861, and later reforms were meant to frame this institution on the guidelines set by the Councils Act of 1892. The membership was gradually raised and in 1913 the council numbered fifteen members: eight officials and seven non-officials.[22] One of the rules laid down that previous sanction of the Dewan was required for all measures affecting the religion or religious rites and usages of any class of people. That particular rule was to remain in force and survived all changes later introduced in the Travancore legislature.

In spite of the importance of having at least some participation in the legislative process at that time, enlistment in the administrative services remained the overriding concern of Travancore's educated middle classes. In 1891 a Malayali Memorial was submitted to the

[18] Quoted in Suresh Kumar n.d.: 62.

[19] RAT 1887–8: 1.

[20] Later a vehement discussion on this subject erupted in the correspondence between the Dewan and Resident of Travancore. The Government of Madras finally acknowledged that the Maharaja had not abandoned his sovereign prerogative of legislation, but thought it imprudent for the Dewan to make any public declaration to that effect. See R/2(894/308) and R/2(894/310).

[21] Baak 1995: 116.

[22] RAT 1903–4: 8; Koshy 1972: 8.

Maharaja, complaining that '[t]he greatest number of appointments is held by foreigners and even among them the number held by Brahmins is more than double that held by the Sudras'.[23]

Asking the Maharaja for a fair share in government appointments for the local Malayali people, the memorial reflected the political aspirations of Nayars, Ezhavas, and Christians.

The Memorial raised for the first time a demand for jobs on the basis of the numerical strength of each caste. For that reason, Kumar calls this movement of the educated middle class for a larger inclusion in the higher grades of the services 'the first political movement of its kind' and even 'the birth of communal politics'.[24] The government responded by accommodating prominent Nayars in the bureaucracy, but that change of policy only served to make the exclusion of the Ezhavas more blatant. Therefore, it was followed by an Ezhava Memorial (1895), asking for the recruitment of more qualified Ezhavas to the services which became increasingly dominated not only by Brahmins but also by Nayars. This time also saw the emergence of several caste associations, the most well-known among them being the Ezhava SNDP Yogam (1903).

To afford his people a more direct opportunity of expressing their wants and wishes, the Maharaja favoured them with a Popular Assembly in 1904, largely meant to meet complaints of under-representation and divert a growing rivalry over what was felt to be an unjust distribution of government employment.[25] This assembly, presided by the Dewan, had no legislative powers at all and was primarily aimed at promoting understanding between the many castes and religious communities whose growing antagonisms were already causing the state much trouble. Although it assembled only one week a year, it formed an important political institution: all its members were non-officials, most of them elected, and it obtained the right to recommend, and thus indirectly elect, the non-official members of the Legislative Council.[26]

In 1914 membership of the Popular Assembly was raised to 100. The election of 77 members took place by constituencies based on taluks, town improvement committees, planters associations, mercantile and trading classes, and landlords paying a substantial annual land

[23] Quoted in Kumar n.d.: 63, see also Table p. 65.

[24] Kumar n.d.: 64, 71.

[25] Jeffrey 1976: 223.

[26] Koshy 1972: 18.

tax. There were no constituencies for castes or religious communities, but in order to ensure the representation of the large majority of disenfranchised, the government carefully spread the 23 nominated seats among Ezhavas, Latin Catholics, Muslims, Pulayas and other weaker sections of the population. In later years the number of nominations from backward castes was increased, Pulayas receiving 3 and, in 1917, 4 seats in the assembly.

Baroda: Starting from Local Administration

As in Travancore, the ruler of Baroda was seen as the source of all power. In the nineteenth century a legal department had been established in Baroda and the legal affairs of the state were directed by a Naib Dewan with the designation of Legal Remembrancer. In 1908, much later than in Travancore but far in advance of virtually all other princely states, a Legislative Council was inaugurated 'to advise His Highness' Government in the arduous task of legislation'.[27]

Much earlier, Baroda had started to develop a system of local administration meant to serve as the foundation for a larger representative framework. In these efforts the government tried as much as possible to leave the ancient system of village government unimpaired. After establishing village panchayats all over the state in the late nineteenth century, the Maharaja's government introduced the elective principle to them (1901), which was further elaborated by later Acts that made their constitution more liberal and extended their resources and powers. In 1904 the system of representative institutions was extended under a local self-government Act, which introduced *mahal panchayats* or district boards, representing groups of villages, and *prant panchayats* representing Baroda's main territorial divisions. Their membership was half elected and half nominated and of those nominated, half were ex-officio members and half representatives of minorities. The elected members of the *prant panchayats* came from the lower boards, including municipalities, and only at the time of World War II were the majority of the members elected on a wide franchise.[28]

Municipalities were granted the right of election in the same way under the Municipal Act of 1892, half their membership being nomi-

[27] BAR 1907–8: 18.

[28] *Gazetteer of Baroda* 1923: 225–9; BAR 1944–5: 18.

nated and half elected. Later Acts increased the elective element. In 1907 there were ten self-governing municipalities. Their powers were mainly in the field of public works, sanitation, education and relief measures. Hardiman is of the opinion that these municipalities and local boards had little effective power so long as they were starved of funds.[29] In 1907–8, Baroda city had indeed less than Rs 3 lakh to spend, but the *Gazetteer of Baroda* was not inclined to attribute the shortcomings of local administration to insufficient funds and pointed instead at a lack of civil responsibility among the representatives of the people.[30]

As a natural sequel to the elaboration of local boards and municipalities, the formation of a regular Legislative Council or *Dhara Sabha* was under discussion in Baroda from the beginning of the twentieth century and—as mentioned above—took definite form in 1908. In that year the legislative council rules were framed by proclamation of the Maharaja. The council that was instituted had a membership fixed at 17, 8 of whom were officials and 9 non-officials. Of the official members 4 were ex-officio members, including the Dewan as President of the Council, the *Sar Suba* or Revenue Commissioner and the Legal Remembrancer. The other 4 official members were appointed by the government from time to time from its principal officers.

'There has been a strong popular element in the Council since its inception, and this idea tends to increase', the *Gazetteer of Baroda* observed with hardly concealed satisfaction.[31] Of the 9 non-official members, however, 3 were nominated by government to represent interests that might otherwise remain unrepresented, like Muslims and Depressed Classes, and the remaining 6 members were chosen by the *mahal panchayats* or district boards from among their own members.

The new Council did not have much influence. It may have been 'endowed with potentialities of administrative power', as the Dewan declared at its opening session,[32] but these potentialities remained as yet largely unused. The majority of the Council consisted of officials and government nominees, and members had only the right of interpellation, moving resolutions and requesting permission for the introduction of Bills. All decisions were in the nature of recommenda-

[29] Hardiman 1978: 117.
[30] *Gazetteer of Baroda* 1923: 236.
[31] *Gazetteer of Baroda* 1923: 242.
[32] BAR 1907–8: iii.

tions to the Maharaja. Real power was vested in the hands of the Dewan and a small number of high officers who together constituted the Executive Council.

In the first decade of the twentieth century there was an extremist nationalist movement centred in Baroda city, which was largely organized by Brahmin nationalists from Maharashtra. They drew inspiration from the Bengali Aurobindo Ghose, a professor at Baroda College (1892–1906), who preached the doctrine of Hindu patriotism exhorting Hindus to reassert the ethics of their feudal past in order to throw-off the British yoke. These extremists organized small revolutionary bands of terrorists to operate within Gujarat, but had to discover that they lacked one vital element: mass backing.

Maharaja Sayajirao, however, had a soft spot for these Hindu patriots and for a long time tolerated their presence in his capital. The ruler of Baroda felt flattered by the laudable, if guarded references made to him by nationalists like B.G. Tilak and V.D. Savarkar and the speculations that an Indian king should head the nationalist movement. As a result, the local Residents suspected him to be in league with the extremist leaders and the Government of India was so apprehensive of his actions that even the slightest lack of tact was seen as a deliberate offence against the paramount power.[33] The British also took a strong dislike at his propensity to travel abroad and Lord Curzon thought he suffered from 'Wanderlust'. When Curzon visited Baroda in 1901, the Maharaja was in Europe.[34] The Political Department met this grave insult with the imposition of severe restrictions on his freedom to travel both in and outside India. In the end, the Maharaja had enough common-sense to distance himself from the extremists to save his throne. Yet the doctrines of a more militant Hindu patriotism remained popular amongst the Marathis of urban Baroda and were to flare up later in the riots of 1939.

Hyderabad: Mulki and Non-mulki Officers

In Mughal tradition the Muslim king was God's shadow on earth or *Zil Allah*. The same tradition prevailed in Hyderabad state but in a more syncretic way, different religions living together under a Muslim

[33] Hardiman 1978: 123 ff.; Gaekwad 1989: 184 ff.

[34] Fatesinghrao 1989: 185; Baroda Affairs 1930–43 in L/P&S/13/1007.

government.[35] Bills were based on Muslim jurisprudence and Hindu Shastras, with special laws binding on a particular community and, in addition, laws in force in British India were consulted. According to Leonard (1978a) the old Hyderabad politics were not pre-occupied with the existence of religious differences, but with the relations between *mulkis* (locals) and non-*mulkis* (outsiders). This *mulki* sense of a Hyderabad identity, irrespective of caste and creed, was continually threatened and reinforced by the large number of outsiders employed in government service.

Under the able leadership of its Prime Minister Salar Jung I (1853–83), the administration of Hyderabad was modernized to prevent the state from being annexed by the East India Company. As part of that modernization programme salaried revenue collectors were recruited from British India: Parsis, Hindus, and many Muslims from north India. Salar Jung viewed these non-*mulkis* as mere employees of the state and in order to preserve Hyderabad's Mughal political traditions and culture, he kept a careful watch to see that they remained separated from the court nobles.[36] Apart from that, only Hyderabadis were entrusted with important political responsibilities.

As in Baroda, the administrative modernization started from the bottom up. Municipal administration was first introduced in 1869 and a local board department was established in 1887. For administrative purposes the whole state, excluding the *Sarf-i-Khas* or Crown lands, was divided into four subas, Aurangabad and Gulbarga in Marathwada, and Medak and Warangal in Telengana, each under a Subadar (Commissioner). The four subas were further divided into 15 districts, each under a Talukdar (Collector), and at the beginning of this century 13 of these districts had their own district boards together numbering 182 members.[37]

In 1892–3 the sixth Nizam of Hyderabad, most probably stimulated by the promulgation of a Council Act in British India, issued a *firman* announcing the establishment of a Legislative Council. Recognizing the right of the people to share in the work of legislation and to representation, the council was empowered to make laws and to call for public opinion on any matter under consideration. In spite of this promising announcement, the council eventually numbered no more

[35] Pernau-Reifeld 1992: 84–5.
[36] Leonard 1978a: 69.
[37] *Gazetteer of Hyderabad* 1909: 51–66.

than six members, all of them leading officials of the main government departments with the Prime Minister as its President. Apart from that, the council had only nominal powers, also because the Nizam had immediately made clear that nothing in the council's regulations should in any manner prejudice the royal prerogatives in the field of legislation.[38]

The regulation establishing a Legislative Council was re-enacted in 1899–1900 as Act III of 1309 *Fasli*, the Hyderabad calendar. The council henceforth consisted of 19 members, of whom, besides the President and Vice-President, 11 were official and 6 non-official members. Of the 11 official members, the Chief Justice, the Judicial Secretary, and the Legal Adviser were ex-officio members, the remaining 8 official members being nominated by the Prime Minister. Of the 6 non-official members, 2 were elected by the landed aristocrats, 2 by the pleaders of the High Court, and 2 were nominated by the Prime Minister from among the residents of the state, of whom one must be from the *paigah* nobles. Membership was for two years, but retiring members were eligible for re-election.[39] Unable to initiate or reject legislation and with an electorate of less than 2,000 voters in a society with restricted freedom of association and expression, the council—in the words of Copland—was a sham.[40]

After the death of Salar Jung I the reorganization of the state was carried forward. Traditionally powerful groups found their positions reduced or abolished and their political power usurped. Urdu, associated with the Muslim community in north India, replaced Persian as the language of administration and the courts. This change, along with the local elite's slow acquisition of western education, further weakened the *mulkis*' opportunities for an official career.[41] From 1886 the Hyderabad Civil Lists showed a steady increase in the number of non-*mulkis* in prominent positions and by the turn of the century there was an unmistakable numerical domination making representation in the services a major political issue. Despite explicit instructions from the Nizam, the 1894 Civil List revealed that the number of non-*mulkis*

[38] RRC 1938: 5–6, 30; Leonard 1978a: 78.

[39] *Gazetteer of Hyderabad* 1909: 53. After that the Council underwent some further changes in composition till it got its final shape in 1905. The slightly different composition as reported by RRC 1938: 36 for 1905 might be due to small alterations introduced by successive *firmans* not affecting its basic structure.

[40] Copland 1988: 787.

[41] Leonard 1978a: 74–5.

among the 680 gazetted officers had increased to 447, whereas that of the Hyderabadis had decreased to 233. Inevitably, the tussle about definitions was not solved by government orders defining non-*mulkis* as a transitional category.

Slightly at variance with Leonard's central argument, the following chapters will elaborate the proposition that with Independence drawing near the *mulki* versus non-*mulki* issue was gradually subsumed by a larger Hindu-Muslim divide. The 1894 Civil List quoted above showed no more than 63 Hindus among the 680 gazetted officers, 20 of them being *mulki*.[42] In view of the large majority of Hindus in the state's population, this numerical disproportion presented aspiring leaders with a welcome opportunity to arouse Hindu consciousness of unjustified neglect.

PROVINCIAL AUTONOMY IN BRITISH INDIA (1919)

The changing conditions at the end of World War I asked for a further advance in constitutional reforms. On 20 August 1917 the newly appointed Secretary of State for India, Lord Montagu, defined in the House of Commons the object of his government's policy as 'the increasing association of Indians in every branch of the administration, and the gradual development of self-governing institutions, with a view to the progressive realization of responsible government in India'.[43]

This important declaration was followed up by a set of reform proposals formulated by Montagu and Governor-General Chelmsford. Their *Report on Indian Constitutional Reforms* (1918) considered separate electorates a hindrance to the development of self-governance. Nevertheless, the authors were strongly convinced that, in view of the pledges given, 'so far as the Muhammadans at all events are concerned the present system must be maintained . . . even at the price of slower progress towards the realization of a common citizenship'.[44]

This insistence on the continuation of separate electorates was at least remarkable, in view of the fact that Muslims—as well as Hindus—were divided among themselves. These internal divisions became poignantly manifest at the end of 1917, when Montagu and

[42] Leonard 1978a: 79–80.
[43] Quoted in Spear 1978: 185.
[44] ICR 1918: 149.

Chelmsford received no less than 44 Muslim deputations, each claiming to speak for the entire community.[45]

The Government of India Act (1919), the outcome of the Montagu-Chelmsford proposals, accepted the principle of direct election as the norm at all levels of political representation. However, the principle of communal electorates was extended more widely both in the centre and the provinces. In distributing the elected seats the subsequent Franchise Committee took the 1916 Lucknow Pact as its guide, with the important result that in several provinces Muslim representation in the new legislatives became considerably larger than its population ratio warranted. Separate electorates were also provided (although not contemplated by the Montagu-Chelmsford Report, which would have preferred nomination) for Indian Christians, Sikhs, Anglo-Indians and Europeans. In this way, in the Madras Legislative Council Muslims received 13 and Indian Christians 5 seats out of a total of 85 general elected seats. As usual, seats were also allotted to special electorates of landholders, universities and chambers of commerce.[46]

The new Act also introduced provincial autonomy by transferring a number of administrative functions to Indian ministers responsible to provincial Legislative Councils. These new councils were unicameral and triennial legislatures with extended powers to legislate subject to certain qualifications. At least 70 per cent of the members were to be elected and not more than 20 per cent were official members. Yet the number of electors remained small, only 2.8 per cent of the population. The executive remained outside the control of this elected non official majority.

As far as election was concerned, the subdivision of the electorate did not stop at the separation of Hindus from Muslims, Sikhs and Christians. Among the Hindus, non-Brahmins had been asking for a greater share of political representation and during the massive anti-imperialist upsurge after World War I their demand was recognized by the British with the same suspicious ease as the Muslim demand was in 1906. Within the general body of non-Muslims a minimum number of seats was reserved and allotted to the non-Brahmins who, though majority communities, might otherwise remain underrepresented. In Madras 28 of the 65 general non-Muslim seats were reserved for non-Brahmins as were 7 for Marathas in Bombay. This was done by

[45] Hasan 1984: 70.
[46] ISC I 1930: 144–5.

establishing multi-member constituencies where at least one of the candidates returned should have the 'reserved' qualification.

Besides elected and official members there remained a third category of members, the non-officials nominated by the Governor. These nominations were meant to secure a spokesman for a class or community which would otherwise go unrepresented or to fill an undesirable gap. Thus the Depressed Classes or untouchables achieved representation, not by reservation but by nomination, in the same way as the *Pulayas* and others were nominated to the Travancore Assembly. The Madras provincial council with 132 members had 23 nominated non-officials including 10 members representing the Depressed Classes. In the Bombay provincial council with 114 members, there were 9 nominated non-officials, 3 of whom were meant to represent the workers in organized industry.[47] Their number of seats increased following the findings of the Muddiman Committee in 1925.

As the Montagu declaration recommended the association of Indians in every branch of the administration, the Montford report devoted a separate chapter to the public services. The training of Indians was thought to be an urgent necessity. The spread of administrative experience among Indians would not only sober their judgement and lessen the burden of imperial responsibilities, but would eventually also 'provide India with the public men versed in the whole art of government'. Unfortunately, there were only a few Indians who had practical experience of the problems of administration, although the report mentioned the Dewans of princely states as distinguished exceptions. Therefore, it made the recommendation that a fixed percentage of the superior posts (33 per cent for the Indian Civil Service) should be recruited in India and that this percentage should be increased annually, the main reason being that 'We are no longer seeking to govern a subject race by means of the services; we are seeking to make the Indian people self-governing.'[48] This recommendation led to the appointment of the Royal Commission on the Superior Civil Services in India, which reported in 1924, and an increasing rate of Indianization. Nevertheless, the ICS numbered a bare 30 per cent of Indians in 1929.[49]

[47] The precise number of nominated official versus non-official seats varied from time to time, since the number of official members was usually less than the maximum laid down in the electoral rules (ISC I 1930: 134).

[48] ICR 1918: 205.

[49] ICS I 1930: 268–70.

THE PRINCELY STATES AFTER THE MONTFORD REFORMS

A special chapter of the Montford Report, re-examining the Crown's relations with what was called 'The Native States', opened with the acknowledgement that although under separate administration, British India and the Indian states were 'in fact, as well as by legal definition, one geographical whole'.[50] The existing relation between the Government of India and the states was described as one of union and co-operation. Yet, the report noted that there were several factors at work to bring the ruling princes into a still closer political relationship with the Government of India. First there was the war in which the states had rendered important services to the Empire in terms of men, material and money, making it perfectly clear 'that our quarrel is their quarrel'. Less forceful but more persistent was the process of growing uniformity by the employment of British Indian officials to revise and supervise the states' financial administration and agricultural organization, their adoption of British Indian systems of education and civil and criminal codes, and the increasing inter-connections across the subcontinent by the construction of railways and telegraphs. The wording makes clear that the process of integration was seen as largely one way.

Looking ahead, the report envisaged a picture of future India 'presenting the external semblance of some form of "federation"'. As a result of its earlier recommendations, the provinces would ultimately become self-governing units, held together by a central government dealing solely with matters of common concern to all of them, like defence, tariffs, railways and so on. The gradual concentration of the government on such matters was thought to make it easier for the princely states, while retaining the internal autonomy which they so eagerly cherished, to enter into closer association with the central government, at least if they wished to do so. However, no attempts to force the pace should be made; the authors of the report only wished 'to open the door to the natural developments of the future'.[51]

In order to strengthen that consciousness of common interests, the report made a very practical proposal, partly elaborating on suggestions considered by earlier administrations, especially those of Lytton and Minto. In previous years the princes had on various occasions met

[50] ICR 1918: 190.
[51] ICR 1918: 192.

in conference with the Viceroy to advise the Government of India on matters concerning the states generally. These meetings depended on the invitation of the Viceroy and at the 1916 meeting at Delhi the Maharaja of Baroda observed, on behalf of the princes assembled, that nothing would be more productive of harmonious relations than 'the establishment of a Council of Princes which will meet at regular intervals'.[52] The authors of the 1918 report now proposed to replace these informal meetings by the institution of a Council of Princes, meant to be a permanent, consultative and advisory body. That council should meet once a year to discuss an agenda approved by the Viceroy. The Viceroy was to become its president, but in his absence one of the princes would take the chair as elected chancellor.

The Council of Princes was free to discuss all questions affecting the Empire as a whole, or British India and the states in common, and its opinion was considered of the utmost value. Although the introduction of a permanent council would do away with the earlier policy of isolation that had been so rigorously imposed upon each state by the paramount power, the affairs of individual states, including their treaty rights, were excluded from discussion and remained the sole responsibility of the Governor-General-in-Council. At that time only the large states of Hyderabad, Baroda, Mysore and Kashmir dealt directly with the Political Department through their Resident, whereas the remaining states stood in indirect relationship with the department through the administration of the provinces to which they belonged. Bombay for instance was entrusted with the supervision of no less than 350 medium and small states. To prevent the more important states, like Travancore, from becoming subordinated to provincial governments that were to become responsible to the new legislative councils, it was recommended as a general principle to place them under the direct administrative control of the Political Secretary to the Government of India.

A major problem mentioned in relation to the states was their great diversity, from patriarchal and feudal to more advanced bureaucracies, with a few showing the beginnings of representative institutions. Future relations with the Crown, so the report suggested, would improve and the establishment of a Council of Princes be facilitated if clearer distinctions could be made between different kinds of rulers enjoying different powers of administration. Nevertheless, whatever

[52] Quoted in Chavda 1966: 159; Copland 1997: 35.

the particular status of a prince, nothing had precluded or was to preclude 'interference with the administration by Government through the agency of its representatives at the Native Courts'.[53] That interference might be required to prevent inhuman practices, to correct flagrant misgovernment, or to guide the hands of a weak or incompetent ruler. This chapter of the Montford report ended, however, on a hopeful note. It expressed the belief that the states would gradually be drawn into the orbit of the Empire and that the processes at work in British India, including the constitutional developments, would not leave them untouched; in time this would affect even the most conservative and feudal elements in them.

After completion of the Montford Report the Government of India asked the governments of the princely states for their opinion on those sections of the report that related to the position of the rulers of the states. The Baroda Darbar sent the Government of India a carefully worded reply, in which stress was laid on matters like the preservation of dignity, *izzat* and honour that were also mentioned in the Montford report. Apart from that, the note argued in favour of free intercourse with brother princes and British provinces on non-controversial subjects instead of always channeling them through the Residencies; it made a strong plea for the autonomy of the state with the least or no interference of the British government's representative in its internal affairs. According to Chavda earlier suggestions of the Baroda government had carried great weight in the formulation of the final proposals relating to the Council of Princes.[54]

The Travancore government too noted with grateful approval the explicit assurances that the rights, dignities and powers of the Indian rulers would be respected and maintained. Therefore, it did not want to raise any objection against the establishment of a permanent Council of Princes which was meant for consultative purposes. It expressed only a warning that what it called 'the popular element' in the proposed constitution for British India was 'not quite in harmony with the political relationship between the Government of India and the Princes' which were based on their own treaties and 'should

[53] ICR 1918: 193.

[54] Chavda 1966: 161–2. Sir Robert E. Holland, Political Secretary to the Government of India at that time, noted more in general that the recommendations made in Chapter X of the Montford report were largely based on suggestions put forward by the princes at Lord Chelmsford's request (Holland, The Indian States, 1925, Vol. II: Chapter IX, R/1/5/59).

remain unaffected by the constitutional changes contemplated in British India'.[55]

The Nizam of Hyderabad refused to have any association with the proposed council. He considered himself an honoured ally of the British Crown and not a subordinate partner. Therefore, he did not seek a more direct channel of communication with the Government of India through a Council of Princes where he could only meet other rulers whom he considered inferior.[56] He was also—fully in line with his brother princes—much concerned for the influence constitutional changes in British India might have on the population in his own state.

There was not the slightest reason for uneasiness, however, as the Montford Report clearly expressed the need for caution in this matter. The report acknowledged that after the great and important services rendered by the ruling princes during the Great War, 'it would be a strange reward for loyalty and devotion to force new ideas upon those who did not desire them'.[57] The doubts that may still have remained were finally removed by the Secretary of State who in 1919 pointed out in the House of Commons that measures of political reform suitable for British India might not be equally suitable for the different conditions in Indian states.[58] Whereas the Montford Report assumed that developments in India, if allowed to follow their natural course, might lead to a gradual convergence of administrative and constitutional arrangements, subsequent events showed that both Indias increasingly went different ways: whereas British India proceeded cautiously on the path of democracy, the majority of princes sought refuge in the principles of autocracy which they saw embodied in their treaties.[59]

In 1921 the Council of Princes, better known as the Chamber of Princes, was formally inaugurated at the Red Fort in Delhi by the Duke of Connaught. In his opening address the Duke, representing the King-Emperor, invited the assembled princes to take on a larger part of the burden of all-India governance and assured them that their

[55] Letter from Dewan of Travancore, M. Krishnan Nair, to British Resident, dated 24.8.1918, R/2(882/128).

[56] Richter and Ramusack 1975: 771; Copland 1997: 46.

[57] ICR 1918: 192.

[58] Letter from Government of India, Foreign and Political Department, dated 10.7.1919, R/2(883/136).

[59] Ashton 1982: 70. Ramusack 1978: 119 ff.

Plate 1: State entry into Delhi at Coronation Darbar: H.H. the Nizam of Hyderabad, H.H. the Gaekwad of Baroda and H.H. the Maharaja of Travancore passing the Jumma Masjid, December 1902 (by permission of the British Library, Curzon Collection 430/78 Nr. 52).

Plate 2: Inauguration of the Chamber of Princes by H.R.H. the Duke of Connaught at the Red Fort, Delhi, 1921 (by permission of the British Library, Harold Wilberforce-Bell Collection 1/17 Nr. 33).

rights and privileges would remain unimpaired.[60] To reflect their great variety in status within the princely order, 108 rulers of states entitled to eleven gun salutes or over received direct membership of the Chamber, while 12 additional members represented groups of smaller states. A standing committee with a chancellor and pro-chancellor was formed to settle current affairs and this small body maintained close ties with the officers of the Political Department.

As an instrument of imperial policy the Chamber turned out to be rather weak. The Viceroy, through his Political Department, remained firmly in control of all proceedings, determining the time of the sessions as well as the agenda. Decisions were not binding on the princes as a body or individually, and the discussions were held in camera. A proposal by the princes to open the sessions to the public in order to counter nationalist allegations that they were plotting against political reform in British India was for a long time held up by the Viceroy.[61] Last but not least, some of the most important princes refused to attend the meetings. Hyderabad belonged to the few major states which refrained from participation, and support from Baroda tended to be minimal because of its ruler's weak physical condition. Travancore also remained in the background but here, apart from prestige-based aloofness, geography also played a part, as the Chamber used to meet in Delhi.

We should however be careful not to overestimate considerations of prestige in explaining some of the larger states' wish to stay away from the Chamber of Princes. The princes were not merely immersed in an irrational preoccupation with status, they also had serious social, economic and political reasons to keep their distance. The Nizam, for instance, suspected the strong Maratha and Brahmin element in the Chamber's organization and its sympathy with the so-called Maratha revival, inspired from Poona, which threatened to affect the loyalty of his own Maratha subjects. When political conditions required, then, considerations of prestige were set aside. On the eve of the Second World War, with independence and federation drawing near, the standing committee of the Chamber was reorganized and in those circumstances states like Hyderabad and Baroda thought it important to have their individual representatives included.[62]

60 Copland 1997: 42.

61 Ramusack 1978: 134–5.

62 Richter and Ramusack 1975; ISC 1929: 20; see also Chapter 4 of this volume.

The 1919 Government of India Act included a provision for periodical parliamentary inquiries to examine the working of the reforms. To that purpose a Statutory Commission was appointed (1927), headed by Sir John Simon. The report it produced was a constitutional masterpiece, but its presence raised a political storm, mainly because an all-British commission was discussing India's future over the heads of the Indians themselves. As federation had become an important item on the political agenda, a representative group of princes asked the Viceroy at Simla in 1927 to appoint another committee to examine and clarify their relationship with the paramount power under the existing treaties. The result was the Indian States Committee under the chairmanship of Sir Harcourt Butler, whose all-white membership seems to have raised no protest.

Another reason for instituting the States Committee was the Nizam's claim, in respect of the management of all internal affairs, to stand on the same footing as the British Indian government. In a carefully worded letter to the Viceroy (1925), the Nizam had called the vexed question of the administration of Berar province 'a controversy between two governments that stand on the same plane without any limitation of subordination of one to the other'. Successive treaties had forced the government of Hyderabad to a permanent lease of Berar, but the Nizam had never relinquished his claim to its restoration; in the 1920s he wanted to re-open the issue. However, as the Nizam had dared to strike at the very essence of paramountcy, he received a strong reply from Lord Reading, reiterating the sovereignty of the British Crown, which meant that no ruler of an Indian state could justifiably claim to negotiate with the British government on an equal footing.[63] This concept of paramountcy was further elaborated by the Indian States Committee, which was to work largely along the lines indicated by Reading's correspondence with the Nizam.

The Committee spent most of its time in India, and visited 15 states in 1928, including Hyderabad and Baroda. In England the case of the princes was presented by Sir Leslie Scott, legal adviser to the Chamber of Princes, but Hyderabad, Baroda and Travancore, critical of Scott's

[63] Correspondence between Nizam and Viceroy, 1925–6, in Sever II, 1985: 413–19; see also Ashton 1982: 110–13, Bawa 1992: 111 ff., and Yazdani 1985: 29, 125 ff. Yazdani observes (p. 142) that Barton's successor, Sir Terence Keyes, took a more sympathetic attitude. He defended the Nizam by stating that the ruler had not claimed exemption from the operation of paramountcy but only claimed to relations different historically from those of other states.

scheme as impossible and his fee as excessive, preferred to state their own case in written replies to the questionnaire.[64]

The report of the States Committee was completed in February 1929 and contained several passages that must have greatly pleased the rulers of the Indian states. Most important among them was the clear statement that paramountcy rested in the Crown and not in the Government of India. As a consequence of that principle and of the history of paramountcy, the report laid down that the princes should not be transferred without their own agreement to a new government in British India responsible to an Indian legislature.[65]

In many other respects, however, the report evoked profound disappointment among the princes. Butler and his committee, following Lord Reading's letter of 1926, stated that the relationship between paramount power and states was not merely a contractual relationship, but a living one shaped by historical circumstances. Rejecting the more restrictive views expressed by Leslie Scott and other council, Butler concluded that rights and obligations in the relationship between states and paramount power not only arose from treaties, engagements and *sanads*, but also from usage, sufferance and other causes. The latter included the right of intervention by the paramount power as the report made unmistakably clear.[66] To make things worse, the paramount power, in Butler's view, was not only bound to protect a prince against all attempts to eliminate him; it was also bound to instruct a prince to remedy the legitimate grievances of his subjects and even to take such measures as would satisfy a popular demand for change without eliminating him. The princes expressed serious misgivings about this at the 1930 session of the Chamber of Princes, but Viceroy Irwin only promised to take up the matter of intervention after the Round Table Conference, the summoning of which had recently been announced.[67]

CONSTITUTIONAL DEVELOPMENTS IN THE STATES UNTIL THE 1930s

Baroda, Travancore and Hyderabad remained free to manage their own constitutional affairs. The paramount power adhered to its 1909 Udaipur policy statement and raised a protective umbrella above

[64] Ramusack 1978: 147.

[65] ISC 1929: 13, 32.

[66] ISC 1929: 23, 16, 29.

[67] Barton 1934: 280; Relations with the Indian States, Note by the Political Department, India Office, 26 July 1943, R/1/5/63.

them, to prevent them from being affected by the national-democratic fervour that was threatening their borders. Fully in line with Minto's Udaipur declaration, the manual of instruction for political officers, quoted above, stipulated that it was not the policy of the paramount power to give open encouragement to the grant of representative institutions by the rulers to their people.[68] Such a call for restraint was hardly necessary, as a widespread demand for responsible government had as yet not been raised. In its comments submitted to the Indian States Committee (1928) the Political Department observed that the people as a whole were little interested in the efforts of the few local intelligentsia to obtain political power and '[T]he latter can easily be won over by a prudent ruler who gives them employment in the State Service'.[69] That was exactly the way in which later Dewans of Travancore, especially Sir C.P. Ramaswamy Aiyar, were going to deal with political opposition.

It was only at the time of the First World War that some signs of modern political activity could be discerned in a few princely states, that is, about fifty years after corresponding developments in British India. The specific background to the formation of *praja mandals* (people's associations) in the states remains obscure, but they very much look like local manifestations not implanted from outside. The earliest *mandals* seem to have been founded in Mysore, Indore and Bhor between 1917 and 1921. As Handa suggests, the Baroda *praja mandal* may have been the first such body in an Indian state.[70] At its 1938 session the President of the Reception Committee stated that this association was established in 1916. Its three main objectives, he cited, were the creation of unity by co-operation, the submitting of wants and grievances of the Baroda people to the officers of the state, and the work for responsible government under the aegis of the Maharaja.[71] Handa is enthusiastic about the *mandals*, but Copland (1985), writing in a more sober mood, reminds us that in the mid-1930s the *praja mandals* existed only in a handful of states and had few active members. Following the assessments of prominent nationalists in

[68] Note by Political Department (P.J. Patrick) on Representative Institutions of Government in Indian States, 1929, in L/P&S/13/886.

[69] Precis of Political Secretary's opinion placed before the Indian States Committee, no date (1928), in R/1/1/4673(1).

[70] Handa 1968: 89.

[71] Sessions of the *Praja Mandal* meetings 1928–39, Confidential File No. 129 HPO Baroda.

British India, he concludes that the vast majority of princely subjects in the 1930s were loyal and submissive.

We should keep in mind that it was not easy for people in the states to initiate political activity. Their freedom of press, speech and political association was severely restricted. Therefore, most work, out of necessity, had to be done outside and for that purpose different *mandals* joined hands in the formation of regional organizations like the Deccan States Conference and the Kathiawad States Conference.[72] Banned from the states' territory and existing largely on paper, they cannot have made a great impact.

Following on these modest beginnings, in 1927, an overarching organization called the All-India States Peoples' Conference (AISPC) was established in Bombay to co-ordinate the work of the local *praja mandals*. Its chief aim and object was formulated as the attainment of responsible government for the people under the aegis of their rulers, and a federal structure as the constitutional basis for *swarajya*. Other, more or less obvious, items high on the agenda were the separation of state revenue from the personal expenditure of the ruler and the establishment of an independent judiciary, separate from the executive, reforms lacking in the majority of states. The AISPC drew much strength from the Servants of India Society (Poona)[73] and was active especially among the Deccan, Gujarat and Rajputana states with some attendance from Travancore and other parts of India.

One of the reasons to build an all-India organization out of the diverse and still hesitant local associations was the wish to place the peoples' case before official authorities like the Simon Commission, which was also considering proposals for a federation of provinces and states.[74] At the second session of the AISPC (Bombay 1929) a resolution, forwarded by D.L. Purohit from Baroda and G.G. Shimoga from Hyderabad, strongly condemned the Butler Committee for consulting the princes but neglecting the people of the states. However, to the great dismay of the AISPC, the Simon Commission did not care for their organization, and Butler and his Committee refused it a hearing. Therefore, resentment at being excluded from all political

[72] Handa 1968: 122.

[73] For the AISPC's organizational preparations and relations with the Servants of India Society, see Abhyankar and Trivedi 1928. All AISPC conferences are extensively documented in L/P&S/13/554. See also Phadnis 1968: 84 ff.

[74] Copland 1985: 122.

consultation and the constitutional progress going on in British India played a major part in the establishment of a central organization. The AISPC expressly stated that it did not want to convert the states into British provinces: 'How can any people wish to exchange indigenous for foreign rule?', one of its presidents asked. Instead, for both British and Indian India constitutional government was upheld as the chief objective. In the states that aim should be attained by the introduction of responsible government for the people through representative institutions under the aegis of the rulers. The Montagu Declaration of 1917, it was claimed, included in its ambit all India and not just British India. This open threat to the absolute sovereignty of the rulers became even more serious by a call for co-operation with political organizations in British India in devising a new constitution for the whole country.[75]

The call for co-operation with organizations in British India strengthened the suspicion among the princes and the British that the AISPC was merely the states' wing of the Indian National Congress (INC); and it was treated accordingly. The AISPC's own self-image was more of an independent counterpart to the INC. In a letter addressed to the Political Department it wrote), 'the [A]ISPC represents seventy five million subjects of the Native States of India and possesses the same status in the Indian States as the INC possesses in British India'.[76]

In its organizational set-up the AISPC closely followed the model established by the INC. The latter's active co-operation was indeed perpetually sought, but to a large extent, the history of the AISPC was occupied by its unsuccessful attempts to induce the INC to render help and assistance to the people of the states in their struggle against princely autocracy. The INC lent moral support, but steadfastly refused to commit men or money to that cause. We will return to that important issue in the next chapter.

The real influence of the AISPC on the people it claimed to represent can only be guessed. Data on the number of people of the states attending the conferences are not always available, or else lack credibility. Apart from that, the AISPC was not the only body in the field and similar though weak attempts were made in other regions. As

[75] Report on the first and second session of the AISPC, Bombay, 17/18 December and 25/26 May 1929, in L/P&S/13/554.

[76] Letter AISPC to Political Department, 2.7.1931, in L/P&S/13/554.

far as local political interest is concerned, Handa asserts that the 1920 non-cooperation had sent a wave of enthusiasm among the states.[77] The general tone of the AISPC sessions however, was one of disgust at the poor response received from the local people, and several AISPC leaders acknowledged that local sentiment and loyalty to the rulers, however undeserved, were still strong. In view of the strict ban on all AISPC activities within the states, the organization had virtually no room to mobilize people for change. The AISPC's main function may well have been to lend its leaders the political respectability needed to claim participation in discussions about the future of India.

Travancore: Nayar Predominance

The princely states remained free to go their own ways. Travancore used this relative freedom to remodel the Legislative Council in several stages till it got its final shape in 1921. The maximum strength was raised to 50 members. There was to be a non-official majority of 35 members, 28 of whom were elected by constituencies based on revenue divisions (23) or special constituencies of planters, landlords, commerce and industry, etc. (5). The franchise was considerably broadened and extended to women, yet the number of people entitled to vote was only somewhere between 2.5 per cent and 3 per cent of the population.[78]

The Dewan of Travancore had informed the British Resident that the political reforms intended to follow the lines adopted in British India,[79] but with the right to discuss the budget, move resolutions and ask questions, the Travancore council had considerably less power than the Montford councils in British India. The most important difference was the absence of any provision for communal electorates or seat reservation. The only comfort for communities who felt unjustly deprived of representation was the possibility that the government might nominate one of their number to the remaining seats. Nomination to the Popular Assembly was another way to redress the communal balance, but the assembly lost its right to recommend members for the council and, without legislative powers or constitu-

[77] Handa 1968: 124.

[78] RAT 1921–2: 39; TPPP 1934: Chapter I.

[79] Letter by Dewan N. Krishnan Nair, to Resident H.L. Braidwood, dated 20.11.1918, R/2(883/136).

tional basis, it failed to satisfy the growing demand for political participation.

As the franchise qualification was mainly based on registered landed property, it was especially favourable to a community like the Nayars. They were evenly spread over the state and the partition of their matrilineal estates had increased the number of land-owners, although their holdings were small and often mortgaged to Syrian Christians. The Syrians, actively involved in plantation industries, banking and general business, were concentrated in a few northern divisions and could count on getting only a small number of seats. Other large groups like the Ezhavas, Muslims and other backward castes, could hardly hope to get representation on their own voting strength. This discrepancy was still compounded by agriculture, the domain of the Nayars, contributing only 17.6 per cent to the state's income in 1931, whereas the revenue from commercial activities had gone up to 34.7 per cent.[80]

In consequence, the Travancore Legislative Council after 1921 was controlled by Nayars, who numbered 16 per cent of the population but held the large majority of the 23 elected seats. Christians, including Syrians and the new converts of the Catholic and Protestant mission, numbered 32 per cent of the population but held only between 4 and 7 seats, and the other communities none or only 1. After the Malayali Memorial Nayars had come to dominate the administrative services, and this imbalance in the opportunity structure was greatly resented by the Christians, Ezhavas and Muslims. Political parties had as yet not emerged, apart from the shadowy existence of a Congress District Committee since 1919, and class distinctions had not crystallized. Therefore, prominent members of these communities articulated their resentment by appealing to ascribed identities of caste and religion to mobilize support.

Early in the 1920s leaders of the underprivileged communities gained a first major victory. No longer ready to acquiesce in their exclusion, they had organized a Civil Rights League to campaign for the opening of the public administration to all castes and creeds (1919). As the Land Revenue Department was also entrusted with the management of temples and temple properties, this combined responsibility offered the government a ready excuse to debar non-Hindus and impure lower castes from admission into the ranks of this most important department. After several memorials and an interview with the Dewan had

[80] Kusuman 1976: 25.

produced no result, a first breach in this high caste bastion was finally made in 1922. Under pressure from especially Syrian Catholics and Ezhavas, government finally acquiesced in a separation of temple management from the Revenue Department, thus removing the ritual barriers that had until then prevented all but the high-caste Hindus from entering this part of the services.[81]

This measure did not really improve the situation and Brahmins and especially Nayars with their long tradition of literacy and government service continued to control official employment. Ten years later, an official enquiry showed that Nayars still accounted for more than half of all official appointments. Out of a total of about 16,000 superior posts in the services Nayars held 8,000 and Brahmins 2,500 as against 600 for Ezhavas and 291 for Syrian Catholics.[82] This uneven distribution of appointments gave rise to the demand that all communities should have proportional representation in all services.

The government land policy was also not particularly suited to remove feelings of alienation among large segments of the population. In 1926 news leaked out that the government was carrying on negotiations with Brooke Bond & Co. on the sale of 2,50,000 acres of land for the production of tea. The Dewan defended this policy by stressing Travancore's urgent need of foreign capital for its economic development, but he did not succeed in setting the country at ease. The Maharani, speaking for the young Maharaja, feared that a deal with Brooke Bond might strengthen local political opposition, 'influenced by the nationalist theories in neighbouring British territories', and the fully elected Popular Assembly was outraged by the suggestion that the Travancorean economy needed the lead of British capitalists. Local planters, most of them Syrian Christians, were making steady headway in the production of tea and rubber, but had to cope with insufficient amounts of land and high rates of land revenue. Thus, the assembly appealed to the government to create equal opportunities for local enterprise and to refrain from signing away large parts of land which in the course of time might be improved by the people themselves.[83]

[81] HFMK II 1972: 289; Jeffrey 1981: 278.

[82] More detailed figures are to be found in *Census of Travancore* 1932 I: 329 ff., TPPP 1934: 20 and HFMK II 1972: 337, but the best source remains TPSRC 1934: 120.

[83] All information for this paragraph has been derived from the file 'Brooke Bond Proposal', R/2(884/163). The case is more fully discussed in Kooiman 1992: 67 ff. and Baak 1993: 85 ff., 1995: 136 ff.

In the end, the Brooke Bond scheme was cancelled, but resentment about the uneven distribution of political and economic privilege only increased.

From the 1920s the main thrust of the struggle against unequal opportunity structures was leveled at the question of legislative reform around which the educated intelligentsia pooled their resources to fight against the political status quo. For this fight they had to rely on their own, as there was hardly any support from outside. In 1928 a Kerala Provincial Congress Conference, held in the neighbouring British district of Malabar, called for the establishment of responsible governments in princely states. The constitution of the INC however, did not permit its provincial wing to interfere in the internal affairs of Travancore and Cochin. One year later a similar demand for a responsible government was raised at the first session of a South Indian States People's Conference. This conference was held in Travancore, but the organization seems to have been short-lived.[84]

Baroda: Patidar Contentment

The total number of members of the Baroda Legislative Council was raised to 26 in 1915–16 and 29 in 1929–30. This increase did not affect the distribution of seats among the different categories of members, but only meant that the number of official members expanded to 15 and that of the nominated non-official and elected members to 4 and 10. The number of ex-officio members could fluctuate, mainly depending on the number of royal princes available for membership.

When in 1926 the council asked for an extension of its powers, the Maharaja convened a State Darbar and told those present that he had introduced earlier reforms of his own free will, and would continue to do so in future, at the appropriate time. In private discussion he added that his people would deserve further reforms when they were more progressive.[85]

For the time being the Dewan remained the centre of administration. He was responsible solely to the Maharaja, and only questions above his individual powers were referred to the Executive Council for disposal within the powers given to it. In the 1920s the Executive consisted of the Dewan as president and four or five other members

[84] Kumar n.d.: 113, 125, 127; Handa 1968: 283.
[85] Sergeant 1928: 194–5.

entrusted with legal, judicial and revenue duties. A more fundamental change of Baroda's Legislative Council had to wait for the new constitution of 1940.

There was, however, one important change in the way members for the 10 general seats were elected. From the inception of the council, members for these elected seats were returned by constituencies corresponding to the *mahal panchayats* or district boards. These boards did not function in a satisfactory way and in 1928 they were abolished. So government had to consider the determination of new constituencies, and in 1931–2 it laid down that the larger *prant panchayats* or division boards were to elect council members, who, on its recommendation, were to be nominated by the government. The *prant panchayats* of the Baroda and Mehsana division got the right to recommend 3 members each and the *prants* of Navsari and Amreli/Okhamandal, each 2.[86] This meant that the popular element in the council was not increased but weakened, as election made way for recommendation and the constituencies were further removed from the people.

The *prant panchayats* were largely the domain of the Patidars, the dominant Gujarati landed proprietors. Insisting on the importance of their interests, they had utilised the new electoral opportunities by capturing more than their due share of seats in the division boards and other representative bodies. In 1931 Patidars, numbering one-fifth of the population, held more than half the number of elective seats in the *prants* (53 of the 102). Only in Okhamandal, Baroda's port-city on the western tip of Kathiawad, Patidars had to give pride of place to Brahmins and Banias, who, numbering 9 per cent of the population, together held a fourth of all elective seats (26 of the 102). The Baroda census noted that this was achieved without much ill-feeling on the part of the non-represented sections, although Brahmins and Banias felt not altogether happy about losing some of their old monopolies and artisan groups began to resent the social ascendancy of the Patidars in the villages.[87] Continuing acceptance of Patidar dominance of the *prant panchayats* perhaps also had to do with the limited influence of the members of these bodies. In 1937, members complained that they were not heard and that officials were completely in command of all affairs.[88]

[86] BAR 1931–2: 20.

[87] *Census of Baroda* 1932 I: 411.

[88] 14th session Baroda State *Praja Mandal*, Visnagar, March 1937, in Sessions of the *Praja Mandal* meetings, 1928-39, HPO, Confidential File No. 129.

Before the 1930s attempts to organize political protest movements in Baroda on lines similar to those in British India were never a great success. The landowning cultivators were in complete command of the situation in the countryside as can be seen from the aborted satyagraha in Petlad district. In 1924 some Gandhian sympathisers tried to launch a satyagraha against the Baroda government over an unexpected raise in land revenue. This campaign came to the notice of the Baroda *praja mandal*, which was largely an organisation of urban intellectuals, many of whom were Gujarati Brahmins. They readily offered their leadership over the Petlad campaign as a way to extend their movement to the countryside, but had to face the fact that they were rather powerless as they lacked support amongst the peasantry. The movement soon petered out.

Hardiman (1978), in describing this satyagraha, explains its failure by pointing at the structural alliance between government and landholders on which the Baroda state actually rested. The vital support of the landed elites was obtained by regular reductions in land revenue and state officials were always sensitive to peasant demands. On the other hand, the peasant elites enjoyed considerable influence in the state bureaucracy and its representative institutions and had more to win from subtle dealings behind the scenes than from outright confrontation. Therefore, Hardiman concludes, the Petlad Patidars had no need for Gandhian satyagraha, the weapon of those who lacked influence in society.

In the end government acquiesced in waiving its right to collect the increase in revenue in Petlad, even though it did not make a public statement to that effect. This flexible stand cut the ground from under the *mandal* leaders' feet. After 1924 the *praja mandal* returned to the shadows, holding its annual conferences and almost ritually passing resolutions demanding reductions in the land revenue and income tax, the uplift of the backward and a ban on the use of liquor.

At the 1928 session of the Baroda *praja mandal* in Petlad, the question of constitutional reform stood high on the agenda. The President, D.L.Purohit (also active in the AISPC), gratefully cited the Maharaja's benevolence shown by the introduction of compulsory education and local self-government. But he went on to say that the people of Baroda were now longing for a government chosen by its own elected representatives, as was the case in the British provinces. Quoting profusively from Spinoza, Locke—and not to forget the *Manusmriti*—he argued that good government was no substitute for self-government and formulated several proposals for the extension of the membership and powers of the *Dhara Sabha* or Legislative Council. Unfortunately for the *mandal*, the Dewan refused to meet the delegation formed to discuss these proposals with the government.

At the same Petlad session the President observed that people in Baroda were not living in British India dominated by foreigners but in an Indian state ruled by fellow-brethren. Then, referring to the high number of Maharashtrians in the administration, he raised this question: 'how is it possible that people who do not belong to Baroda should carry on the administration?'[89] That question was to become a major theme in the years to come.

Hyderabad: Muslim Rule under Attack

As we have seen, all authority in the state of Hyderabad was centred in the Nizam. Since 1892 there was a Legislative Council, but the extension of its membership and powers was extremely slow. The British Indian government, though never relinquishing its formal right of intervention, refrained from any pressure on the Nizam's government to introduce more responsible forms of administration. That policy yielded important results. During World War I Hyderabad sided with the British and the Allied Forces against the Turkish Sultanate and proved itself a faithful ally. Yet, the political alliance with Hyderabad seemed to have been more highly valued than the modernization of its government.

From an early date, the British had been able to establish their influence on the appointment of the Prime Minister. As a consequence the Nizams usually had a strained relationship with the chiefs of their administration whom they never fully trusted. Therefore, the strong autocracy of Hyderabad was permanently infested by what Pernau-Reifeld has called a *Dualismus an der Spitze,*[90] or a split at the top. That strained relationship became manifest soon after the last Nizam, Mir Osman Ali Khan, assumed power in 1911. Drawing strength from the imperial partnership proclaimed by the Udaipur declaration and the emergency created by World War I, he decided to break the power of officialdom embodied in the person of the Prime Minister. After the

[89] Sessions of the *Praja Mandal* meetings 1928–39, HPO, Confidential File No. 129.

[90] Pernau-Reifeld 1992: 64.

resignation of Salar Jung III he did not appoint a new Prime Minister but decided to take the administration of the state into his own hands (1914). At that time the Residency did not object. A few years later the Nizam, flattered by the title 'His Exalted Highness', tried further to strengthen his grip on the state administration by selective appointments. But whereas Ashton emphasizes that he wanted to replace Hindu and British officials by Muslims, Yazdani only stresses the ruler's wish to surround himself by people whom he personally trusted.[91]

When the war was over Lord Chelmsford, the Viceroy, in a personal interview with the Nizam, told him that the experiment to rule without a Prime Minister had been a costly mistake. Thereupon, the Nizam was obliged to accept a constitutional scheme which transferred the principal duties of government not to a new Prime Minister but to an Executive Council presided over by a Prime Minister. That council, established in 1919 'for the good government of the State',[92] consisted mainly of officials, with non-*mulkis* holding the most important positions. Sir Ali Amin, a former member of the Viceroy's Executive Council, became the new Prime Minister.

In the same year the Nizam asked by *firman* for 'a thorough and complete investigation of the conditions most favourable to the enlargement of the Legislative Council and the expansion of its usefulness', including a substantial introduction of the elective element combined with effective protection of minorities.[93] The British Indian government followed these cautious steps towards reform with great interest, but refrained from open encouragement. In 1920 the Political Department asked the Resident to report on the constitutional situation in Hyderabad, but insisted that recourse should be had to information already available at the Residency and that the Nizam should not be disturbed by direct enquiries on this subject.[94] In pursuance of the Nizam's *firman*, the Prime Minister was authorized 'to collect all necessary materials on which a liberal scheme for the attainment of the above mentioned objects may be based'.[95] For that

[91] Ashton 1982: 84; Yazdani 1985: 79–80.

[92] RRC 1938: 33.

[93] Quoted in RRC 1938: 33.

[94] See file R/2/70/76 on Constitutional Reforms in the Hyderabad State, especially letter from Foreign and Political Department, New Delhi, to Lennox Russell, Resident Hyderabad, 10.1.1920.

[95] RRC 1938: 33.

purpose Mr. Rai Balmukund was appointed and in 1921 he submitted a detailed report suggesting that the Legislative Council be enlarged on the Morley-Minto model in British India. But before his proposals could be considered Ali Imam retired from service and his proposals (as well as some other reports) with recommendations were shelved.[96]

The experiment with the Executive Council failed and the effect of this British intervention soon wore off. In 1925 a new British Resident was appointed, William Barton, who earlier had served as Resident in Baroda and Mysore. Barton attributed that failure basically to the ruling prince who continued to interfere with the proceedings of the Executive Council. The personal machinations of the Nizam had reduced the council, in the words of Barton, to mere constitutional camouflage designed to screen the arbitrary acts of the ruler who represented 'the most complete absolutism in history, an absolutism untempered by fear of danger from without or within'. On his arrival the Resident found that the Executive Council had practically ceased to function. As a result the estrangement between the Nizam and his nobles and subjects had increased, oppression and corruption were rampant everywhere and the wide-spread sale of appointments was infecting the services with corruption.

In a rather personal tirade against the Nizam, Barton added that the prince's rapacity in the collection of *nazars* had been growing with the years and was 'now border[ing] on insanity'. Hindus had to bear the brunt of that rapacity, as they made up the larger part of the peasantry and ultimately had to make good the contributions by officialdom to the ruler. The severe criticism of the ruler and the quite unflattering comments on his character are remarkable for a Resident who had just arrived at his post. Perhaps they have to do not only with personal incompatibility but also with Barton's local but unnamed informants among whom we suspect a large number of discontented and dispossessed nobles eager to intrigue.

A final factor explaining the existing state of misrule according to Barton's memorandum was the decline in the prestige and the influence of the Residency. Barton observed that his predecessor, Sir Lennox Russell, had adopted an attitude of comparative detachment to many of the existing abuses and adhered to the view that existing treaties forbade interference. Several years later, the same

[96] SFHS 1938: 3; Bawa 1992: 93.

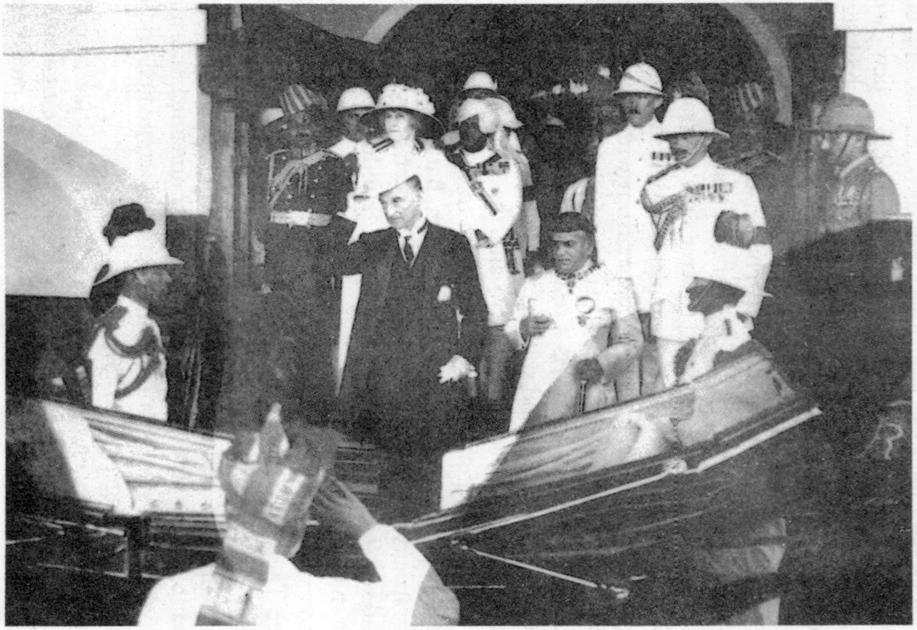

Plate 3: Visit of Lord and Lady Reading to Baroda: the Viceroy and the Gaekwad of Baroda getting into the state carriage, January 1926 (by permission of the British Library, Reading Collection 10/11 Nr. 4).

Plate 4: Lord Reading's visit to Hyderabad: Darbar at Chow Mahalla Palace with Viceroy and Nizam seated in the centre, 1923 (by permission of the British Library, Reading Collection 10/7 Nr. 10).

criticism was levelled in the political notebook prepared by the local Residency.[97]

As may be inferred from this summary of his secret note, Barton made a strong case for another intervention. After consultations with the Viceroy and the Political Secretary (May 1926) his recommendations were largely accepted. The Nizam, already hurt by Reading's March 1926 letter on the Berar issue, was forced to appoint an efficient president and Executive Council, to acknowledge the independent responsibilities of that council, and to appoint one member of the council, the Director-General of Revenue and the Director-General of Police from among the British officers nominated by the Political Department in Delhi. Barton had succeeded in convincing the Viceroy that intervention would have no evil effects on Muslim opinion in India, provided that it was made clear that it was not intended to prejudice the system of personal rule in general and that of the Nizam in particular.[98] Bawa asserts that the new appointments were welcomed by the population at large.[99]

One of these British officers was Sir Theodore Tasker, who became Revenue and Police Member of the Executive Council (1928–42). Whereas the Nizam resented his presence as an infringement on his royal prerogative, Tasker in his confidential diary argues that the Nizam himself, by his persistent failure to rule in the spirit of the 1926 arrangement, made continuation of the British in key positions inevitable for the full twenty years. Tasker also testified to the wide gulf between palace and council as it became manifest in the process of decision-making. Departmental proposals that had received the council's recommendation were sent up as a formal Urdu *arazdasht* (petition) to the Nizam's *Peshi* Office over which the council had no control. 'It was at this unpredictable stage that intrigue had its opportunity. One member of council described the Nizam as "the permanent opposition".'[100] For British officers, that lack of control,

[97] Memorandum from W. Barton, Resident Hyderabad, 11.12.1925, R/1/1/1465. *Hyderabad Political Notebook*, Vol. II, 1945: 6, in Lothian Papers, Mss. Eur. F 144 Nr. 63. Russell had been forced to retire when it came to light that he had been showing the Nizam his confidential official correspondence, Copland 1997: 51.

[98] Barton's Memorandum, 11.12.1925, and recorded discussions between Viceroy, Barton and Political Secretary, in the Viceregal Lodge, 8 and 11 May 1926, in R/1/1/1465.

[99] Bawa 1992: 117.

[100] Tasker's introduction to his confidential diary, kept when Member of the Hyderabad Executive Council, Mss. Eur. D 798, Vol. 6. The *Peshi* was the Nizam's personal adviser at the palace.

compounded by the high degree of unpredictability of a self-willed monarch, was difficult to stand, as their reports clearly show.

PRELIMINARY ASSESSMENT

Looking back on this brief discussion of constitutional reforms we may conclude that systems of political participation, election and communal representation were introduced in British India much earlier and on a much larger scale than in the princely states. Especially after World War I and the introduction of partially responsible government in the British provinces, the two Indias grew apart. Nevertheless, the progress made by highly literate states like Travancore and Baroda was not inconsiderable. From an early date they had their own representative institutions and in that respect they were quite exceptional: the only other state to institute a Legislative Council which could be compared with those in British India was Mysore (1907).[101] Even so, the powers of these councils remained limited and served to soften rather than reduce the royal absolutism that was still predominant.

The councils in Travancore and Baroda had a non-official majority and even included a substantial number of elected members, although their election in Baroda was only indirect. As a result of the limited franchise, the councils in these states largely reflected the existing power structure with Nayars and Gujarati Patidars dominating the elected seats in the representative institutions. In Travancore, this dominance evoked increasing resentment among the less privileged in society, whereas in Baroda the under-represented sections were as yet more prepared to accept the existing situation.

In Hyderabad, reform was extremely slow with the Legislative Council firmly in control of an official membership and local people left with hardly any influence on its composition. Though the question of reform was taken up for consideration, the authorities, faced with a large Hindu majority in the population, shrank from attempts to make the council more representative. Proposals for the introduction of the elective principle were shelved. An important point to note, in view of the questions raised in the first chapter, is that none of these Indian states had provided for separate electorates, neither for Muslims nor for other communities.

Another notable difference with the situation in British India was

[101] For a discussion of constitutional developments in Mysore, see Manor 1978: 24 ff.

employment in the public services. The Montford report and the ensuing Civil Service Commission (1924) had recommended a gradual Indianization of the services which, however slow, placed Indian interests against those of Europeans along a nationalist dividing line. Within the states that process was more complicated with other Indians, often perceived as outsiders, dominating the official bureaucracies. In Travancore Nayars had succeeded in breaking the virtual monopoly of foreign Brahmins only to establish their own grip on the services which they eagerly guarded. Here, rivalry for entry into the services had already started around the beginning of the twentieth century. In Baroda as well as in Hyderabad the voice of protest against outside dominance was raised much later, mainly in the 1920s, while in Hyderabad agitation against the so-called non-*mulkis* was compounded by the growing division between Hindus and Muslims.

3

Baroda, Travancore, and the Question of Separate Electorates

A NEW CONSTITUTION FOR BRITISH INDIA

THE LONG and arduous process of political devolution in British India, marked by the installation of the Indian Statutory Commission and the Round Table Conferences in London, resulted in the Government of India Act of 1935. In spite of Congress opposition the 1935 Act accepted communal representation and assigned it a firm place in the new constitution, both in the legislature and in the public services. Thus the number of separate electorates for Muslims and other minority communities were not only maintained but even extended.

The Depressed Classes, treated as untouchables, received no separate electorates, in spite of the promise held out by the Communal Award of August 1932. Criticized as another expression of divide-and-rule, the British had then declared themselves ready to grant that privilege. The INC insisted on an amendment of the award in consultation with the minority communities concerned, but Gandhi emphatically rejected it. Fearing that the grant of a separate electorate for the lowest Hindu castes would only serve to perpetuate the evil of untouchability and divide the nation, he started his fast unto death. After hectic deliberations with B.R. Ambedkar, leader of the 'untouchables', a compromise was reached which was embodied in the 1935 Act: instead of separate electorates the untouchables received an increased number of reserved seats to be elected from joint electorates.[1] The term Scheduled Castes was henceforth adopted to indicate the lowest-ranking or depressed Hindu castes who were listed in a schedule appended to the Government of India Act for purposes of statutory safeguards.

[1] Galanter 1984: 31.

The new constitution laid down that at the centre Indian ministers responsible to a central legislature were to control the whole administration except for defence and foreign affairs which were placed in the reserved part of the administration. The main advance over the reforms of 1919 was the grant of full provincial autonomy, which meant that for the first time Indian politicians had the opportunity of winning real power at the provincial level. After the elections of 1937 in eight of the eleven provinces Congress governments came to power, appointed by the Governor but responsible to a popularly elected assembly. All members of the provincial assemblies—with second chambers added in six provinces—were elected and officials were no longer eligible for membership. The electorate was expanded from 6.5 to 30 million voters, which meant that a tenth of the population, or nearly a sixth of the adult population, became enfranchised.

Under the new Act the principle of nomination was abolished. In the Madras Legislative Assembly the number of elective seats increased to 215. No less than 69 seats were assigned to separate electorates of Muslims (28), Indian Christians (8), Anglo-Indians (2) and to categories like landholders (6), commercial interests (6) and labour (6). Members for the remaining 146 seats were chosen from general constituencies but included 30 seats reserved for Scheduled Castes. In the same way the Bombay Assembly, which now numbered a total of 175 members, had special seats for Muslims (29), commerce (7), labour (7) and other categories, whereas 15 of the remaining 115 general seats were reserved for Scheduled Castes.[2]

This meticulous parcelling-out of seats to specific social categories illustrates the essentially static view of Indian society prevailing in official circles. It is also of direct relevance to our investigation into the relationship between electoral arrangements and social consciousness. Right from the beginning of constitutional reform, landholders, merchants and industrialists were grouped together in separate electoral bodies, soon to be followed by the nomination of special labour representatives. Under the 1935 Act the number of elected labour representatives was increased to 38 and workers were organized into their own labour constituencies. These provisions directed electoral

[2] I adopt the figures as presented by Chiriyankandath (1992: 52, Table 3) which are based on the official report on the results of the 1937 elections. Slightly different figures can be found in the original proposals of the so-called White Paper (PICR 1933: 79) and in Baker 1976: 293.

and legislative politics into economic channels with employers and workers each voting for their own representatives. Yet nobody has ever argued that the class consciousness of planters, millowners or workers was aroused by these provisions. The special electorates were meant to serve an existing class consciousness, and did not create it.

In the Introduction we have referred to the widely-assumed causal relationship between separate electorates and the rise of communalism. Bipan Chandra, for instance, is of the opinion that British policies bear special responsibility for the growth of communalism in British India and singles out separate electorates as a particularly strong instrument of British divide-and-rule: 'one of the poisonous trees which was to yield a bitter harvest in later years'.[3] Sumit Sarkar admits that nationalists are inclined to exaggerate British responsibility in dividing Indian elite groups along communal lines, but also agrees that separate electorates inevitably hardened the lines of division by forcing political leaders to cultivate only their own religious followings.[4] Recent work however, tends to downplay the element of a deliberate strategy to divide the nationalist opposition to colonial rule and Chakrabarty (1994) acknowledges that the British may have been prompted by a genuine concern to be fair to the many caste and religious communities they had so scrupulously counted and measured. But the effect was the same. Kaviraj alludes to considerations of fairness, but he makes no effort to conceal his personal doubts. Towards the end of the colonial empire, he writes, the colonial government 'showed considerable ingenuity in finding unexceptionably noble principles of political morality whose practical consequences would be to irreparably damage nationalist consolidation'.[5]

Among the practical arrangements which inclined in this direction, Kaviraj mentions the establishment of communal electorates, apart from the more significant encouragement of the idea that groups with different religions could not live together.

The authors quoted above all refer to the situation in British India and not to the princely states. Therefore, in this chapter we will study electoral arrangements implemented within the narrow constitutional confines of the Indian states and look for possible connections

[3] Chandra 1988: 408–9, quote p. 142.
[4] Sarkar 1983: 20–1, 59.
[5] Kaviraj 1997: 232.

between these and emergent communal feelings. For that purpose we will concentrate on developments in the states of Baroda and Travancore in the 1930s.

BARODA

Civil Disobedience on the Borders

From 1875 Baroda was ruled by Sayajirao III, an energetic and enterprising prince. He was an enlightened man who openly broke the most blatant practices of caste and religious exclusivism. He invited depressed class people to dinner at his table, financed the study abroad of B.R. Ambedkar, and shared food with Muslim friends at a mosque.[6] All these could have been empty gestures but are illustrative of a social climate that was quite different from Travancore where the rulers till recent times did not touch food in the presence of ritual inferiors, even if they happened to be the Governor of Madras. Govindbhai Desai, member of the Baroda Executive Council in the 1920s, confirmed this remarkable openness in social relations. At the end of his long career he observed that Hindus who earlier would not have tea together at a table had come to eat dinner without any distinction to caste or religion. Due also to the personal influence of the Maharani, women were no longer required to remain in purdah.[7]

Sayajirao III was also a declared autocrat who resisted any limitation of his personal power. Although his state was well administered, the British kept him under close surveillance, as they suspected him of seditious tendencies. He was a member of the Indian State Delegation to the Round Table Conference in London, where he spoke in support of an Indian federation, but growing sadder, and with his pride hurt, he gradually retired from political life. Spending the larger part of his time in Europe, he left the administration in the hands of his Dewan, Sir V.T. Krishnamachari (1927–44), a most able Brahmin who combined orthodoxy with a modern and rational outlook.[8]

Under the leadership of these men, Baroda was a picture of political tranquillity in the early 1930s, even though it was not free from occa-

[6] Sayajirao III 1938: 863.

[7] Desai 1929: 10–11.

[8] In that way he was described by Lothian who knew him personally when temporarily posted in Baroda, Lothian 1951: 122.

sional tension and conflict. When in 1930 Gandhi launched his Civil Disobedience campaign from Sabarmati Ashram, the national political movement came very near to Baroda's borders. Afraid that the movement might make use of Baroda as a safe haven, the Government of India was watching developments in Gujarat very closely. It was not content with the Baroda Darbar's adherence to a position of strict neutrality and insisted on the state's active cooperation in preventing border-crossings by political activists who wanted to avoid arrest or to start their campaigns from the Maharaja's territories.[9] The demand for strict border control was strongly supported by officers in the neighbouring British districts who complained of a stream of Baroda subjects making mischief in their territory. The collector of Kheda, for instance, accused the Baroda government of 'living in a fool's Paradise' by thinking that there were no organized centres of agitation and propaganda in their state.[10] Part of the problem, British officials acknowledged, was the artificial character of the boundaries with centres located just across them and within sight of the villages from which the activists originated.

Authorities in Baroda asserted in defence that state officials were giving all necessary assistance to their counterparts in British India. In a confidential letter the Dewan declared that the Civil Disobedience movement found no support with the bulk of the people of Baroda and that the situation was fully under control. He added that he had a list of people in Baroda who had joined the Civil Disobedience movement in British India. There was not a single Patidar leader among them, apart from a few young Patidars who were in close touch with activists in British India. Going one step further, the Dewan complained that agitators from British India were entering Baroda in large number, flooding the state with their pamphlets and propaganda.[11]

The British were not impressed. They decided to respond to the complaints received from Bombay. Accordingly, the Resident was instructed to impress upon the Baroda government that it would be spared interference in its internal affairs, as long as it was ready to

[9] Correspondence between Government of India, Foreign and Political Department, and Resident of Baroda 1930–1, L/P&S/13/1007.

[10] Quoted from report from Kaira to Home Department by Alfred Master, Collector, 4.9.1930; see also report 29.1.1931, R/1/1/1993.

[11] Confidential letter from Dewan of Baroda, August 1930, enclosure in letter by D.G. Wilson, Resident of Baroda, 13.9.1930, R/1/1/1993.

cooperate in ensuring that no activities of the Civil Disobedience movement were allowed on its territory.[12] The Dewan stuck to his assertion that there were no organized centres on Baroda territory, but offered his co-operation in having all illegal migrants sent back to British India. About the same time, a memorandum, circulated by the Government of India and listing a number of recommendations and suggestions for the prevention of communal strife,[13] could be filed away unused.

When in January 1932 Civil Disobedience was resumed, there were some manifestations of political unrest, including a movement among students in schools and colleges. The Dewan, Sir Krishnamachari, had some Congress leaders arrested, but was not disposed to take any measures to end demonstrations in support of Congress in Baroda. Although Baroda had proved to be a reluctant ally, the Bombay government felt satisfied with the course of events and reported to the Political Department in Delhi (1932) that 'the Baroda Darbar, after failing last year, are now supporting the British Government staunchly'.[14]

The greatest challenge to Baroda's government came indeed from outside its boundaries. In 1931, a meeting of Baroda state subjects in Bombay issued an appeal, praising Baroda for its progressive administration, but criticizing the Gaekwad's absentee rule with its many consequent evils, adding that 'Baroda subjects' plight [was] nothing if not miserable under an irresponsible bureaucracy' (1931). The Political Department in London was inclined to attribute these indications of dissatisfaction to propaganda from Congress quarters and the large number of temporary immigrants from British Gujarat.[15]

[12] Letter from Secretary to Government of Bombay to Secretary to Political Department, 30.1.1931, and from Political Department to Resident of Baroda, 7.1.1932 and 18.2.1931, R/1/1/1993 and R/2/508/168.

[13] Government of India, Home Department, circular letter dated 13.4.1931 on Prevention of Communal Strife, R/2(508/167). In 1933 the Baroda government replied to the Resident that it had no objection to supply him with timely information of any communal trouble, but would appreciate information about similar troubles in neighbouring British India, Political General Correspondence, Section 34, File 55, HPO Baroda.

[14] Quoted from letter by Political Department Bombay, to Charles Watson, Political Secretary, Delhi, 2.5.1932, R/1/1/2216. See also related correspondence in this file.

[15] No further information on the status of this Baroda subjects meeting available; see *Times* 9.6.1931 and Political Department note by P. Patrick, 9.6.1931, L/P&S/13/554.

In a different guise, but not less constructive, support for the nationalist cause came from the Baroda government itself. Sayajirao was an enthusiastic supporter of Gandhi's swadeshi movement. The Baroda *Administration Reports* extensively document government loans to industries, tax concessions, the easy acquisition of land and the construction of harbour and railway facilities. Local entrepreneurs like the founders and developers of Alembic Industries and Hindustan Tractors and Bulldozers were able to capitalize on these favourable conditions; they were relatives or close associates of Vallabhbhai Patel and Gandhi. Even though these new non-textile firms did not always turn out to be an immediate success, Erdman concluded in 1971 that most of Baroda's post-Independence industries, including some of the giants, date from Sayajirao's time.[16]

Nevertheless, Civil Disobedience does not seem to have passed the people of Baroda completely unnoticed. It raised the Baroda *praja mandal* from its erstwhile slumber and young Patidars, Brahmins and Banias, inspired by Gandhi's campaign in British India, began to gather wider support for the people's association. From the beginning of the 1930s members of the *praja mandal* toured the districts to enlist members and establish village branches preaching the gospel of swadeshi, boycott of foreign cloth and total prohibition. As yet they met with a poor response. In 1930 Sardar Patel had become president of the executive committee of the *mandal* and paid frequent visits to Baroda to build up his contacts with the organization. Under his influence and that of his local associates the *mandal* became a more Patidar-dominated body with a better chance of linking up with the peasantry of the state.[17]

Local British Residents were easily inclined to regard the *mandal* as an organization directed against the state. Nonetheless, from their own reports it becomes clear that the leadership did their utmost to maintain good relations with the state authorities. The *mandal* worked for the improvement of the conditions of the people by all legal and constitutional means and only in exceptional circumstances was the usual spirit of cordial co-operation abandoned and replaced by a more critical attitude. That was for instance the case in 1936 when its leaders wanted to conduct an enquiry into the real burden of land

[16] Erdman 1971: 7–12; Tripathi and Mehta 1990: 119 ff.

[17] Fortnightly Reports from Baroda for these years; *United India and Indian States* 16.8.1930; Hardiman 1978: 129–30.

revenue in view of the fall in agricultural prices during the economic depression. The government resisted this initiative as uncalled-for, but in the end an understanding was reached which permitted the mandal to conduct its economic enquiries.[18]

In spite of the growing influence of Sardar Patel and his political supporters in the affairs of the *mandal*, the organization managed these years to maintain a formal political independence. There were strong Congress leanings present within, and when Jawaharlal Nehru visited Baroda, the *praja mandal* took care of the necessary arrangements for his reception. But publicly most leaders declared that their organization was not aligned with the INC or any other body. This was probably prompted by tactical considerations, as an open declaration in favour of the Congress would make it virtually impossible to remain in the good books of the government. The Baroda State Police Commissioner, a Maratha, declared that the National Congress had no support among the general populace, but the British Resident did not wish to be deceived. He reported a strong sympathy, perhaps latent, among all Gujarati Hindus for the Congress. Gujaratis, both officials and general people, were beginning to be infected with the slogan 'Gujarat for Gujaratis' which was associated with Congress policies. Maratha officials, the Resident wrote, felt uneasy about this growing sentiment and were likely to take up a more hostile stand against Congress and to underplay its influence.[19] The *praja mandal* commented in these years that government officials and especially the Police Department were working against their organization and secretly tried to dissuade the people from cooperating with it. 'The service of the people is a path of thorns', the chairman of the reception committee told the *praja mandal* delegates in 1937.[20]

The Haripura Congress and the States (1938)

The INC adhered to its established policy of a guarded distance from the states. Gandhi was convinced that the India of the states was an integral part of geographical India. But he often repeated his favourite

[18] Fortnightly Reports from Baroda for the first half of July and the first half of August 1936, R/1/1/2790.

[19] Fortnightly Report from Baroda for the second half of February 1932, L/P&S/13/1007.

[20] Jayashankar B. Bhojak, Chairman, Reception Committee at 14th Session Baroda State *Praja Mandal*, Visnagar, March 1937, in Confidential File No. 129, HPO Baroda.

theory that the princes were trustees of the people over whom they ruled, drawing for themselves only a small fixed percentage for their private expenses. It was moral persuasion that should raise among the rulers a consciousness that they were servants of their people and that their destiny was bound up with the larger India. He added a more pragmatic consideration to this policy of non-interference, when he acknowledged that it was not want of appreciation alone that compelled Congress' attitude but also 'our helplessness'.[21]

Apart from that, many senior Congressmen regarded state-based organizations as simply too weak to be of any use in their fight against imperialism. The *praja mandals*, represented in a handful of states, were short of funds, left-wing dominated and bitterly divided.[22] The Congress itself deemed it below its dignity to have local committees which could not function in a constructive way because of the numerous restrictions imposed by the rulers.

Nevertheless, there was much disappointment with Congress aloofness from the affairs of the states. In 1934, Congress Committees in adjoining British provinces had stressed that it was the duty of the INC to carry on a campaign in the Indian states in the same way as in British India. Elaborating on that sense of duty, the *Servant of India*, a strong champion of the cause of the Indian states, claimed that in many cases the Civil Disobedience movement had received more manpower support from the states than even from British India.[23]

At successive annual sessions, starting in Calcutta in 1928, Congress had assured the people of the states of its sympathy with their legitimate and peaceful struggle for political rights. But it was always assumed that the burden of that struggle should fall on the people themselves. In February 1938, however, the Congress session at Haripura, immediately adjoining Navsari division of Baroda, decided for the first time to lend more than moral support to movements in the states asking for responsible government.

This Haripura session, under the presidentship of Subhas Chandra Bose, has been hailed as a momentous occasion: it was the first time that Congress extended not only goodwill but also support, at least to a certain extent, to political movements in the states. However, from the text of the resolution on Congress policy towards the states, we have to agree with Jeffrey and Copland that it amounted to no more than

[21] Gandhi 1941: 64–5.
[22] Copland 1985: 125–6.
[23] *The Servant of India* 20.9.1934: 439. See also File Reforms, L/P&S/13/554.

an elaborate restatement of existing policy without committing the Congress to active help.[24]

The Haripura Congress declared that it considered the states integral parts of India and stood for the same political, social and economic freedom in the states as in the rest of India. Nevertheless, it reiterated that the burden of the struggle for that freedom ought to be shouldered by the people themselves. Congress was not in a position to work effectively in the states because of the many limitations imposed by the rulers and the British authorities. The name and the great prestige of the Congress may have raised hope in the minds of the people, but its inability to live up to expectations could only result in disillusion and thus hamper the natural growth of the freedom movement in the states. Another consideration expressed by the Haripura session and closely resembling British Indian policies was that the general policy of the Congress was often unsuited to the different conditions prevailing in the states.

Therefore, Congress was ready to extend its goodwill and support to freedom movements inside the states, if carried on in a peaceful and legitimate manner. But under existing conditions, help would inevitably be limited to moral support and sympathy. The only significant departure from established policy was that '[I]ndividual Congressmen . . . however, will be free to render further assistance in their personal capacities. In this way the struggle can develop without committing the Congress organization and thus unhindered by external considerations.'

As part of that policy, local Congress committees should henceforth function under the direct control of the Congress Working Committee. Yet the internal struggles of the people must not be undertaken in the name of the Congress. For that purpose independent organizations should be started or continued where they existed.[25]

The Haripura Congress was no watershed, but in actual practice, there was a change of policy.[26] Gandhi and other Congress leaders, already on record as favouring a more active policy, agreed to guide the political agitations for responsible government that erupted in several princely states, not only in Baroda and Travancore, but also in

[24] Jeffrey 1978: 13 ff.; Copland 1985: 123 ff.

[25] Text of Congress resolution, 21.2.1938, in Sever Vol. II, 1985: 572–3.

[26] This change of policy is discussed more extensively by Copland 1997: 164 ff.

Mysore, Jaipur and Rajkot. The movement in Hyderabad, also related to the issue of federation, will be discussed in more detail in the next chapter. The Congress Working Committee's decision at Wardha at the end of 1938 to lend these agitations its influence was fully in line with this new spirit.

Confidential notes circulating within the Political Departments in New Delhi and London also stressed that the Haripura resolution was less harmless than appeared at first sight. The Congress still focused on the centre, but it was acknowledged that as far as responsible government in the states was concerned, Congress leaders had gone considerably further than they used to do. It was a departure from the old policy of non-interference, a note by the London department stated, most probably emanating from secretary P.J. Patrick. Therefore, in the summer of 1938 Political Agents were instructed by the Political Department in Delhi to pay the closest attention to deficiencies in the internal administration of their states, as defects that earlier went unnoticed could now be seized upon as part of a campaign against the states.[27]

The state governments also realized that times had begun to change. After the Haripura session they convened a conference attended by the Prime Ministers of many states, including Baroda, Travancore and Hyderabad. In a memorandum drafted at this conference, the new Congress interest in the states was branded as a mere bid for power and the paramount power was asked to make a statement that it did not insist on the grant of partial or complete responsible government as a condition precedent to entering a future federation. But such a statement was more than the British were willing to give.[28]

Employment and Representation

The outcome of the Haripura Congress became immediately apparent in the political resolutions of the Baroda *praja mandal*. In August 1938 the Mehsana branch of the *mandal* asked not only for the usual reduction in land revenue and total prohibition, but also for responsible government. Since then, the latter demand—raised more casually

[27] Very confidential demi-official note with annexes by C.G. Herbert, Political Department, Simla 17.6.1938, L/P&S/13/887.

[28] Phadnis 1968: 121–5. See also reply to a question in the House of Commons, 16.12.1938, discussed in Chapter 4.

on earlier occasions—became a recurrent theme at meetings all over the state.[29]

One year before the Haripura Congress, the 14th session of the Baroda *mandal* had already expressed its confidence that 'at the proper time the subjects of Indian States will get active help from the Congress to reach their goal'.[30] At the next annual meeting of the *praja mandal* (Bhadran, October 1938) 'the proper time' was thought to have arrived. In a bid to gain more control of the organization and bring it into line with Congress policy and program, Patel managed to be elected as president of the Bhadran meeting. In his presidential address he invited the rulers of Indian states to study the Haripura resolution and to take steps to establish popular institutions in their territories. One of the main resolutions requested the Baroda government to make a public declaration that responsible government was the final goal of state policy. As a first step to that end, the Maharaja's government should appoint a committee, half its membership from the *praja mandal*, to frame a suitable constitution for the state.[31]

Also at the Bhadran session a report was read out by one of the secretaries dealing with the question of official employment. On this the *praja mandal* had issued a pamphlet and from that pamphlet the secretary concluded that of the 218 officers drawing a salary of Rs 300 or more per month, 71 belonged to the state whereas 147 were outsiders. We may infer from his words that those who 'belonged' were Gujaratis, and the 'outsiders' were Marathi speakers. Earlier, the *mandal* had accused many of these outsiders of caring only for their salaries.[32]

This report touched a sensitive issue. Under the old regime

[29] Fortnightly Report from Baroda for the second half of August 1938, R/1/1/3046, and Personal and Confidential Demi-official from Dewan of Baroda to Resident, 15.11.1938, L/P&S/13/1007.

[30] Presidential address by Pranlal Munshi, 14th Session Baroda State *Praja Mandal*, Visnagar, March 1937, Confidential File No. 129, HPO Baroda.

[31] Sessions of the *Praja Mandal*, Confidential File No. 129, HPO Baroda. In an open letter to *The Times of India* (24.12.1938) a certain Mr. Panwala raised the question whether people in Baroda were really ready for responsible government. He observed that the main legislation was initiated by Maharaja Sayajirao III, as members of the *Dhara Sabha* did not make use of the powers conferred on them. When His Highness, by way of experiment, invited public opinion on the state budget, only one of the non-official members of the *Dhara Sabha* took the trouble to study it, whereas the local newspapers did not care to give any comment.

[32] Chairman Reception Committee, Baroda *Praja Mandal*, Visnagar, March 1937, Confidential File No. 129, HPO Baroda.

Maharashtrian Brahmins, following in the wake of the Gaekwads' conquests, used to dominate the top levels of the state bureaucracy. However, as a result of progress in education, the higher ranks of the Baroda administrative service were increasingly filled by Gujaratis. According to the Census, from 1875 to 1921 the Maharastrian share in the number of gazetted government posts had fallen from 64 to 17 per cent, whereas the share of Gujarati Hindus and Jains had risen from 24 to 62.5 per cent. The presence of Gujarati Muslims had meanwhile increased from 2 to 14 per cent.[33]

The distribution of government positions was not as eagerly watched as in Travancore, where the political elite was pressing the government to grant them a larger share in official employment. Nevertheless, many Gujaratis seem to have felt uneasy about what they considered to be official neglect, even though the community-wise composition of the services was not widely known. The census figures, for all their shortcomings, showed that in 1931 the Marathi share of top level appointments had indeed increased from 17 to 24 per cent, but this growth was largely achieved at the cost of the Muslims, and the share of Gujarati Hindus and Jains had remained stationary at 62.5 per cent.[34] Since the 1920s a Public Service Commission advised the Government on all appointments and there was a Clerks' Training Class each year, with a hundred students selected by that commission to be trained in general administration; the government claimed that all successful candidates were absorbed in the services.[35]

In an open letter to *The Times of India*, B.Z. Panwala, a Baroda citizen, countered the criticism of Gujarati under-representation. First, he contended that as many as 25 state officers had been wrongly described as outsiders in the *mandal* report. Next, drawing the line on the state service list a bit lower at the level of Rs. 100 per month, he pointed out that 60 per cent of the officers were Gujaratis. The remaining posts were occupied by Maharashtrians together with Parsis, Muslims, Christians and others. Marathas, according to him, were

[33] Figures for 1875 are derived from Hardiman 1978: 118–19, but my own counts from the 1921 Census differ from his. I have included Prabhus in the Marathi speaking category, since succesive census reports describe them as immigrants from the Deccan (Maharashtra).

[34] *Census of Baroda* 1921 II: 114–21 and 1932 II: 78–83.

[35] BAR 1929–30: 7–8.

numerous only in the army and the household departments, and in the lower services Gujaratis claimed more than 80 per cent of the posts.[36]

At the Bhadran meeting Sardar Patel also spoke about the question of government employment. He is quoted by the *Bombay Chronicle* (30.10.1938) to have 'complained that outsiders had been imported into the state and sons of the soil kept out of the administration which had created distrust among the people. It was time that the voice of the people was allowed to prevail in administrative matters. . . .'

In a personal communication to the Resident, the Dewan reported that the Bhadran meeting was attended only by a small section of people from the state. Most of those present were said to have come from the neighbouring British Indian district of Kheda. The Dewan, who had no reason to write flattering accounts about Patel's political interference in his state, mentioned also that *mandal* members were unwilling to pass resolutions in the manner in which Patel wanted but 'by repeated personal appeals (including in private talks, appeals to the Marathi-Gujarati feeling) he had them adopted'.[37]

Whatever the truth of the Dewan's assessment, derived from personal informants, when Patel visited Baroda in January 1939 the city became the scene of communal riots. Baroda city numbered a large minority of Marathi speaking people and Muslims, among whom the Sardar was not popular. He was alleged to have attacked the Maharaja and his government and a general impression prevailed, spread by the Marathi press, that Patel as a Gujarati was bitterly opposed to Maharashtrians. Spokesmen of these communities, together with Gujaratis like B.D. Amin of Alembic Chemicals, had tried unsuccessfully to persuade Patel to cancel his visit.

On 20 January Patel arrived in Baroda. His tour through the city led to black flags along the route and cries of 'Vallabhbhai go back'. The *pandal* erected for his reception by the *praja mandal* was destroyed and a terrorized Vallabhbhai hid in his car and asked to be driven away as fast as the car could go.[38] The general meeting had to be postponed till the next day. On 21 January Patel was able to make a

[36] Open letter from B.Z. Panwala, Baroda, in *The Times of India*, 20.1.1939, in Confidential File No. 129, HPO Baroda.

[37] Personal and Confidential Demi-official from Dewan of Baroda to Resident, 15.11.1938, L/P&S/13/1007; Fortnightly Report from Baroda for the second half of October 1938, R/1/1/3046.

[38] Quoted from Jayakar Papers by Copland 1985: 130.

public speech. He called the Maharaja a wise and great ruler, protested against the land assessment which was said to be higher than in British India, and strongly condemned all forms of communal or provincial conflict. His words did not have the desired result. After the meeting large-scale violence broke out and local millhands, mainly Marathis and Muslims, joined the fighting, leaving many injured and one Maratha killed.[39]

What these disturbances made clear was that the National Congress had to reckon with strong opposition, at least in Baroda city. Patel as a leading representative of that Congress was seen as an enemy of the Maharaja's government which still could count on wide-spread support among large parts of the population. Even more controversial were Patel's public references, in his Bhadran presidential address quoted above and later in Bardoli, to the communal distribution of appointments in the state administrative services. In an open letter to *The Hindustan Times* (28.1.1939) he tried to make his position clear. Since the communal tension that had erupted in Baroda city was mainly to be attributed to his comments on the administrative services, he wanted to repeat to the public at large the exact wording of his hotly disputed speeches. 'The only thing I have said', explained the Sardar, is 'that the people claimed responsible government . . . [and] . . . that they could never be satisfied with a system under which most offices of responsibility were filled by people coming from outside Baroda State, and that they should insist on having them filled by people who are residents of the State.'

Gandhi's private secretary, Mahadev Desai, also entered the public discussion. Referring to similar incidents in Travancore, he wrote that in Baroda meetings of the people were disturbed and broken up by state-hired hooligans acting in connivance with the police. According to Desai, Patel's public statements could hardly be said to have caused the riots in Baroda city. Patel had only called upon the government to encourage local talent instead of always importing men from outside. Nonetheless, Desai's article sounded a note of bitterness when it ended,

[39] Report on the disturbances in Baroda 20–2 January 1939, by Sir V.T. Krishnamachari, Dewan, in Confidential File No. 134, HPO Baroda and R/1/1/3282. Whereas the *Times* of 26.1.1939 reported that in Baroda 'a new form of communalism' had come up between people from different provinces, the 1979 Vadodara District Gazetteer observes that the hostile reception of the Sardar revealed 'the anti-national attitude of the State' (*Gazetteers, Vadodara District* 1979: 137).

by referring to the Maharashtrian population of Baroda as a microscopic section that monopolized most of the high offices.[40]

Representatives of the *praja mandal* accused Marathi leaders of organizing the incidents in Baroda city, and Gujarati papers from British India levelled bitter attacks on the state administration. A judicial inquiry into the disturbances was demanded, but the Dewan, Sir Krishnamachari, had serious doubts about its effect on public opinion. In a letter to B.G. Kher, Chief Minister of Bombay, he explained that his investigations had resulted in evidence which, if published, would lead to increased bitterness between the communities instead of allaying the existing tension.[41] Another note in the same file, without date or author, warned that a judicial inquiry would lend this local question an all-India importance which could only hamper the common struggle for the independence of India. Nevertheless, in March 1939 the appointment of an official enquiry committee was taken up for consideration, but its terms of reference were so restricted that it was not able to make a real start.[42]

When these communal riots broke out in Baroda city, Maharaja Sayajirao was laying ill in Bombay. He died on 6 February 1939 and His Majesty the King-Emperor was pleased to recognise the succession by his grandson, Pratapsingh Gaekwad.[43] The new Maharaja immediately declared to support the recommendations of the committee instituted the previous year to consider constitutional advance. This committee consisted of members from different communities and schools of thought including the general-secretary of the Baroda *praja mandal* and had submitted an unanimous report. On the auspicious occasion of his ascending the *gaddi* the new ruler—who solemnly declared to have 'come to realize that the agriculturist is the backbone of my State'[44]—also announced that the reduction of land revenue, sanctioned by the late Maharaja for five years on account of low prices, was to be made permanent. In that way, the threat of political unrest

[40] The paper cuttings are from L/P&S/13/1007. The cutting with Desai's article mentions a date (22.1.1939) but no source.

[41] Letter from V.T. Krishnamachari, Dewan of Baroda, to B.G. Kher, Chief Minister of Bombay, Baroda 9.2.1939, in Confidential File No. 134, HPO Baroda.

[42] Appointment of a Committee to conduct Judicial Inquiry into the Disturbances in the City on 20–22 January 1939, Confidential File No. 69, HPO Baroda.

[43] Letter from the Viceroy, Lord Linlithgow, New Delhi 15.2.1939, R/2(534/305).

[44] Quoted in Pendse 1940: 4.

spreading to rural areas was bought off at the cost of Rs 20 lakh or 22.3 per cent of state revenue.[45]

The recommendations for constitutional reform promulgated by Maharaja Pratapsingh emphasized once more the complete identity of interests between the ruler and the ruled. They provided for a Legislative Council (*Dhara Sabha*) with a majority of elected members, general constituencies and constituencies for special interests (landholders, commerce and industry), but neither for communal electorates nor for responsible government. Although the council received some more powers, the executive appointed by the Maharaja remained responsible only to him. The Political Department declared to approve of the recommendations and the Political Adviser (the new title of the Political Secretary) commented in an internal note that 'the reforms are conservative in character but with the strong Maharashtrian element in the capital they will probably be accorded a reception sufficiently favourable to justify ignoring Congress demands for greater liberalisation of the Government'.[46]

As soon as the recommendations for reform became known, the Working Committee of the *praja mandal*, meeting in Bombay under the presidentship of Sardar Patel, issued a public statement criticizing the proposals as reactionary, unsuited to reflect public opinion, and worthy only of rejection. As its main objection the Working Committee cited the complete lack of any reference to 'responsibility in Government, remote or elementary'.[47]

Emphasis on the issue of responsible government was noteworthy but not altogether unexpected. Much more remarkable was the change that took place among the Muslim minority of Baroda state. Before 1939 their poorly-attended political meetings had passed resolutions protesting Italian atrocities on Muslims in Tripoli and criticizing British policies in Palestine. But with the growing Congress interest in Baroda state affairs, and especially after the announcement of forthcoming constitutional reforms, Muslims started to worry about their future place in the politics and society of Baroda and of India in general. From December 1938 the local Muslim Conference passed resolutions on the line of Muslim League demands in British India and appealed to Muslims to press for their distinctive rights as a

[45] Hardiman 1978: 14; Pendse 1940: 16.

[46] B.J. Glancy, Political Department, Minute Paper, no date, L/P&S/13/1007.

[47] *Bombay Chronicle* 7.3.1939.

religious community. After the riots in Baroda the president of the meeting of the Navsari District Muslim Conference exhorted those present to demand separate Muslim representation in the new state council and all local bodies. Since then the novel demand for communal representation became a standing subject on the agenda of all Muslim meetings held in different divisions of the state. Trade-union leaders joined the chorus and demanded on behalf of labour that workers should get one-tenth of all seats in the new legislative.[48]

The Government of Baroda Act (1940) inaugurated by state proclamation in 1940 differed only slightly from the original recommendations made public by the Maharaja a year earlier. In its order on the delimitation of constituencies the government claimed it had given 'most anxious consideration' to the many memorials urging the introduction of some form of communal representation. But since the new constitution was based on an identity of interests among the different classes of people, the Maharaja's government did not accept the suggestion for separate electorates or reservation of seats.[49]

That stand was maintained in spite of a communal disturbance during municipal elections in Sidhpur (May 1939), a town with important sections of Hindu and Bohra merchants. In a keen contest between Hindu and Muslim candidates in the same wards for the same votes, both parties were waiting for voters outside the polling-booth. Angry words were exchanged, which ended in serious fighting leaving 40 people wounded and a large number arrested.[50] But Sidhpur remained an exception.

A contemporary lawyer called the lack of any provision for communal interests 'one of the brightest spots in the new constitution'.[51] The *Amrita Bazar Patrika* wrote that the Indian nationalists had long been demanding such liberal reforms in their own constitution and now 'they must congratulate the people of Baroda for getting them in advance'.[52] Nevertheless, the new reforms were far from liberal. The new Legislative Council (*Dhara Sabha*) consisted of 60 mem-

[48] Fortnightly Report from Baroda for the second half of December 1938, R/1/1/3046; Idem for March, April 1939 and later months, R/1/1/3394.

[49] Government of Baroda, Order on the Delimitation of Constituencies, 1940, quoted in Pendse 1940: 32–3.

[50] Disturbances at Sidhpur, Mehsana district, Confidential File No. 150, HPO Baroda; Agitation in Baroda State 1939, R/1/1/3282, and *The Statesman* 7.6.1939. For earlier disturbances at Sidhpur see HPO Baroda, Confidential File No. 317.

[51] Pendse 1940: 31.

[52] Reception by the public of the scheme of reform embodied in the Government of Baroda Act, 1940, Confidential File No. 76, HPO Baroda.

bers. Of these, 23 members were nominated, 6 of them ex-officio as members of the executive and 17 non-officials, appointed to represent minorities like the untouchables and other backward communities.[53] 10 members represented industry, commerce, labour, cooperative societies and holders of landed rights as special interest. The remaining 27 members were elected by territorial constituencies on a wide franchise (Appendix II) and the number of persons on the voters' list at the election of 1940 was about 8.5 per cent of the population.[54]

The *Dhara Sabha* had the power to initiate and pass legislation, and to discuss and vote on the budget. Members might also ask questions and move resolutions on matters of public interest, subject to certain limitations. But the vital condition remained that all legislation required the previous assent of the Maharaja. In a public speech the Dewan of Baroda explained that the rejection of responsible government was also meant to keep the state free of communalism. He warned against political and communal influences from British India that could harm Baroda in developing its own form of democracy and he pointed out that the British Indian provinces did have responsible governments but also suffered from the most acute communal problems.[55]

The Act laid down that the executive should consist of the Dewan and such other members as His Highness might appoint. One member was to be chosen from the non-official members of the *Dhara Sabha*, but all members were responsible to only the Maharaja and not removable on a vote of no-confidence. After 1940 the executive numbered 6 members, including the Dewan, each in charge of a number of departments in respect of which they exercised clearly defined administrative powers.

After the enactment of the new constitution the nationalist press complained that the *Dhara Sabha* remained a mere advisory body and that the executive was in no way responsible to the people. Sardar Patel maintained that the reforms fell far short of the expectations of the public, but advised against opposition to the reforms. The *mandal* decided indeed to accept them 'as far as they went'. An appeal was made to all people of Baroda to vote at the 1940 elections and the

[53] Article 11 of the Government of Baroda Act (1940) laid down that not more than 3 of the 17 nominated members should be officials, but in actual practice virtually all nominated members were non-officials.

[54] Full text of the Government of Baroda Act (1940) in L/P&S/13/1007. See also Pendse 1940: 28 ff. and BAR 1944–5: 7–8.

[55] Reception by the public of the scheme of reform embodied in the Government of Baroda Act, 1940, Confidential File No. 76, HPO Baroda.

mandal secured 24 elected seats including most of the special constituencies in the new legislative.

The Muslims in Baroda were less willing to work the reforms. In the absence of separate electorates they feared standing no chance of being elected to the *Dhara Sabha* and therefore they reiterated their demand for separate representation. At the sixth session of the Baroda Raj Muslim Conference in Mehsana Division (1940), the main speaker called the provision for general electorates and nominations harmful to the interests of Muslims and other minorities. He claimed no less than one-third of the total number of seats in all elected bodies in the state for Muslims as well as their representation in the state bureaucracy in proportion to their numerical strength. All people present at the meeting were urged to join the Muslim League and to refrain from contacts with the National Congress or the *praja mandal*. In a resolution the Muslims in Baroda were called upon to abstain from participation in the 1940 elections and this call for abstention was repeated in various meetings in different Muslim localities in Baroda city.[56]

The dissent voiced by Muslims did not prevent the *Dhara Sabha* from convening for the first time later that year. On that occasion the Dewan, Sir V.T. Krishnamachari, proudly referred to Baroda's long record of civil unity and social justice which offered a solid foundation for further progress. Subsequent events seemed to prove him right: the communal riots in Bombay and Ahmedabad of 1941 did not spark across the state borders, in spite of a large influx of refugees from these troubled places.[57] At the end of the first session, a leader of the *praja mandal* spoke in appreciation of the working of the reforms.[58] During the war the *mandal's* ultimate aim continued to be responsible government with complete loyalty to His Highness the Maharaja. It remained an independent organization with no formal links with the INC or the AISPC, though the Congress in 1940 had finally resolved to assist the people's movement in the states in all possible ways.[59]

[56] Fortnightly Report from Baroda for the first half of May 1940, R/1/1/3504.

[57] Fortnightly Report from Baroda for the second part of April 1941, L/P&S/13/1007.

[58] Reception by the public of the scheme of reform embodied in the Government of Baroda Act, 1940, in Confidential File No. 76, HPO Baroda. See also intelligence reports, Political Department, R/1/1/3519.

[59] Fortnightly Reports from Baroda for the first half of March and the second half of April 1940 and the second half of May 1941, R/1/1/3504 and L/P&S/13/1007. See also intelligence reports in R/1/1/3519.

After the War

When the war was over and elections had to be held for a new legislature, the Muslims of Baroda were still considering their attitude towards the new constitutional arrangements. As in 1940, Muslim League supporters were asked to boycott the elections and the *praja mandal* achieved a sweeping success (February 1946). That result meant a further encouragement to the *mandal* which, with Independence drawing near, had also to face a first wave of communal riots in Baroda city (September 1946). It resumed its campaign for more responsible forms of government and disagreed with His Highness's view that responsible government could not be granted so long as the British exercised paramountcy in India.[60]

In the meantime, the government of Baroda had appointed a committee under the presidentship of Chief Justice Sudhalkar to consider a revision of the 1940 reforms (June 1946). The form of government had to be on democratic lines, but not necessarily an imitation of the British system. Public comment was invited and the committee received a large number of requests for separate electorates and reserved seats, especially from Muslim and Scheduled Caste organizations.[61] A Kshatriya organization in Mehsana even urged that the appointment of office bearers in a provisional government 'should be made from all castes in proportion to the population'.[62] But Independence overtook Baroda's last reforms committee and after 1947 caste-based representation had no place in the new political system.

The Indian Independence Act of 1947 released the princely states from all their obligations to the British Crown. Shortly before the transfer of power, Maharaja Pratapsingh had agreed to sign the Instrument of Accession to the Republic of India. A Constituent Assembly was set up to frame a new constitution for Baroda state and to serve as interim legislature under a provisional popular ministry. Responsible government was finally established in April 1948 and in January 1949 the Maharaja announced the merger of his state with the new Bombay state.[63] The several straggling blocks of intermingling territory inter-

[60] Fortnightly Reports from Baroda for 1946 and 1947, L/P&S/13/1008.

[61] Constitutional Reforms, Government of Baroda Act 1940, Confidential File No. 75, HPO Baroda.

[62] Quoted in Shah 1975: 92.

[63] According to Wood (1984: 75) the incorporation of Baroda and the Gujarat states in the Province of Bombay was already effected in March 1948. Here I adopt the chronology as given by Menon (1985: 423) who served as Secretary to the Ministry of States during this crucial period of national integration.

spersed between the former British districts now became consolidated in a single administrative unit. When the Maharaja had second thoughts and tried to reverse decisions which he had earlier approved of, the Government of India summarily derecognized him as ruler of Baroda and deprived him of his privy purse.[64] For princely India there was no going back.[65]

However, the new administrative structure that had emerged in 1949 was soon challenged by strong linguistic movements demanding a separate state for both the Gujarati and Marathi speaking communities. The demand was granted in 1960 with the bifurcation of Bombay state into Gujarat and Maharashtra. Yet, when the language problem had been solved by the formation of a separate state, the number of Hindu-Muslim riots began to increase. More and more cities and towns in Gujarat were falling prey to communal violence and the new state became plagued by a long series of violent incidents and movements. Local observers agree, however, that Ahmedabad and Baroda, the old capitals of British Gujarat and the Gaekwad state, share the dubious honour of being the preferred habitat of communal violence, though of late Surat seems to outrival both of them.[66]

Ahmedabad was swept into the movement for a Gujarat state but had seen no major riots. A few years later, an insignificant incident burst into an orgy of violence that lasted for three days. More than one thousand people lost their lives and thousands of shops and houses were destroyed by fire. These worst communal riots in Ahmedabad's history seem to have caught the authorities completely by surprise and totally unprepared.[67] The same happened in Surat, a town that for decades had prided itself on the peaceful coexistence of its religious communities. However, after the demolition of the Ayodhya mosque in December 1992 the city exploded in a ruthless anti-Muslim pogrom with riots characterized by a brutality never seen before.[68]

[64] See Menon 1995: 429–33. Though there was no question of maladministration, the British had problems with the private character of the ruler who during the war had married a second wife in spite of recently passed Hindu Monogamy Act, discussed in L/P&S/13/1008 Baroda Affairs 1943–8.

[65] The ruler's *titular* successor, Maharaja Fatesinghrao P. Gaekwad, entered politics. At successive elections from the 1950s he won a seat in the national parliament from a Baroda city constituency, first on a Congress ticket, later as a member of the Congress-O (Pantham 1976: 207).

[66] Chandra 1993: 1883; Lobo and D'Souza 1993: 152.

[67] Shah 1984.

[68] Breman 1993; Lobo and D'Souza 1993: 152.

The outbursts of violence in Ahmedabad and Surat were entirely unexpected. On the other hand, since Independence the city of Baroda has earned itself the reputation of being a hotbed of communalism prone to the eruption of religious passion on the slightest pretext. None the less, when after the Ayodhya drama violence raged in large parts of India and the urban population was preparing for the worst, Baroda remained virtually undisturbed.

The intricate territorial mingling of directly and indirectly ruled areas before 1947 makes it very difficult to trace later communal disturbances in Gujarat to one or the other political heritage. Wood (1984) has tried to separate British from princely legacies in post-Independence Gujarat politics, but unfortunately he did not include communalism in his analysis. Historians studying contemporary records may not be able to detect the phenomenon of communalism in its silent, almost imperceptible form. They seem to share this unenviable position with their fellow social scientists and even with responsible authorities on the spot who are also absolutely helpless when it comes to anticipating potential communal confrontations in the present context. This unpredictability may have less to do with the sources of information used than with the special characteristic of the phenomenon itself. The basic cause of communal conflict is a feeling of mutual threat and distrust that may be simmering right below the social surface where more often than not it escapes the attention of most interested observers.

TRAVANCORE

Constitutional Reforms and Abstention

In 1924 the old Maharaja of Travancore had died. Having no sisters, he had adopted, in accordance with the matrilineal custom of his family, two relatives as his nieces, who became the senior and the junior Maharanis. After his death the senior Maharani became Regent by right, but the junior Maharani was the mother of the still minor heir to the throne. The resulting tensions inside the palace were only increased by the senior's apparent preference for Christians in positions of authority and the junior's turn to Hindus for support.

When the young Maharaja was invested with ruling powers by the British Resident,[69] representing the Viceroy (1931), the junior

[69] Actually, his title was not Resident but Agent to the Governor-General.

Maharani was determined to rule through her son, who was too weak to resist. She felt restricted by conventions at court and was fond of travelling abroad, taking her son with her and often visiting the theatre. A declared sympathizer of the Hindu cause, she nevertheless had her tonsils removed by missionary doctors in a Christian hospital at Nagercoil. She was feared more than loved.[70]

In her ambition to rule, the junior Maharani received the able assistance of Sir C.P. Ramaswamy Aiyar, an outstanding administrator. In his speech of investiture the new Maharaja announced that he had decided to avail himself of the services of Sir Ramaswamy Aiyar as legal and constitutional advisor. At that time, Sir C.P., once described by Lord Willingdon as the most brilliant Indian statesman of his day, was making a distinguished career in British India, serving as Indian representative at the League of Nations and Law Member of the Viceroy's Executive Council. In Travancore he was attracted not only to the almost unlimited power which service in a princely state offered; he was also motivated by an unshakable devotion to the Hindu dynasty, and its junior Maharani in particular.[71] He was the all-commanding personality of Travancore politics in the 1930s assuming formal responsibility as Dewan in 1936.

The Civil Disobedience movement in the British provinces (1930) roused hardly any excitement in Travancore. A few volunteers marched to Payyanur in British Malabar to join a salt satyagraha, while inside the state there was some propaganda for *khaddar* and burning of foreign cloth.[72] The main effect may have been that some Nayars used the Congress stress on temperance as a cloak for agitation against Ezhavas who had grown rich on toddy.[73]

There was however a growing agitation for legislative reform, also stimulated by the Maharaja's announcement on his ascent to the *gaddi* that he intended to enlarge the powers and functions of the legislature. In response to that agitation the Travancore government decided to publish the main outlines of its reform proposals which were meant

[70] Several issues of *Princely India*, 1932, and Fortnightly Report from Travancore for the first part of January 1933, R/1/1/2338.

[71] Ouwerkerk 1994: 71 ff. For critical comments on the appointment of Sir C.P. see Fortnightly Report from Travancore for the first part of October 1932, R/1/1/2224.

[72] Kumar n.d.: 127.

[73] Kumar n.d.: 127. See also the Fortnightly Reports from Travancore for this year in R/1/1/1889.

'to secure adequate representation of all interests and all points of view and to fit the constitution into the scheme of Federation now under contemplation in India'.[74]

As these proposals did not allude to any communal safeguards, Ezhavas, Muslims and different Christian sects immediately forwarded their claims for a representation commensurate with their numerical strength in the population. They demanded separate electorates, or at least reserved seats, and, in case adult franchise was impossible, a widening of the existing franchise so as to guarantee proportional representation. Their main argument was that communalism was 'so strong and deep-rooted' that without its own champions in the representative institutions a community could hardly hope to have its claims satisfied.[75] Their agitation drew encouragement from the Communal Award promulgated for British India in August 1932.

The constitutional reforms that were published in Travancore a month later fell far short of the political aspirations that had been rising among many disadvantaged communities.[76] The main disillusionment for the politically active Christians, Ezhavas and Muslims was the government's forthright rejection of communal electorates and even reserved seats. From the outset, the government made it perfectly clear that it considered such measures to be unsuited to conditions in Travancore, where they could only contribute to the creation and multiplication of existing communal cleavages and to the promotion of sectional interests, endangering the larger interests of the state. In its stead the government preferred direct election combined with the compensatory principle of nomination.

The reforms introduced a bicameral system consisting of an assembly and state council. The (*Sri Mulam*) assembly became the main legislative body. It numbered 62 non-official members, of whom 43 were elected by general constituencies and 5 by special constituencies representing the landlords, planters, commerce and industry. 14 seats were reserved for the nomination of members from communities who were considered unable to secure adequate representation by general election. Half this number was ear-marked for groups like the Ezhavas who got at least 4 seats by nomination, and the Muslims

[74] Travancore Government Communiqué 2.6.1932, quoted in Ouwerkerk 1994: 83.

[75] HFMK II 1972: 334 ff.; TPPP 1934: 4; Chiriyankandath 1985: 224.

[76] Full text of Travancore Government Communiqué 29.10.1932 in L/P&S/13/886.

who got 2. A similar arrangement applied to the council: it had 27 non-official members of whom 16 were elected by general constituencies and 5 were nominated. Women had equal voting rights with men and two seats were reserved for them out of those filled by nomination (see Appendix I). Franchise for both houses was on the same footing but at higher rates for the council. In all, only about 3 per cent of the population was enfranchised which was hardly an increase compared to the 1921 reforms.[77]

Both houses had the power to initiate and pass legislation, but the assembly, with the right to vote on the budget, succeeded the old legislative council as the main legislative body. They had no control over the executive which remained firmly vested in the sole authority of the Dewan. In the 1930s several British Residents complained that centralization in the Dewan was top heavy and only resulted in an extremely slow moving and inefficient bureaucratic machinery. Their suggestions for the establishment of an executive council, or the introduction of secretaries above the heads of departments but not co-equal to the Dewan, were ignored, and the Political Department saw no reason to press the matter. In 1931 the Resident cautioned that too much pressure on the Maharani-Regent might hurt her feelings 'which is just what the Government of India desire to avoid'.[78]

Consequently communal organizations of Christians, Ezhavas and Muslims held protest meetings and decided to send deputations to the Dewan to represent their grievances. Realizing that their interests might be better served by joining forces, their leaders established a Joint Political Conference (*Samyukta Rashtriya Samiti*, December 1932), modelled on the non-Brahmin Justice Party in Madras. Hailed as the first political party in Travancore, this was in fact a common platform for a number of communal organizations. Nevertheless, these organizations had been able to create a space where they could meet and develop a common stand *vis-a-vis* the government.

In January 1933 a deputation of this Joint Political Conference (JPC) warned the Dewan that the published electoral rules would 'result only in the accentuation of communal bitterness in the state and the prevention of the formation of popular parties on political lines'. The JPC rejected representation by government nomination as an inadequate compensation for representation by election. The demand for com-

[77] TPPP 1934: Appendix 64 ff.

[78] The quotation is from a letter by H.R.N. Pritchard, British Resident, to Political Department, 16.3.1931, L/P&S/13/1283. See also the Resident's Confidential Memorandum, 26.11.1935 in R/2(888/207).

munal electorates was dropped but the deputation argued instead with increased vigour for reservation of seats in joint electorates (or multi-member constituencies) for the major communities in proportion to their share in the population. Finally, to lend more strength to their argument, the deputation referred to British India where the principle of reservation had been accepted by the Communal Award. The government, also following British Indian policies, suggested the holding of a Round Table Conference to discuss a rearrangement of the constituencies, but the leaders of the JPC wanted to draw up a larger agenda before they were ready to join such a conference.[79]

Some weeks later representatives of the constituent organizations of the JPC met again and passed the important abstention resolution, saying that the Christian, Ezhava and Muslim communities 'should abstain from taking part either by voting or by standing as candidates in the elections or by accepting nominations to the reformed Legislative Bodies so long as Government do not make provision for the representation by election of all considerable communities proportionate to their populations in the Legislature'.[80]

In a few long letters exchanged immediately after the start of the Abstention Movement the different positions were clearly marked out. The government refused to grant reservation of seats, primarily because it understood reservation as special protection to certain minorities. The concession of reservation to all communities in the state, including the Brahmins and Nayars, as advocated by the JPC, was a contradiction in terms having no counterpart anywhere else. The JPC found this lack of a counterpart no ground for refusing reservation and stipulated that in case of the Nayars, reservation was actually meant not to protect them but to prevent their long-standing but undue predominance in the legislative bodies.

The government and JPC also held radically different views on the possible effects that seat reservation might have on future political developments in the state. The government said it feared the reservation of seats would only increase communal bitterness and hinder the growth of popular parties on political lines. The JPC, on the other hand, contended that the reforms proposed by the government in fact placed all other communities under the dominance of one group, the Nayars, and that this unequal distribution of power was the basic cause of the intensification of communal strife and division. Only the

[79] TPPP 1934: 35 ff., Appendix 115 ff., Ouwerkerk 1994: 85 ff.
[80] TPPP 1934: 36–7; HFMK II 1972: 343–5.

institution of multi-member joint electorates with reserved seats and a well-balanced representation in the legislature would create a suitable climate for the formation of political parties transcending communal limitations.

Apart from these fundamental differences, there was the practical problem of how the territorial extent of constituencies could be so arranged as to secure exact proportional representation between all sections of the population. These and other reasons made the government conclude that the proposed electoral reforms should first be given a fair trial before alterations could be raised for consideration. The JPC, however, was not convinced that the administrative difficulties in delineating the large multi-member constituencies were so great as the government tended to suggest. Also, it did not think a trial could serve any useful purpose. Therefore, abstention was and remained the JPC's final stand. But it deliberately refrained from using the term non-co-operation with a view to dissociate itself from what non-cooperation had come to mean during recent events in British India.[81]

In spite of strenuous efforts on the part of the government to make them a success, the Travancore elections of 1933 turned out to be a poor show. Only a handful of Christians, Ezhavas and Muslims could be persuaded to stand as candidates, only a quarter of the general electorate voted, and in most constituencies candidates were returned unopposed. As the abstentionists had predicted and in fact laboured for, the Nayars gained a large majority in both houses (35 of the 59 elected general seats), Christians won 10 seats in both houses but the other large communities only had a few representatives. The British Resident reported grudgingly that the abstentionist movement had achieved a considerable measure of success,[82] though the Viceroy in a banquet speech in Trivandrum at the end of the year still called abstention from participation in the constitutional changes 'ill-advised'.[83] Attempts by the opposition to have the legislature dissolved met with no success.

The inauguration of provincial autonomy in British India served as an incentive to the struggle for responsible government in the states. In the same year (1935) the Government of Travancore announced its intention to reconsider the thorny question of the revision of the

[81] All texts in TPPP 1934: 135–61.

[82] Fortnightly Report from Travancore for the second half of June 1933, R/1/1/2338.

[83] Viceroy's banquet speech at reception in Trivandrum, 10.12.1933, L/P&S/13/1283.

electorates in order to bring about a just and equitable representation in the legislature.[84] Upon hearing this news Christians, Ezhavas and Muslims resumed their agitation against 'the caste Hindu monopoly of political power' and reiterated their demand for 'the establishment of equal opportunities for all classes and communities in the state'.[85] However, they were still in the dark about the specific reforms the government had in mind. The British Resident who had been consulted in private by the Dewan, Sir Habibullah, welcomed the reform proposals as sound measures and felt especially satisfied that they did not contemplate the introduction of communal representation on any large scale.[86]

A few months later the Travancore government made its reforms publicly known. In a covering communiqué the government explained that it could not conceive of a legislature in which the elected seats were parcelled out in strictly mathematical proportions among no less than 12 to 14 communities. Therefore, the major contingent of seats remained to be filled in open competition which would involve a trial of strength between the Nayars and the Syrian Christians. Communities who were small or backward, however, would continue to have their interests served by the door of nomination. The government also thought it necessary to introduce seat reservation for those communities who were numerically strong and politically conscious and yet, by the manner of the distribution of their population in the state, unable to command a majority in any constituency.

Following these broad guidelines, Ezhavas, Muslims and Latin Catholics lost virtually all their nominated seats in the assembly to Scheduled Castes, Protestant Christians and female representatives. In return they were given an increased number of reserved seats (14) in the general constituencies. The same applied to the council where these communities received fewer nominations but were allotted four reserved seats where previously they had held none. Altogether Muslim representation rose from 2 to 4 seats in the assembly; in the council their number remained at 3, but now including the special seat for Commerce (Appendix I).

[84] Fortnightly Report from Travancore for the first half of June 1935, R/1/1/2645; text of Government Press Communiqué in R/2(888/212).

[85] Statement to the Press by Joint Political Conference, dated 15.7.1935, R/2(888/212).

[86] Letter from W.A.M. Garstin, British Resident, 15.7.1935, to Secretary to Political Department, R/2(888/212).

On account of their geographical distribution even universal suffrage would not help Ezhavas, Muslims and Latin Catholics secure the minimum number of seats in both Houses as promised under the reforms. To ensure them that minimum it would have been necessary either to take recourse to the principle of separate electorates or to reserve them seats in multi-member constituencies. The Travancore government was definitely of the opinion, and in this it was supported by the British Resident, that the second possibility was 'less objectionable'. Therefore, it appointed a Commissioner for Franchise and Delimitation and instructed him, in line with these general considerations, to make detailed proposals regarding the principles of franchise and the delimitation of constituencies.[87]

One year later the Commissioner submitted his report. On the strength of his recommendations the government passed orders widening the franchise and regrouping the constituencies. All persons paying a land tax of no less than one rupee, or any municipal tax at all, were enfranchised and so were the poor fishermen who held a certificate for fishing. This raised the percentage of the enfranchised population to 10–12 per cent, about a sixth of the adult population, and a proportion similar to that in British India following the Government of India Act. The 43 existing electoral divisions were dissolved and the state was divided into 17 new multi-member constituencies returning 43 members to the assembly and 10 similar divisions returning 16 members to the council. These multi-member joint electorates included a number of seats having a reserved qualification. The Quilon and Kottakara constituency, for example, returned 3 members to the assembly but 1 seat was reserved for a Muslim and 1 for an Ezhava. In constituencies returning only 1 member, no reservation was made.[88]

Although no definite assurances were given to all of the many Christian sections, the supporters of the Abstention movement reacted favourably. At least a large part of their demands were conceded. The delimitation of the new constituencies was such that, in view of their voting strength, 10 of the 29 generally elected assembly seats were likely to go to the Nayars, 10 to the Syrian Christians, and 4 to other Hindu castes, leaving only 5 seats for really open competition. That meant that the Nayars especially, who till then had controlled

[87] Travancore Government Press Communiqué, 17.8.1935, L/P&S/13/1283.

[88] Travancore Government Orders of 20.8.1936, L/P&S/13/1283 and R/2(888/217); RAT 1935–6: 100–1; Ouwerkerk 1994: 88; Chiriyankandath 1985: 263.

most of the elected seats, had to face a painful loss of influence, which they accepted, at least for the moment, 'with remarkable good grace'.[89] Deputations by Nayars who on second thoughts came to the Dewan to vent their misgivings over the recent electoral reforms, were set at ease by the assurance that in case the new regulations would not give them an equal opportunity for self-expression the government would not be a party to perpetuating that kind of injustice.[90]

The 1937 elections took place in a quiet atmosphere that was free of the more extreme manifestations of communal tension. The JPC captured 25 of the 48 elected seats in the new assembly and became the largest single party. The protected communities gratefully secured their reserved seats and both Nayars and Syrian Christians succeeded in sending 12 of their number to the assembly. However, there was no change in the constitutional set-up of the state. The powers of the legislature remained as they had been under the 1932 constitution and the executive offices of the government remained firmly in the hands of the Maharaja and Dewan. Whereas in the provinces of British India provincial autonomy was being introduced, the Travancore political forces were aligning for a new contest: the demand for responsible government under the personal rule of a hereditary monarch. That was the main challenge facing the erstwhile JPC, now reorganized with some Nayar support into a larger body called the Samyukta Party.

The Public Services

In another field the communities behind the Abstention Movement were more successful. After the investiture of the new Maharaja the government had appointed a Public Service Commission to investigate official recruitment and the principles to be observed.[91] Its findings confirmed the strength of communal preference by establishing that caste Hindus held a number of appointments three times higher than their share in the total population, whereas Ezhavas, as numerous as the Nayars, held only 3 or 4 per cent. The Christians with 31.5 per

[89] Letter by W.A.M. Garstin, Resident, Quilon 28.8.1936, to Political Department, L/P&S/13/1283 and Fortnightly Report from Travancore for the second part of August 1936, R/1/1/2791.

[90] Fortnightly Report from Travancore for the first half of November 1936, R/1/1/2791.

[91] Fortnightly Report from Travancore for the second part of August 1932, R/1/1/2224.

cent of the population held 16.6 per cent of the jobs. The Mar Thoma (Syrians) Christians as a highly literate group were overrepresented and the overall Christian shortfall was caused by the poor representation of the Catholic and Protestant converts from the lower Hindu castes.

To remedy this imbalance the Commission did not think it practical to make provision for the representation of every individual community. Therefore, its report listed only 14 major communities and recommended that each have its share of appointments to the lower services. In the superior services the majority of the posts should be filled under a complicated scheme of selective examinations within rotating communities.[92] The government, not entirely convinced, took no immediate action, but after a year of indecision, placed Dr G.D. Nokes, an European judge of the Travancore High Court, on special duty to study the recruitment problem afresh.

This appointment was probably provoked by an unexpected development. In July 1934 the Chief Secretary to the Government had asked all heads of departments and offices to return the total number of persons employed in each department, their salaries and communal background according to a schedule. This schedule listed nine communal categories and grouped Hindus and Christians of untouchable caste origin together into one and the same category as distinct from the Christians of higher status. In September a local paper published a copy of this schedule and alleged that government had already accepted it as a means of distributing official employment.[93] Official spokesmen hastened to emphasize that the schedule was purely for departmental use and issued merely to collect statistics, but the harm was done.

The news aroused a storm of protest and made several communities express their particular concerns. Syrian Christians objected to separation from the Latin Catholics and insinuated that this bureaucratic division was solely meant to prevent them from getting a share in the services on the strength of the total number of Christians in the state. The Latin Catholics, formed out of the lower Hindu castes and fishermen along the coast, resented the loss of status implied by their

[92] TPSRC 1934: 87, 120.

[93] *Yuvabharati* 1.9.1934, quoted in *Weekly Secret Bulletin* 1.9.1934; note by Garstin, Resident, about alleged re-classification of Christians in Travancore, 16.4.1935, L/P&S/13/1291.

suggested classification with the untouchable or so-called depressed classes. The archbishop of Trivandrum even spoke of religious persecution as Ezhavas and other low castes on becoming Christian would go further down on the social scale.[94]

Echoes of this uproar reached London, where the schedule was rather thoughtlessly perceived by some politicians as a measure directed against Christianity as such. From his correspondence with Travancore Lord FitzAlan, a Catholic member of the House of Lords, concluded that the Maharaja's government had grown alarmed by the growth of Christianity and wanted to reduce its influence. His Lordship asked, and was granted permission, to question the government whether it was true that the Catholic Christians in Travancore were classified and treated as depressed classes.[95] Informed about the Lord's intentions, the Political Department in London lamented, 'if there were such a thing as being out of order in the House of Lords, this would be out of order'.[96] The matter was considered an internal one over which the Political Department had no jurisdiction. Nevertheless, in order to deal with Lord FitzAlan more effectively, the department asked the government of India for more detailed information, emphasizing that it would obviously help them, if they were in a position to point out that not only the Travancore government but the churches too made some distinction between Christians from different caste communities.[97] And here, the department touched upon a weak spot, pointing at divisions not so much between Hindus and Christians as among the Christians themselves.

The major Christian churches in Travancore had their own built-in communal tensions. These tensions became manifest not only in matters of worship and burial but extended also to the field of employment. Most of the public service positions allotted to different categories of Christians were occupied by Syrians who as a literate community dominated the Catholic and Protestant church organizations.[98] Therefore, Christians from a lower caste background had

[94] Statement by president All Kerala Catholic Congress in *Indian Express*, 16.3.1935; letter from Archbishop of Trivandrum to Garstin, Resident, 8.3.1935, R/2(888/213).

[95] Question by Lord FitzAlan, 13 March 1935, in House of Lords, R/2(889/236).

[96] Correspondence W.O. Croft, India Office, 18.2.1935, L/P&S/13/1291.

[97] Correspondence W.D. Croft, India Office, with Board of Education, 7.3.1935, L/P&S/13/1291.

[98] See for instance the LMS, Travancore Correspondence, Box 32–3.

appealed to the government urging that they should be differentiated from the other Christians. As a result, the government had in 1933 introduced for purposes of employment a separate category of Christians, those belonging to the Depressed Classes.

This information enabled the government in London to give Lord FitzAlan an adequate reply. Viscount Halifax, president of the Board of Education, could quote from a statement made by the government of Travancore to inform the House of Lords that the existing classification of Christians was made after consultation with leading representatives of the Christian communities. Latin Catholics as well as Protestant churches claimed as a right to be considered a separate but formerly untouchable community for purposes of educational and other concessions. FitzAlan was far from satisfied with this answer but for the moment had to give in.[99] The same proceedings took place in the House of Commons where questions were raised by the Duchess of Athol, a Scottish member and sister of the Viceroy.

The majority of the Travancore press commented adversely both on the interpellation by FitzAlan and the reply given by Halifax. The Nayar papers vehemently condemned the Christian 'agitators' who were held responsible for getting Travancore a bad name abroad, while a public meeting of depressed class Christians at Trivandrum denounced the intervention in Parliament as solely meant to discredit a government which was giving them such valuable assistance. Only a section of the Latin Catholics, while requesting they be treated as a separate community, recorded its gratitude to Lord FitzAlan and the Duchess of Athol for the political interventions made on their behalf.[100]

The day after FitzAlan asked his questions in Parliament, Nokes, entrusted with the task to offer new recommendations on the recruitment problem, submitted his report to the government of Travancore. Based on his recommendations the government promulgated an order regulating recruitment to the various classes of service and the communal proportion. The principle of communal representation was accepted, inevitably, but only to a certain extent. For that purpose the new rules recognized eight Hindu caste groups, the Muslims and six Christian denominations. The Syrian and Latin Catholics were split

[99] Reply by the Government of Travancore, 10.3.1935, forwarded by the Government of India, Political Department, New Delhi 12.3.1935, to Secretary of State for India, London CRR/2(889/236). For a more detailed discussion of this question, see Kooiman 1993.

[100] *Weekly Secret Bulletin* from 23.3.1935 to 18.5.1935.

into two distinct categories and the classification of Christian converts along with Hindus as depressed classes was abolished. The term 'Depressed Classes' was studiously avoided.

The order introduced a three-tier division in the administrative service. In the higher division efficiency was to be the primary criterion with only a vaguely defined safeguard against communal underrepresentation. In the intermediate services 60 per cent of the posts were to be allotted to the best qualified candidates with communal preference for the remainder. In the lower division all recruitment would be on the basis of communal representation and rotation. In all divisions promotions would be determined by merit and years of service.

Nokes was appointed the first Public Service Commissioner under the new scheme of recruitment. Henceforth all appointments to the public service would be made on the advice of the Commissioner. All the communities recognized by the government order, with the exception of the Brahmins, Nayars and other caste Hindus, Jacobite and Mar Thoma Syrians, were considered inadequately represented and therefore entitled to preferential treatment. Only the temple department and the military remained excluded from the purview of the new rules. Government had made a major concession in the sphere of employment and in a confidential report Garstin, the British Resident, assured the Government of India that the new scheme, closely following similar legislation in British India, was undeniably on the right lines. He called it 'an unbiased and earnest scheme free of favouritism and communal bias'. The succeeding Resident agreed and reported that Nokes was doing a very conscientious job.[101]

Still, it was not long before the underrepresented communities started to complain that most of the key positions were still falling to the Brahmins, Nayars and the more established Syrian Christians. There was certainly some ground for concern, as actual appointments were still being made by the heads of the departments in utter disregard of all government recommendations. The resulting disappointment led a Latin Catholic member to move a resolution in the legislature urging the government to guarantee that all recognized communities were duly represented in the bureaucracy.

[101] Government Order No. 893, published in *Government Gazette*, 25.6.1935, pp. 1243 ff. Confidential report by Garstin, Resident, to Glancy, Political Secretary, 28.6.1935, L/P&S/13/1291. Notes by Skrine, Resident, June 1938 and 26.3.1938, R/2(889/236) and L/P&S/13/1291.

The heated discussion that followed only disclosed the deep-rooted communal bitterness that prevailed among the various representatives. In an exhaustive reply the Dewan argued that there was no cause for complaint. He could refer to the latest report of the Public Service Commissioner which showed that the till then inadequately represented communities, like the Ezhavas, Muslims, and Latin Catholics, had received 38 per cent of the available appointments in the intermediate division and more than 66 per cent of the appointments in the lower division. The resolution was withdrawn.[102]

An adequate representation in the public services was also a prominent issue in the abstention movement that was discussed above. There was a strong personal overlap between the movements for political representation and official employment, and largely the same communities, especially Nayars and Christians, stood lined up in this fierce rivalry for official benefit. Stray references in the Resident's reports mention attempts by small groups to use the public employment issue to exacerbate communal feelings on a larger scale. The main difference between both movements was that in the fight for the small number of legislative seats Christians were better able to close rank and pose as a homogeneous community. In the fight for the much more numerous places in government service however, Christians were split in a number of distinct, mutually competing sub-communities, as was already clear from the Latin Catholic refusal to be grouped together with the Syrians. Another example may serve to illustrate this point.

A long-considered scheme of union between two Protestant churches, established by the Anglican and Independent missionary societies, was rejected by the latter. The rejection was couched in doctrinal and organizational terms but the main reason had to do with their separate entitlement to a certain proportion of public appointments under the 1935 government order. If union were effected with the Anglicans in northern Travancore, it was feared that 'the plums of office and appointment' would go to the small but more advanced section of Syrians that was present in the Anglican but absent in the Independent mission church. The decision was a purely Indian affair, leaving the missionaries to lament that their converts were becoming more and more communal in outlook.[103]

[102] SMAP 26.11.1937.

[103] Account of Travancore Church Council (Independents) 1935 and letter by Eastaff, missionary, 10.7.1935, in LMS, Correspondence Box 33. Sinclair, missionary at Martandam, 15.10.1936, to Garstin, Resident, R/2(888/219).

Civil Disobedience 1938–1939

On 2 February 1938 a motion in the assembly to discuss the urgent need for the establishment of reponsible government was ruled out of order by the Dewan. According to Sir C.P. Ramaswamy Aiyar, the Travancore constitution exhibited all the characteristics of a fully responsive (as differentiated from a responsible) form of government. Apart from that, a fundamental change of the constitution was impossible in view of the existing treaty obligations of the ruler to the paramount power.[104] The vehement debate that followed remained inconclusive, but a definite answer came across the seas when an important question was raised in the House of Commons. Drawing attention to the Dewan of Travancore's statement that the power of an Indian ruler to grant measures of responsible government was restricted by the necessity of obtaining the explicit consent of the paramount power, Captain Heligers asked what the policy of the British government was in this matter. On the day that the Haripura Congress adopted its resolution on states, the Under Secretary of State for India answered in reply: 'It is not the policy of the Paramount Power in ordinary circumstances to intervene in the internal administration of full-powered States. In particular, I can assure Captain Heligers that the Paramount Power would certainly not obstruct proposals for constitutional advance initiated by a Ruler.'[105]

This was another stimulus for local politicians to start a campaign for the introduction of responsibility in government and the removal of a high handed and controversial Dewan.

The Haripura session had defined *purna swaraj* for the whole of India, inclusive of the states, as its final end in view. It had directed however, that the struggle in the states should not be undertaken by Congress committees but by independent local organizations. In consequence, a Travancore Congress Committee, formed the year before, was disbanded and discussions to form a local organization were resumed with renewed vigour.

The Congress resolution on states, endorsed by the annual session at Haripura, had earlier that month been drafted by the Congress

[104] See Fortnightly Reports from Travancore, January 1938, L/P&S/13/1283; Ouwerkerk 1994: 126–7.

[105] Question by Captain Heligers in the House of Commons, 21.2.1938, R/1/1/3060 and L/PO/5/20; Pernau-Reifeld 1992: 282; Ouwerkerk 1994: 128. Copland observes that the wording of the reply even suggested that government was in favour of constitutional change, Copland 1997: 165.

Working Committee at Wardha. In these first weeks of February several meetings took place at Trivandrum attended by many of the leading public figures, members of the legislative, lawyers and journalists from different communities. They resolved to start a common political organization to work for responsible government. On 23 February, another preliminary meeting was held which in the light of the Haripura resolution decided to form an independent Travancore State Congress. The attainment of responsible government under the aegis of His Highness the Maharaja by all peaceful and legitimate means was defined as their major objective.[106] In its first press statement the Travancore State Congress (TSC) disputed the Dewan's refusal to concede major reforms and welcome of the recent statement of the British government in Parliament.[107]

Building on the foundations laid by the Samyukta Party the TSC aimed at creating as broad a coalition as possible. Apart from Brahmins it contained a cross-section of the major communities of Travancore, including a strong Syrian Christian element and a few individual Nayars. Pattom Thanu Pillai (Nayar) was elected president, T.M. Verghese (a Mar Thoma Syrian) deputy president, and C. Kesavan (Ezhava), who was involved in the Abstention movement and the JPC, became a prominent member. Most of the leaders maintained their links with their respective communal organizations. These double affiliations were forbidden by the INC, but the constitution of the TSC remained silent on this point. Yet this Travancore Congress was more than a communal association. By bringing constituents from different communities together on a shared platform it may be called a supra-communal organization with people ready to work together for common goals and to forget their petty quarrels, at least for the moment.

The formation of the TSC came at a timely moment. The year 1938, as Copland has emphasized, witnessed a vast popular awakening in princely India, even though the reasons are not yet fully understood.[108] British authorities saw in this awakening a deep Congress plot and the Travancore government reacted by imposing rigorous restrictions on

[106] The same objective had been laid down by a provisional State Congress meeting as far back as 1930, see Fortnightly Report from Travancore for the second part of December 1930, R/1/1/1889.

[107] *The Hindu* 28.2.1938; Chiriyankandath 1985: 285; Daniel 1985: 38-40; Kumar n.d.: 157; Ouwerkerk 1994: 113, 136.

[108] Copland 1985: 127.

TSC activities like membership recruitment, press publications and public meetings (March 1938). Louise Ouwerkerk, an eye-witness to many of these events, describes what she saw as a recurrent pattern at authorized TCS meetings: disturbances were created by rowdies who, unhindered by the on-looking police, abused or even physically assaulted the individual TSC leaders. The resulting chaos and confusion were attributed to the inflammatory speeches of these leaders who were accused by the government of subversive activities.[109]

In May 1938 the TSC addressed a memorial to the Maharaja, petitioning for a cabinet of ministers responsible to a legislature elected by adult franchise. As an important step towards that end the memorial asked for a declaration of civil rights with freedom of press, speech and assembly. Added to the memorial was a memorandum which contained an elaborate attack on the Dewan, asking for his immediate dismissal from the service of the state and an independent inquiry into his administrative and financial transactions as Dewan. As government refused acknowledgement of these documents signed by 21 leading members of the TSC, they were published in Cochin under the title *Travancore Today: Her Struggle for Freedom*. Although the Resident made efforts to make the signatories prove their evidence in courts, there were no arrests and no public tribunal.[110]

In spite of a temporary ban on the TSC, its leaders refused to submit. Gandhi sent a personal messenger to Travancore, Rajkumari Amrit Kaur, a Christian lady with royal background (Kapurthala state). She found no desire on the part of the Dewan to come to a settlement and left the state, according to the Resident 'thoroughly depressed',[111] to report failure to Gandhi. Gandhi was not convinced that the TSC was disloyal or subversive, but rejected the personal attacks on the Dewan as contained in the memorial.[112] He wanted the TSC to focus on the principles of democracy and freedom and urged the signatories to withdraw their charges unconditionally.[113] Mrs Amrit Kaur left the state on 25 August and the same day the TSC was declared an unlawful association. Nonetheless, the next day it held a meeting on

[109] Ouwerkerk 1994: 136, 139.

[110] Fortnightly Report from Travancore for the first part of June 1938, L/P&S/13/1283; Ouwerkerk 1994: 142.

[111] Fortnightly Report from Travancore for the second part of August 1938, L/P&S/13/1283.

[112] *The Hindu* 3.9.1938.

[113] Ouwerkerk 1994: 144–5, 154.

Trivandrum beach where its leaders Pattom and Verghese were duly arrested.

Civil Disobedience had started in earnest. The movement was fought in a campaign full of bitterness and personal recriminations. Leaders when arrested nominated their own successor as the next 'dictator', but with the restraining hand of most leaders removed, events were getting out of hand. Police interventions left a number of people wounded, school life was interrupted, and the press rigidly controlled. The Resident reported that most of the Congress support came from the largely Christian areas in north and central Travancore. There were a few demonstrative processions in sympathy for the TSC from Madras and Cochin but they played an insignificant part. The government of Madras noted that the political agitation in Travancore was conducted entirely by subjects of that state and it was not being materially reinforced from outside.[114]

Perturbed by the growing agitation and public attacks on his personal integrity, the Dewan resorted to a policy of divide and rule, demonstrating that this strategy was not the exclusive property of the colonial power. First of all he tried to isolate the local Christians by denouncing the demand for responsible government as the Christian version of communalism, in utter disregard of the important non-Christian participation in the TSC and similar demands raised in states without a significant Christian minority. Also, he tried to instil fear in the minds of the Hindus by accusing Christians, whose share in the population was still increasing, of an ulterior motive, 'from time immemorial', to take over Travancore and change it into a Christian state. In his conversation with Amrit Kaur he harped on the same subject and explained that he was opposed to responsible government, as it would definitely mean a Christian oligarchy.[115] During the viceregal visit to Travancore (January 1939) he pressed the same point, and apparently not altogether in vain: after his visit Lord Linlithgow took a slightly more favourable view of Sir C.P. and wrote privately to the Secretary of State that the Travancore state was finally taken well in

[114] Confidential letter from Chief Secretary to Government of Madras to the Secretary to the Crown Representative, 15.12.1938, L/P&S/13/1283.

[115] Copy of a Statement on Travancore by Rajkumari Amrit Kaur, 29.8.1938, in Ouwerkerk Collection, Nr. 48. Ouwerkerk 1994: 153. Apparently, the Resident was so impressed by the Dewan's representations that in one of his reports he referred to the 'Christian State Congress', see Fortnightly Report from Travancore for the second part of September 1938, L/P&S/13/1291.

hand by a Dewan who had 'cut the claws of the important, well-educated and intelligent Syrian Christian element'.[116]

The Civil Disobedience of 1938 only deepened the existing hostility between the Dewan and the TSC, especially the Syrian Christian part of it. During the campaign their largest bank, the Travancore National and Quilon Bank Ltd. went into liquidation. There were strong suspicions that this bank crash was orchestrated by the Dewan, as the bank managers, two Syrian Christian businessmen, had incurred official displeasure by joining the opposition and financing the State Congress. One of them, K.C. Mammen Mapillay, had taken a prominent part in the founding of the JPC. Announcing its closure Mammen Mapillay attributed the bank's difficulties to the malicious propaganda carried on by Sir C.P.[117] This incident, which had long after-effects, offers an additional explanation why local capital shied away from large-scale investments in the economy of the state.

About the same time Sir C.P. encouraged the Hindu Mahasabha to come to Travancore. The Hindu Mahasabha (HM) was not a religious body but a communal organization that championed Hindu political interests whatever they might be. As we shall see, it played a dubious role in Hyderabad politics, in spite of vigorous attempts by the government of that state to curtail its activities. Sir C.P., on the other hand, welcomed its president, V.D. Savarkar, in Travancore and blessed his efforts to establish a local branch of the HM 'in order to infuse among the Hindus the consciousness of a pan-Hindu solidarity and strength'. From Savarkar's presidential address to the next HM annual conference (Nagpur, December 1938) we may glean what he had learned about Travancore. In that address he stated that, though the Christians posed no threat to India as a whole, in Travancore they had to be closely watched and kept in check, as 'the Christians seem to cherish political designs against the Hindu state'.[118] The Travancore branch of HM however, never amounted to more than a handful of Brahmans and Nayars who backed Sir C.P.'s policies.

In 1936 government temples had been opened to all Hindu castes. This 'spiritual fall of the Bastille', as it has been characterized by Louise

[116] Private letter Lord Linlithgow to Lord Zetland, Secretary of State, 17.1.1939, L/P&S/13/1283.

[117] The bank case has been discussed very extensively by Ouwerkerk 1994. C.P. Mathen, the other director of the bank, recalled his bitterness in a booklet with the revealing title *I Have Borne Much* (1943).

[118] Quotations from Ouwerkerk 1994: 172.

Ouwerkerk, was not only meant to proclaim the universality of the Hindu faith, as Sir C.P. would have it in his public utterances on this subject.[119] It was also, and maybe primarily, a deliberate move to reduce receptivity among lower castes like the Ezhavas to other, particularly Christian, religious influences and to wean them away from the anti-government coalition. Not content with the mere opening of temple gates, the government also took charge of the training of Hindu priests in Sanskrit and the scriptures.[120]

As part of this strategy to consolidate the Hindu body in the state, Sir C.P.'s government extended considerable patronage to a Kerala Hindu Mission. This mission, meant to reconvert those who had gone over to Christianity, received financial support and land grants out of the Hindu Charitable Endowment Fund.[121] Measures already under contemplation were now implemented, like the withdrawal of school fee concessions from depressed class children who became Christians, and the amendment of the Educational Code prohibiting the running of schools in church buildings and prayer houses. The resulting indignation led to new questions being raised in the British Parliament. The government pleaded financial and practical motivations in taking these steps,[122] but could not deny that they affected almost exclusively the education by Christian missions among the lower castes. In a pamphlet printed in connection with the Hindu Mission the authors praised the government and called the Christian missionaries their 'chief enemies in this *Kali Yuga*'. They said, 'The spectacle of Hindu boys whose faces shine with the throb of Aryan blood in their veins entering a mission school is indeed unbearable.'[123]

These various measures, obviously impelled by a desire to check conversions of Hindu subjects to Christianity, did not greatly hurt the interests of the Syrians who generally were not eager to embrace

[119] Iyer II 1945: 323–4.

[120] Ouwerkerk 1994: 98–9.

[121] It should be remembered that at the same time Christian missions in the state were receiving government grants-in-aid to an extent that would be unthinkable in the British ruled Indian provinces.

[122] Press Communiqué Government of Travancore, 17.12.1937, explaining revision of fee concessions, L/P&S/13/1291. Amendment Educational Code, R/2(888/219). In reaction to the many protests, government consented not to apply these measures retrospectively. For a more detailed discussion, Kooiman 1996.

[123] *Christian Missionaries: we do not want them anymore* (1936), enclosed in letter by Garstin, Resident, 29.4.1936, L/P&S/13/1291. A handwritten comment in the margin of this pamphlet reads: 'This might have been a Nazi pamphlet'.

converts from the lower classes. But it increased the feeling among poor and lower-class Christians that they might incur government displeasure by associating too closely with the Syrian opposition and that they had their own cause to defend.

Finally, the Dewan made use of his power of nomination to the public services and legislatur to reward loyalty. Nayars were most prominent among those so privileged, but Ezhavas, after a period of threat and alienation, were also honoured with selective appointments, changing erstwhile staunch opponents into government henchmen. The oppositional state Congress, the Dewan was fond of observing, was a communal organization, whose leaders were self-seekers in as much as practically all of them had applied to him for jobs and had been refused.[124] But when occasion required, their applications were accepted. Resident C.P. Skrine observed that the Dewan ruled by dividing, and bribed with offices and other favours, with the result that communalism was rampant and intruded into every department. Even, so the Resident, who was never known as a great critic of C.P. Ramaswamy Aiyar, considered 'the judicious distribution of the loaves and fishes among the adherents of Government . . . a perfectly logical and indeed inevitable feature of the policy of an administration which regards the demand for responsible government as dangerously revolutionary'.[125]

On the Maharaja's birthday in October a large demonstration was held in Trivandrum. Louise Ouwerkerk, who clearly sympathized with the local Congress, saw thousands of people dressed in *khaddar* and wearing Gandhi caps, and concluded that the TSC commanded huge popular support. The Resident, on the other hand, following Sir C.P., had a poor opinion of the TSC and called it 'a thoroughly selfish and parochial movement based on hatred, falsehood [and] communalism . . .'.[126] He saw no excitement or public interest in the TSC.

On this festive occasion the Maharaja released all Civil Disobedience prisoners and the State Congress regained its legal status. The TSC however, had become a house divided. Most of the Christian members wanted to continue the struggle and refused to withdraw the

[124] Sir C.P. quoted in A Statement on Travancore by Rajkumari Amrit Kaur, 29.8.1938, in Ouwerkerk Collection, Nr. 48.

[125] C.P. Skrine, Resident, in Note on the Travancore Disturbances, 11.10.1938, and Fortnightly Report for the first part of June 1938, L/P&S/13/1283.

[126] Fortnightly Report from Travancore for the second part of November 1938, L/P&S/13/1283.

memorandum, with allegations against the Dewan. The other side was more inclined to follow the policies advocated by Gandhi and saw their only chance of success in the forging of a link between their local grievances and a larger all-India movement. In December 1938 the signatories to the memorandum were arrested and threatened by a trial for sedition to be held in camera. Urged by Gandhi they decided to withdraw the controversial memorandum. Just before the viceregal visit the prosecution was dropped and an impartial inquiry avoided. But the deep split within the ranks of the TSC could no longer be concealed.

The Dewan managed to hold its own and responsible government was not drawn any nearer. When the Dewan asked the Political Department (October 1938) whether there was any likelihood of pressure by the British authorities to introduce a further advance in the matter of constitutional reforms, the answer was that the Maharaja's government was free to grant further constitutional concessions or to refrain from doing so.[127] But no pressure was applied, perhaps also because Resident Skrine advised against a delegation of the Maharaja's powers to the elected representatives of his people. In British India, the Resident opined, the able assistance of British or British-trained civil servants and police officers might make experiments in democracy work. But in Travancore, with its inefficient administration, it would be difficult for His Majesty's representative, with his small staff and no authority whatsoever, to help in any material way to make democracy a success. And in case of failure, the Resident warned, the ruler would have a good deal of justification in throwing the blame on the British government.[128]

Sir C.P. also had no cause for triumph. In preparation for the viceregal visit to Travancore he had travelled to New Delhi to discuss the draft speech of the Maharaja at the banquet. The Dewan wanted the ruler to state that the recent constitutional reforms presented the maximum that could safely and properly be given and that the state's subjects now enjoyed practically the same constitutional advantages that British Indians enjoyed under the Montford reforms. Tacitly, he took

[127] Note by B.J. Glancy, Political Department, about his conversation with Sir C.P. Ramaswamy Aiyar, Dewan of Travancore, 8.10.1938, and extract private letter from Lord Linlithgow, Viceroy, to Lord Zetland, Secretary of State for India, dated 20.12.1938, L/P&S/13/1283.

[128] C.P. Skrine, Resident, in Note on the Travancore Disturbances, 11.10.1938, L/P&S/13/1283.

for granted that political developments in Travancore were lagging more than twenty years behind those in British India. However, the Viceroy refused to accept that statement, and the sentence was deleted from the proposed speech.[129]

TSC leaders were planning a new Civil Disobedience in March 1939 aimed at the usual ends. Gandhi however opposed any further Civil Disobedience in the princely states and urged 'to suspend it till I advise resumption'.[130] The TSC maintained only superficial links with the INC in the form of personal messengers (Amrit Kaur, G. Ramachandran) and the display of national symbols (*khaddar* and Gandhi caps). Nevertheless, Gandhi's advice demonstrates his long-distance influence: the TSC leadership, weakened by new arrests, decided to postpone Civil Disobedience indefinitely. The movement was now irretrievably split. Many of the youngsters, disillusioned by the moderate policies of the State Congress, became communists and devoted themselves to work among factory workers and landless labourers. The Indian National Congress proved unable to establish a strong local power base. Prohibition had been a failure, only alienating the important Ezhava community, and *khaddar* and cottage industries had achieved poor results.[131]

In this situation some Nayars, dissatisfied with the 1936 reforms, approached the government and asked for a change in the existing electoral arrangements. Government came a long way to meet their demand and announced that instead of a single non-transferable vote in multi-member constituencies, with reservation of seats every elector would become entitled to as many votes as their were reserved seats in addition to one vote for the general seat. The change implied that the whole electorate could vote for the seats reserved for a particular community. Minority communities like the Muslims and Latin Catholics, who had not been very prominent in the recent political agitation, were granted a special concession whereby any candidate who secured more than 60 per cent or more of the votes polled from his community was declared elected.[132]

As a result of this change, the franchise became communalized,

[129] Private letter Lord Linlithgow to Lord Zetland, 20.12.1938, L/P&S/13/1283; Ouwerkerk 1994: 190.

[130] *The Statesman* 24.3.1939.

[131] Ouwerkerk 1994: 177.

[132] Travancore Press Communiqué (April 1939) in Fortnightly Report from Travancore for the second part of April 1939, L/P&S/13/1283 and 1298.

with electors labelled as of a particular community. Even more important for our central problem is that actually a restricted form of separate electorates was introduced in Travancore: if Muslims and Latin Catholics could muster more than 60 per cent of their vote for one candidate from their community, he would be elected irrespective of the vote by the general electorate. The TSC refuted the measure as an attempt to destroy the small measure of communal agreement that people had been able to build up,[133] but the protest was in vain.

As the approach of war cast its heavy shadows over India and the world, Gandhi was looking for an understanding between the contending parties in Travancore. Towards that end he exhanged telegrams with Sir C.P. and held discussions with Pattom and Verghese. The Dewan and the Maharaja's mother were however determined to keep the TSC isolated from infection by the INC at all costs. Therefore, in a personal interview with TSC leaders, Sir C.P. had made them understand that there could be no question of either outside intervention or responsible government. Gandhi was hurt and accused Sir C.P. of robbing the people of their self-respect. The Dewan remained adamant to the Mahatma's protestations. He insisted on having agreed with the TSC leadership that there was no objection to any private advice so long as it was clearly understood that the responsibility for any action was not of an outside body or individual. He appreciated Gandhi's position as 'one of the great moderating forces in Indian politics' but would not tolerate his intervention in the matter of agitation in Travancore.[134] Another inconclusive interview of TSC leaders with the Dewan followed at the beginning of September, but war had broken out, giving him a welcome excuse to stop all further negotiations.[135]

The War and After

Divided on the attitude to take towards Gandhian politics and the war effort, the TSC was unable to regain strength. Formerly accused by the Dewan of being a Christian communal organization, it was now labelled as a body riddled with communists. It was consequently harassed by the police and struck by temporary government bans. The

[133] *The Hindustan Times* 27.4.1939, 2.6.1939.

[134] Correspondence between Gandhi and Sir C.P., 10.8.1939 and 15.8.1939, R/1/1/3316.

[135] Ouwerkerk 1994: 180.

allegations were never proved, but Sir C.P. successfully weaned a number of leading Ezhavas away from the ranks of the opposition by granting them scholarships or nominations in the state council. At the silver jubilee meeting of the Nayar caste organisation, Savarkar of the Hindu Mahasabha, who was invited to preside, made a strong plea for strengthening the Hindu states and for the consolidation of all Hindu communities in Travancore. Sir C.P. took an active part in the celebrations and promised active cooperation.[136]

In the summer of 1941, Sir Francis Wylie, Political Adviser to the Crown Representative, toured the southern states. He was not impressed by the constitutional position in the states he visited. In Travancore, he noted, the legislature was dominated by government people and was without real power. There was no executive council and Sir Wylie discovered that the Dewan was in fact 'the sole King of the Castle . . . playing upon the innumerable communal differences which are the most conspicuous feature of life on the Malabar coast'.[137] In spite of all obstructions put in its way by this king of the castle, the TSC succeeded in winning 11 seats in the assembly and 3 in the state council during the elections of 1944.[138]

After World War II Travancore became the scene of another conflict when government tried to take over the management of Christian schools as part of its attempt to introduce free and compulsory education. Amidst this turmoil, Sir C.P. Ramaswamy Aiyar launched his plans for a new constitution, patterned on the American model. It provided for an assembly, popularly elected by universal franchise, and a council, composed of representatives of various bodies, interests and professions. The plans did not include a reservation of seats or any other method of securing representation of minorities. There was also no trace of responsibility in the proposed constitutional set-up. The rights and privileges of the Maharaja were to remain unaffected and the Dewan was not removable by vote of the legislature. It was the last bid to save the dynasty and after a failed attempt on his life, the Dewan, the most loyal servant of princely Travancore, had to flee the state in disgrace.[139]

136 Ibid.: 203–7.

137 In another frank comment, he thought the Dewan 'rather like a clever businessman running a farm in England', see Note by Sir Francis Wylie of his visits to Travancore, Cochin and Mysore, 1941, R/1/1/3728.

138 Ouwerkerk 1994: 219–22.

139 Ibid.: 265 ff.

In September 1947 Travancore was granted responsible government. The following year a popular ministry headed by Pattom Thanu Pillai assumed office. Travancore was merged with the state of Cochin and until 1956 the last Maharaja of Travancore served as *Rajpramukh* (Governor) of the new state. In that year, Travancore-Cochin, together with the former directly administered district of Malabar, was incorporated into the new Malayalam-speaking state of Kerala.

This new state, made up for the larger part of former princedoms, has been more or less free from the violent communal outbursts that have plagued large parts of northern India. Nevertheless, less overt but deeply ingrained, Kerala politics are governed by community-based political organizations and votebanks. The state is marked by the peculiar phenomenon of various communities launching their own political parties to promote their particular interests. Therefore, some scholars contend that Kerala politics should be understood as the extension of caste and religion to the public domain.[140]

The several manifestations of communalism in the new Kerala state do not come as a complete surprise. They may be seen as a continuation of the tensions and conflicts that have plagued Kerala, particularly the former Travancore part of it, for a much longer time. George Mathew (1989) has argued that, from a long-term perspective, Kerala has taken the communal road to a secular society. However, such statements remain extremely risky in view of the flexibility of our definitions and the unpredictable twists and turns of the communal phenomenon. Over the past few years Kerala has become a fresh recruiting ground for the Rashtriya Sevak Sangh, a communalist party which has established powerful strongholds especially in Trivandrum, the former capital of Travancore.

COMPARATIVE OBSERVATIONS

Separate electorates were introduced in British India as early as 1906 along with the first cautious steps towards direct elections. They were easily granted to Muslims who as the former ruling minority feared that constitutional reforms might reduce them into insignificance, and

[140] There may be elements of each community in all political parties (with the exception of the Muslim League), yet all parties can be associated with particular communities and within each party factionalism expresses the deeper divisions of religion and caste, see Hardgrave 1979: 209, 211; Varughese 1987; Oommen 1995.

in 1919 extended to the Sikhs, Indian Christians and Anglo-Indians. There was no great struggle needed to get these communal claims conceded and Indian Christians even had serious misgivings about them.[141]

In Travancore, on the other hand, no separate electorates were ever granted, although several communities joined in a desperate campaign to wrest them from a reluctant government.[142] In Baroda there was nobody who even cared to ask for them and only on the eve of Independence did some Muslim groups, echoing the policies of the Muslim League in British India, start to demand separate representation in defence of their political rights.

Seat reservation was introduced in British India in 1919, first for the large group of non-Brahmins and later (1935) for the Scheduled Castes. In Travancore seat reservation had to wait for the reforms of 1935 and applied to Muslims, Ezhavas and Latin Christians only and never to the numerous Scheduled Castes, although Ezhavas might be reckoned to that category. In Baroda there was no reservation of seats at all before 1947.

Nomination, initially the only way to council membership, came later to be used as a principle of distributive justice by allotting seats to groups that might otherwise have no representation. In British India nomination to council membership was abolished in 1935. In Travancore and Baroda, on the other hand, the system of nomination was maintained and even after 1935 nominated members constituted a substantial part of council membership.

There were no separate electorates in Baroda and also communalism was practically unheard of prior to 1947. There were occasionally minor conflicts between Hindus and Muslims, but the only major trouble occurred in 1939 when there were riots in Baroda city between Gujarati and Marathi speakers. One of the few minor Hindu-Muslim conflicts that were reported had to do with municipal elections at Sidhpur in the north. Significantly, the trouble started in a general constituency that had one Hindu and one Muslim candidate. So, until 1939–40 the *Baroda Administration Report* could proudly state that the 'spread of modern education and of liberal ideas is steadily softening the edges and angularities of different faiths and the resulting broad sense of

[141] *The Servant of India* 12.1.1939; Manohar 1992: 153–5.

[142] As mentioned earlier, a restricted form of separate electorate was granted to a few minority communities in 1939.

toleration reduces the chances of religious tension which was never acute in the state'.[143]

This same statement recurs in earlier and later reports and its routine character clearly affects its credibility. Nevertheless, the reports of the British Residents contribute to this picture of traditional communal harmony.[144] One may question the diligence of the average British Resident in writing his fortnightly and other reports on local political events. However, even after the Government of India had in 1933 expressly asked the Residents for timely intimation of communal trouble that might arise in their states,[145] the general thrust of the Baroda reports did not change. One might argue for a latent but powerful communal tension hidden somewhere below the social surface, but the conclusion must be that this tension never led to explosions serious enough to leave an imprint on the available documentary evidence. The prevailing impression is one of quiet and peaceful communal relations.

Like Baroda, the state of Travancore was never forced to follow the constitutional experiments of British India. Yet, in spite of the important fact that no separate electorates were ever introduced, we have seen that there were fierce communal rivalries, not only in the field of council membership but also in that of government employment. Communal associations and conferences were mushrooming, from Nayars down to the depressed classes, both Christian and non-Christian. Most of them had their own daily or weekly newspapers serving as their mouthpiece and launching scurrilous communal attacks on the others. The reports of British Residents and Indian visitors abound with complaints that the population was 'unhappily stricken with the plague of communal animosities' and that communalism was 'a deep-seated disease in Travancore'.[146] The Dewan, Sir C.P. Ramaswamy Aiyar, who never shrank from using these

[143] BAR 1939-40: 2.

[144] The same conclusion in *United India and Indian States*, 22.4.1939, which is also supported by Banu 1989: 72–3 and Lancy Lobo of the Centre for Social Studies in Surat, personal communication.

[145] Supplying information about communal troubles in Indian States, in HPO, Political Department, Section 34, File No. 55.

[146] Quotations from Resident Field's Confidential Memorandum, 26.11.1935, R/2(888/207) and copy of a Statement on Travancore by Rajkumari Amrit Kaur, 29.8.1938, in Ouwerkerk Collection, No. 48. See also Field's Confidential Report to the Government of India, 2.1.1935, in R/2(888/210) and Garstin's demi-official letter, 16.6.1936, L/P&S/13/1291.

internal social divisions to his own advantage, complained to the Political Department that people in Travancore were much more inclined to think and act in terms of a specific communal identity than was usual in British India.[147]

Therefore, the question that remains to be answered is why there was such a striking difference in communal relations between the states of Baroda and Travancore. And how can we explain the prevalence of deeply-entrenched communal feelings in Travancore where no invidious electoral arrangements can be blamed for creating social enmity?

In northern India the incidence and potential eruption of communal tension had much to do with the presence of large groups of Muslims and their former role as rulers of India. The south-western part of the subcontinent also accommodated a Muslim minority. These Muslims had not come overland as part of a Muslim conquest, but had peacefully settled as traders on the coast, especially in Malabar, at a much earlier date. After the arrival of the European trading companies they had been ousted from their commercial strongholds and driven inland, where they eked out a marginal existence as small traders and land labourers. Travancore numbered only a small number of these Muslims (about 6 per cent). They cherished no memories of a glorious past as former rulers and had made no contribution to local state formations to boast of. In Baroda too Muslims were a small minority. Some of the more prominent among them, like the Bohras and Memons, were active in trade and enjoyed the same status as the Banias from whose ranks they had most probably converted. Yet, the large majority worked in agriculture or had joined the public force as sepoys and constables. They never had much political power and showed no great eagerness to get it.

One of the main features of Travancore society, which sets it clearly apart from the situation in British India and Baroda, is the large number of Christians, especially the Syrians, there. When in the eighteenth century Travancore rose as the single most powerful force on this coast, it was Syrian Christians who joined the caste Hindus in the centre of the new political order. As Susan Baily (1989) has shown, they proved to be trusted allies of the state as commercial agents, warriors and office-holders. In the nineteenth century this political system collapsed under the restrictions imposed by British paramountcy,

[147] Note on a discussion between Dewan of Travancore and Sir Bertrand Glancy, Secretary to the Political Department, somewhere in 1938, L/P&S/13,1283.

and as part of the resulting disintegration the Syrians lost much of their privileged position. Supported by British Residents and Christian missionaries, who mistook Syrian decline as caused by age-long heathen oppression, they were able to exploit the new opportunities and emerged as the state's most literate and enterprising community.

Shut out from the centre of the administration, the elite of Syrian Christians made sustained efforts to use their educational and economic achievements to regain a share of political power. Leaders from various Syrian sections, but especially from the Jacobites and Mar Thomites, started to clamour for electoral safeguards and legislative participation as a way of doing justice to their neglected community. The Roman Catholics and Protestant missionary churches, although even more outside the political establishment, were much less involved in the agitation of the 1930s.

The Syrian demands found no favourable response from the Travancore government. Whereas in British India separate electorates to Muslims and other minority communities might help to sustain the Empire, political concessions to Syrian Christians, one of the most prominent communities of Travancore society, were viewed as threatening the kingdom that became increasingly associated with Hindu orthodoxy. Census figures from the nineteenth century show a steady increase in the number of Christians in the state. This increase was almost exclusively due to an inflow of converts from the lower Hindu ranks to Latin Catholicism and Protestantism, but it created an atmosphere of distrust and fear that Christians were going to take over the kingdom.

It would be unfair to accuse the Travancore government of religious intolerance, for Christian missions had received generous grants-in-aid to finance their charitable projects, especially in the field of education. Also, the official permission that was required for the building of places of worship, whether Christian, Hindu or Muslim, was seldom withheld. Syrian Christians frequently protested against rejection by government of applications for new churches.[148] But Sir C.P. could boast that during his tenure of office the government was sanctioning the building of nearly three new Christian churches every month.[149] In several cases, a refusal of permission was caused by

[148] Fortnightly Report from Travancore for the first part of May 1935, L/P&S/13/1283.

[149] Press conference, 1.3.1944, R/2(890/246).

problems among the Christians themselves. Government initially withheld permission for a separate Catholic church for 400 new Pulaya converts, as it considered the existing building large enough. In another case, the building of a new church was refused by a government official who belonged to a different Christian denomination.[150] The struggle was not about religious issues but about the distribution of power.

The issues at stake in that power struggle were not only legislative seats, which though prestigious were small in number, but also the much more numerous positions in the administrative services. With an elaborate and growing bureaucracy, the state of Travancore had much to offer its subjects in the field of educated employment. In 1931 no less than 60 per cent of all educated people worked in government service. There was an intense competition to enter that service, also because of the world-wide economic depression. Many people, both skilled and unskilled, working with plantations and export firms, were losing their jobs. The only ones not affected, or not in the same way affected by the depression, were those working on fixed incomes, such as government servants.[151]

There was however a marked predominance of Nayars and a few foreign Brahmins in the state's administrative services. That uneven situation was challenged by other aspiring groups, first of all Christians but later also Ezhavas and Muslims. That does not mean that the Christians were altogether without political influence. Though ritually excluded from the temple department, they were overrepresented in the educational and medical departments. The more advanced Syrian sections could refer to a general Christian underrepresentation to justify their demands for a redistribution of political privilege and they actively fostered an all-Christian solidarity to serve that purpose. As the administration had become the virtual property of a few high caste communities who were the Maharaja's most loyal supporters, the struggle for power assumed almost inevitably a more directly communal character.

In Baroda locally dominant groups had much less reason to mobilize for opposition against the government. The Patidar peasant elite, as Hardiman (1978) has pointed out, was well represented in the state bureaucracy which looked adequately after their interests. What was

[150] Note by Skrine, Resident, 24.6.1938, R/2(889/236).

[151] TEDEC 1931: 13–21; Chiriyankandath 1985: 218.

still more important, government proved most eager to comply with their wishes, as it could ill afford to lose their support. Apart from that, Patidars occupied the best part of all seats in the local bodies, especially the *prant panchayats*, which from 1931 had the right to select members for nomination to the legislative council. Therefore, the peasant elite was well-entrenched in the bastion of power and had no need for communal agitation to press for more democratic systems of government as was the case in Travancore. Demands for more representative institutions came chiefly from a select circle of urban intellectuals which the government chose to ignore.

The same contrast in political behaviour may be observed between the economic middle class in Travancore and Baroda. Travancore with its extensive potential for plantation development welcomed foreign capital, which soon dominated the principal spheres of commercial and financial activity. The local entrepreneurial classes, largely composed of Syrian Christians and a few Ezhavas, could not depend upon a similar preferential treatment on the part of the government and had to compete with the European coastal firms on very unequal terms. They felt thwarted in their efforts by their own state, which they perceived as one of the main obstacles on their way to economic progress. This feeling of alienation was only strengthened by the proposed sale of cultivable waste land to a foreign tea company (Chapter 2) and the controversial crash of the Travancore National and Quilon Bank. It is true that local capitalists were gradually able to extend their influence in the estate economy, primarily in rubber, but they had to fight their way up all alone. An appeal to a separate communal identity and organization, partly reflective of class interests, was an obvious method to get their voices heard in the right places and to wrest concessions from an uncooperative government.

In Baroda, on the other hand, government was very active in creating conditions favourable for the emergence of local industry. As we have seen, Banias and some Patidars were quick to respond and even though many results at first were rather disappointing, economic life was overwhelmingly dominated by 'home-grown' industrialists who saw the state as their chief ally and were as a result not inclined to challenge government policies. Erdman observes that in the 1960s some of Baroda's older industrialists were still looking back somewhat nostalgically on the good old days of princely rule.[152] This feeling of

[152] Erdman 1971: 7.

contentment offered barren ground for political opposition, communal or otherwise. Those industrialists who associated with the *praja mandal* generally pressed for caution and emphasized the importance of good relations with the administration.

It has been argued that the introduction of separate electorates in British India has greatly increased, if not caused, communal tension and conflict, as under this electoral system people came to perceive themselves primarily as part of a particular community rather than as citizens of a larger national state. Yet, one might wonder how far this reasoning really holds true.

In case of separate electorates people are indeed grouped together in one constituency on the basis of religion, generating conditions in which religious distinctions might harden into much broader antagonisms. There is, however, no compelling need to appeal to religious symbols, as both voter and candidate move within the same social boundaries and there are no rival communities competing for the same seats. As the 1937 elections in British India clearly demonstrated, separate electorates did not create strong feelings of solidarity within the Muslim community which spread its electoral support over several Muslim parties and candidates, leaving the Muslim League with less than 5 per cent of the total vote.

On the other hand, in general constituencies with open competition candidates in search of votes may feel more easily tempted to invoke religious or caste affiliations, especially if they happen to belong to the majority community. Of course, such a strategy is a risky and ambiguous venture, attracting some and alienating other people.

However, the system introduced in Travancore in 1936 had an inherent need to mobilize sentiments of religion and caste. The constituencies were delimited in such a way that major communities like Syrians and Nayars might gain a number of seats commensurate to their population ratio—if only all Syrians and Nayars in their respective majority constituencies would vote for a candidate from their own community. The results of the 1937 elections proved that this message was not lost on the enfranchised members of these communities. In addition, in 1939 the electoral rules were changed, guaranteeing Muslims and Latin Catholics a representative of their own choice, if they could muster more than 60 per cent support for one candidate. The principle of separate electorates was never granted, but the delimitation of constituencies and electoral arrangements went a long way in enabling political leaders to build their own communal votebanks.

The principle of communal reservation was introduced in the Travancore public service, at least in the lower and intermediate ranks. Stricter regulation of the access to the state bureaucracy was demanded by communal leaders, not only to safeguard their own employment but also to curtail government power to divide their ranks by a judicious use of the patronage at its command. As politics in Travancore were still largely based on personal networks and status considerations, the government could, by a calculating distribution of official favour, appease certain opponents, buy them over, or split them. In this way, the astute Ramaswamy Aiyar could succeed in carrying through much of his controversial policies and the Political Department referred with admiration to 'the skill with which they [the Travancore government] "divide and rule" '.[153]

One of the main conclusions to be drawn from this chapter is that in the emergence of communalism separate electorates as well as the demand for them may have been an effect rather than a cause. Both Baroda and Travancore had important elite groups in agriculture, commerce and industry. But in Baroda, the landowning and industrial elite was well represented in the administration and the legislature, and its interests were well served by a sympathetic government. In Travancore, on the other hand, an important part of the elite was not so favourably situated and in its fight for political power and status it had to deal with a government that was much less cooperative and mainly in the hands of a rival elite. This situation meant a clear invitation for the elite that felt excluded from privilege to press their demands by mobilizing their own community and stressing their separate identity. Here, separate electorates were not an instrument in the hands of the government to weaken the ranks of the opposition, but they were eagerly sought by the underprivileged communities themselves as an important means to wrest a minimum number of council seats from a reluctant government.

[153] Note 1938, Indian States General Questions, L/P&S/13/886

4

Hyderabad and the Process of Globalization

TOWARDS FEDERATION

SINCE WORLD WAR the colonial government had committed itself to a policy of progressive realization of self-governing institutions in British India, and it was increasingly faced with the problem of what kind of future it envisaged for the princely states. Official opinion expressed the belief that the trend of political events must necessarily draw the states closer and closer into the orbit of the larger Indian Empire. But the conviction grew that for an increasing association between British India and the states there should be a constitutional framework that had to contain proposals for federation.

The British did not make light of their responsibility in this matter. As far as Hyderabad was concerned, colonial officials were convinced that this state would have been swept away from the Deccan by its Maratha enemies but for the timely appearance of the British on the scene. Left entirely to himself, the Nizam would not have been able to maintain himself for any length of time. Thus future independence needed a firm federal basis. Otherwise, 'the inevitable result of casting loose a multitude of States and irreconcilable entities without a firm Central Government would be a return to the chaos of the century that preceded the conclusion of the Maratha wars . . .'.[1]

Therefore, all efforts were directed at creating a political structure that could contain the many divergent forces that were thought to make up Indian political life. Following the Montford Report the constitution-making process slowly went its way through Round

[1] Letter from Sir Terence Humphrey Keyes to Foreign and Political Department, New Delhi, 15.4.1930, L/P&S/13/548. See also Barton quoted in Menon 1995: 388.

Table Conferences, a White Paper and joint parliamentary committee till it got its final shape in the 1935 Government of India Act. In this new constitution the federal principle formed an important new element. The princely states, till then under separate treaty obligations to the Crown, were to be integrated with the directly administered provinces of British India in a federation entrusted with wide central powers. In a bicameral Central Legislature members directly elected by the people in the British provinces were to take their place side by side with members representing the states. The far-reaching implications of the Act can be gleaned from the fact that it was going to a large extent shape the later constitution of independent India.

The provincial part of the Act could be introduced as a legislative enactment and did not need approval of the parties concerned. As we have seen in the previous chapter, that part of the new constitution was being worked by the formation of provincial ministries after the 1937 elections. The Congress took a prominent part in forming these ministries, but only with a view to strengthening the nation's struggle for independence. But the federal part of the 1935 Act proved much more difficult to implement, being subject to the important condition of a majority consent by the rulers of the states. The princes, however, were prey to serious doubt and hesitated, feeling uncertain as to what federation would mean to their personal prerogatives as guaranteed under the treaties.

Another possible consequence of prospective federation and of more concern to us here is the effect it might have on the relations between different communities. Therefore, this chapter will first examine the particular communal situation in Hyderabad and the forces working for the preservation of what was increasingly being called a Muslim state. Then, elaborating on the three-tier political structure as explained in the opening chapter, I will investigate the all-India policies, both British and Indian nationalist, which each in their own way were making attempts to bring the states into some kind of a political union with the provinces. Facing these centralizing forces were more localized movements threatening the state from below by their appeal to religion and language. Nationalism in the states has been defined as a movement aimed at a shift in the centre of allegiance from ruler to people and claiming a share in public life to all those who somehow belong. Very often 'those who belong' were identified by a reference to shared cultural symbols, foremost of which were religion or language, threatening the larger unity of state or nation.

The main focus in this chapter will be on the 1937–9 period with its federation proposals, political reform and communal politics. We will see that at the outbreak of the War the Nizam, Osman Ali Khan (1911–48), was still able to frustrate all attempts to bring Hyderabad into a federation and to change his autocratic regime into a more responsible form of government. He was to be the last Nizam and this was also his last victory. In 1948 Hyderabad was incorporated into the Union of India amidst scenes of communal bloodshed, comparable to what happened on the India-Pakistan border at the same time.

PRESERVATION OF HYDERABAD, A STATE IN DANGER

In spite of its size, for a long time Hyderabad led a rather secluded existence, apparently unaffected by developments outside. According to Akbar S. Ahmad, the Nizams skilfully kept Hyderabad out of the turbulence of larger politics, thus creating an island mentality for their subjects. Thus, when India was beginning to demand greater participation in government, Hyderabad, maintaining its island mentality, remained isolated from the mainstream of politics.[2] In the 1930s this situation began radically to change, especially so after 1937. In the words of Swami Ramananda Tirtha, a prominent Congress leader from Hyderabad, 'true political life started during this period'.[3]

Muslim rule in Hyderabad was not based on religion, nor did it mean that there was systematic oppression of non-Muslims, as Hindu communal organizations like the Arya Samaj and Hindu Mahasabha are wont to claim. First of all, Muslims and Hindus presented no solid monolithic blocs, but were internally divided by sect, caste and language. Muslims were divided into Sunnis and Shi'as with some minority groups like Bohras and Khojas. There were continuous rumours that the Nizam contemplated conversion from Sunni to Shi'a. The resulting unrest and suspicion at court most probably were the main reason for the issue of official declarations (1935 and 1936), stating that the ruler did belong to the Sunni and that the state religion was Hanafi (Sunni).[4] Hindus were split not only by caste but also by

[2] Ahmad 1988: 177, 180.

[3] Tirtha 1967: 74.

[4] In 1935 a *firman* of the Nizam declared the state religion to be Sunni, according to the Resident the first time that such declaration had been made. One year later, a

language, the Marathi, Kannada and Telugu speaking citizens of the state tending to look beyond the frontier to their fellow-speakers for support.

Hyderabad's seventh Nizam has become associated with political conservatism and religious obscurantism. Nevertheless, at the beginning of his reign the British Resident reported favourably about the young prince's determination to shape his own policies and to form his own opinion.[5] Only later, when his independence of mind had brought him into conflict with the British, did the tone of the reports change.[6] Yazdani considers the seventh Nizam a statesman tolerant in religious matters.[7] Resident Barton, the main but far from sole critic of the Hyderabad ruler, agreed that the Nizam did not discriminate between the different classes of his subjects but only in the sense that Hindus and Muslims suffered alike from his various schemes for extorting money. Nevertheless, Barton drew attention to the disturbing circumstance that oppression fell most heavily on the Hindus who made up the bulk of the peasantry.[8] According to his successor, Sir Terence Keyes, the Hindus paid 95 per cent of the state's revenue and were bitter at the high expenditure on Muslim institutions and personages.[9]

Under this ruler some non-Muslims managed nevertheless to obtain leading positions. British officials were convinced that there was a career for educated Hindus in certain fields of government, 'though they were shut out from the plums'.[10] Maharaja Sir Kishen Pershad, to

---

Gazette Extraordinary was needed to explain that the Nizam really was a Sunni, Resumé of Events in Indian States, Hyderabad 1934–5, L/P&S/13/1200; Hyderabad Affairs, R/1/1/3222; Copland 1988: 789.

[5] Yazdani 1985: 54, 58.

[6] This critical tone was not the exclusive property of William Barton's writings, but can also be gleaned from later Resident's reports, see for instance Duncan Mackenzie in Resumé of Events in Indian States, fortnight ending 15.12.1935, L/P&S/13/1200.

[7] Yazdani 1985: 53, 78. Bawa mentions that the Nizam used to give donations to Christian churches, Bawa 1992: 82.

[8] Memorandum by W. Barton, Resident Hyderabad, 11.12.1925, in Hyderabad Affairs, R/1/1/1465(1).

[9] Keyes quoted in Bawa 1992: 128. See also note by Resident Mackenzie, 1936, R/1/1/3222.

[10] Internal note (1939) by P.J. Patrick, India Office, London, after conversation with Th.Tasker, Revenue Member Hyderabad, L/P&S/13/667.

quote one illustrious example, for a long time served as Hyderabad's Prime Minister (1925–36). An old-style aristocrat, he had married women of Hindu and Muslim families and from his privileged position he assured his brother Hindus that Hindus and Muslims were 'the two arms of these Dominions'. In an open letter he referred to the freedom of religion that the Hindus had always enjoyed and the generous *jagirs* (revenues) granted to their temples. He exhorted the Hindus to be happy and satisfied under the rule of a king who so highly valued all forms of life that he even took a wounded goat in his own car to be treated.[11] Government also tried wherever possible to respect Hindu sensibilities, as evidenced by the restrictions placed on cow slaughter, a sensitive issue that elsewhere in India created a great deal of unrest.

Still, there was a clear preponderance of Muslims in the state services. Many of the leading positions in government were filled by Muslim administrators recruited from outside. The old Mughal Empire used to employ a large number of people from Persia and beyond, who were attracted by lucrative *jagirs* in the service of the emperor in Delhi. In the same way, Hyderabad attracted many qualified people from northern India, especially Aligarh, to staff its administrative departments. These outsiders not only reinforced the Muslim element in the state but also brought with them many ties to the religious and political movements of north India which were increasingly divided along communal lines.[12] As already indicated, this difference between *mulkis* (locals) and non-*mulkis* (outsiders) formed a persistent problem in Hyderabad politics; but when independence drew near, this issue was overshadowed by a larger Hindu-Muslim divide.

I have already quoted the numerical disproportion of Muslim and Hindu representation among the gazetted officers in the 1894 Hyderabad Civil List. My own count from the Civil Lists of 1896 and 1923 shows an increase of the Muslim share in major appointments from 55 to 71 per cent and of the Hindu share from 7 to 15 per cent over the same period, due to a considerable fall in the number of European and Parsi officers. In 1936 the Hindu figure had further risen to 20 per cent, whereas the Muslim percentage showed a slight

[11] Open Letter Bahadur Sir Kishen Pershad 'To Brother Hindus' (no date), L/P&S/13/1232.

[12] Ashton 1982: 87.

fall to 67 per cent.[13] The Census of 1921, adopting a different calculation, mentioned 3,521 employed in public administration, 1,711 of whom were Hindu and 1,376 Muslim.[14] But if we restrict public administration to gazetted appointments, Muslims enjoyed more than 77 per cent of these positions (864 of the 1,112 in 1931).[15] From these and other sources we may safely conclude that Civil Lists and Census reports, for all their imperfections and lack of compatability, clearly point in the same direction: Muslims dominated the higher echelons of the government and their share of administrative positions was much larger than their percentage of the population. They also clearly dominated the state-run schools which, apart from their more urban concentration, may explain their higher literacy.

Sir Akbar Hydari, Prime Minister after 1936, tried to explain this Muslim preponderance as not the result of a deliberate policy but 'an accident of history'.[16] To balance this picture, however, one should add that Hindus were well represented in the professions and clearly dominated agriculture, trading and banking. The 1931 Census did not even mention trade as an occupation followed by Muslims and there was practically no Muslim peasantry. For that reason, the government also tended to consider the Muslim hold on the public administration as a kind of justified compensation for the fact that Hindus owned most of the private wealth in the state.[17] The *Deccan Times* (22.5.1938) took another line in defence of the Muslims. It pointed out that government service, just like agriculture and industry, belonged to communities that possessed 'special flair' for that particular occupation. In Hyderabad these communities happened to be Muslims and Brahmins who had furnished candidates for government service for generations. It concluded that more openings in the services for Hindus would only benefit the Brahmins who constituted a negligible

[13] These percentages are derived from counting the main appointments to the Hyderabad civil departments, excluding the military (mainly Muslims with a number of Europeans in commanding positions) and the officers in the districts (see H.E.H. the Nizam's Government's Lists for the years mentioned). The quite arbitrary choice of the years 1896, 1923 and 1936 was determined by the question which copies of the Civil List the clerks of the Andhra Pradesh State Archives were able to trace for me. Bawa, quoting figures from the 1931 Civil List, arrives at 75 per cent Muslims and 20 per cent Hindus in all departments (Bawa 1992: 151).

[14] Census of Hyderabad 1921 II Table 10.

[15] Copland 1988: 788.

[16] Quoted in Ramesan IV, 1966: 172.

[17] Copland 1988: 789–90.

proportion of the population but served as the main instigators of the Hindu communal movements.

These arguments failed to convince those who felt unjustly left out of power. Swami Ramananda Tirtha, according to his own account 'a Congressman to the core', born in Hyderabad but educated at Sholapur and Poona, complained of the enslavement of the Hindus: '(I)t was all a communal Muslim hierarchy that controlled life. To be a Hindu meant all humiliation'.[18] The Hyderabad government asserted that it were mainly Hindus who benefited from the liberal remissions in land revenue, amounting to about Rs 50 lakhs annually, and the large sums of money spent through the cooperative societies on the countryside.[19] Yet, the most vocal Hindu representatives were not impressed. They kept contending that Hindus were paying heavy revenues to maintain a system that was only out to oppress them.

Federation was another question that loomed large in Hyderabad politics. According to contemporary observers Hindus were generally in favour of a federal scheme, whereas most Muslims were opposed to it. That opposition was inspired by the uncertainty as to what extent the new constitutional arrangements envisaged for the centre were going to apply to Hyderabad state. If federation implied a government that reflected the composition of the population, it might mean the passing of power into Hindu hands.

At first the Nizam's government seemed not averse to the principle of federation. Both Ashton and Yazdani ascribe this open attitude to the influence of Terence H. Keyes, Resident from 1930.[20] Apart from that, in view of the Nizam's claim to be the leader of the Muslim community in India, he could not afford to ignore the discussions on federation. Realizing the importance of the forthcoming Round Table Conference (RTC), the Nizam decided to join the activities of the Chamber of Princes in preparation of it and granted a substantial donation to its treasury. Nevertheless, he sent his own delegation to London, separate from that of the Chamber of Princes, led by Sir Akbar Hydari, at that time Finance Member of the Executive Council. The instructions issued by the Nizam enjoined his delegation to adopt an attitude 'of sympathy but also of wise caution' towards an all-India federation. Their main charge, apart from the preservation of

[18] Tirtha 1967: 50.

[19] Printed pamphlet, no date, most probably a government publication, in Hyderabad: Arya Samaj Agitation 1939, L/P&S/13/1232.

[20] Ashton 1982: 131; Yazdani 1985: 159.

Hyderabad as the premier Indian state in any federal union, was to uphold all the existing treaties with the British paramount power, in particular its guarantee of military protection.[21]

At the first RTC (1930) the princes formally accepted the idea of an all-India federation of British India and the princely states, and declared their readiness to take a position of honour and equality in the British Commonwealth of Nations. The wish to safeguard their relation with the Crown was one of the main considerations inducing Hyderabad and other states to take this stand. The British government was greatly satisfied with Hyderabad's close cooperation, and Barton later acknowledged that '(h)ad Hyderabad . . . stood aloof, it is unlikely that federation would have come into the sphere of practical politics'.[22]

After coming back to India, Hydari and other state delegates proved to be much less enthusiastic about federation. At an informal conference at the Viceregal Lodge (1932), they asked for more clarity about the scope of paramountcy and the distribution of seats in the federal legislative, but the Viceroy was unable to meet their demand. The uncertain financial implications also served as a serious hindrance, although Hydari wished to be clearly understood that Hyderabad was in no way blocking federation.[23] In 1936 Hydari became Prime Minister of Hyderabad with the arduous task of preserving as much of the state's political integrity as possible in the face of the on-going federal process.

Among the forces at the intermediate level, working for the preservation of Hyderabad, mention should be made of the Hyderabad State Political Conference (HSPC). At several of its sessions opinions were articulated which strongly urged the independent and continued existence of the state. These objectives of the HSPC were fully in line with the views of Hydari who in a radio broadcast stated that the Deccan with its cultural unity might set an example to the conflicting 'races and cultures' of India.[24] But the HSPC strove for a continued exist-

[21] Instructions issued by H.E.H. the Nizam to his Delegation, L/P&S/13/548.

[22] Sir William Barton in *Western Morning News*, 28-8-1939. A similar opinion can be found in Lothian 1951: 149.

[23] Minutes of an informal conference with a number of states, including Hyderabad, Travancore and Baroda, at Viceregal Lodge Simla, September 1932, R/1//1/4690; Barton 1934: 300.

[24] Quoted in Yazdani 1985: 192.

ence of the state at the price of reform. Its conferences had to be held outside the state which led to the charge of external agitation, although the HSPC had no partners in the larger India.

The first HSP Conference was held during the 1923 Congress session at Kakinada. About 500 visitors and delegates from Hyderabad used this session to conduct their own conference on Hyderabad affairs. The only Muslim participant opposed the proceedings[25] and subsequent conferences turned out to be rather critical of what was called Muslim oppression.

The fourth HSP Conference (Akola 1931) especially expressed a strong local nationalist sentiment. Emphasizing its unswerving loyalty and devotion to the Nizam's government the conference adopted resolutions calling for the '[i]deal of united nationalism and citizenship of the State'. This combination of nationalism and Hyderabad citizenship meant, as we can glean from the proceedings, an emphasis on village education, reservation of employment for qualified Hyderabadis and encouragement of indigenous manufactures. It is not enough, so it was stated, to have an industrial department; successful industrialists should be especially honoured and on state occasions it should be made compulsory for every Hyderabadi to wear clothes of state-made materials.

The HSPC at Akola also raised the demand for fundamental civil rights, the early introduction of responsible government and popular representation in state and federal legislatives. The presidential address stressed that Hyderabadis could not behave differently from others 'when they live in the same atmosphere and are influenced by the same ideas'. In case one might suspect that these demands were meant to benefit Hindus and prejudice the position of Muslims, it was expressly stated that the HSPC rejected all kinds of 'religious and communal squabbles'. It asked for a textbook comprising the high principles of all religions to be used for religious and moral education. Although the conference was largely Hindu, there were a few Muslims attending.[26] Later conferences, increasingly dominated by Marathi speaking politicians, reiterated the demand for responsible govern-

[25] Bawa 1992: 102–3.

[26] Resolutions and speeches of the 1931 Hyderabad State Political Conference, L/P&S/13/554.

ment and extension of the legislative.[27] The impact of these HSP Conferences on Hyderabad is difficult to estimate.

A similar movement, but operating within the state, was the Nizam's Subjects League or *Mulki* League (1935). It shared many objectives with the HSPC, like the introduction of responsible government and the reservation of the services for the sons of the soil. The league sought its basis in a united Deccani nationalism without any distinction of caste and creed, and rejected all forms of communalism as outside attempts to create division. Its state nationalism was said to exclude support from British India but was combined with the proposal of Hyderabad joining the federation. In spite of its loud profession of loyalty to the ruling house, the Nizam's Subjects League did not find official approval. Its demand for reform and protest against a north Indian predominance in the administration were considered a threat to the established order and thus this middle course organization remained short-lived.[28]

What becomes clear from these political movements is first, that it was becoming more and more difficult for Hyderabadi Muslims to work for political reform. Being a small but dominant minority, a more popular form of government would surely reduce their influence. Secondly, beneath the declarations of loyalty, there was an unmistakable shift from the traditional view that the Nizam derived all authority from himself to the view that he embodied the sovereignty of his people, being their ruler because they had declared him to be such. In this shift in allegiance from top to bottom the emergence of an nascent feeling of nationalism becomes manifest.

INCREASING PRESSURE FROM ABOVE

Before 1935 the INC did not occupy itself very much with the federal scheme. It expressed agreement with the principle of federation, if acceptable to the representatives of British India as well as of the Indian states. At the time of the RTCs in London, the Congress

[27] According to Raghunadha Rao 1988: 137, the Akola conference was the last one. The Resident reported another Hyderabad State (Subjects) Political Conference in Poona, 1935, see Resumé of Events in Indian States, Hyderabad, fortnight ending 15.12.1935, L/P&S/13/1200. See also Bawa 1992: 105.

[28] Hasan 1935; Bawa 1992: 137–43.

Working Committee made accession of the states to a federation conditional upon the grant of fundamental rights to the people, including their right to elect their own representatives.[29]

The Congress was interested in political reform rather than federation. It wanted to attack the states by raising political consciousness among the people. From 1920 there was a Congress District Committee in Hyderabad, but left to its own resources it never was in a flourishing condition. Yet, even this rather innocent committee was considered potentially dangerous: the mere fact that three men with *khadi* shirts and Gandhi caps were propagating the *charkha* and preaching intemperance made police officers report immediately to the highest authorities.[30]

From the beginning of the 1930s, journals like the *Servant of India* and *United India and Indian States* urged the Congress for more active support. Provincial Congress Committees in Maharashtra and Karnataka joined the demand. Referring to earlier Hyderabadi participation in Congress campaigns in British India,[31] they called it a Congress duty now to carry on similar agitation in Hyderabad and other states. The Congress Working Committee (CWC) did acknowledge that people in the states should have the same political rights as those in the rest of India. But it stressed that the responsibility to fight for these rights must necessarily fall on the people of the states themselves. Greatly disappointed, the *United India and Indian States* (April 1936) concluded that it was better to call the Indian National Congress the British Indian National Congress.[32]

Another organization working at the all-India level was the All-India States Peoples' Conference (AISPC). As we have seen, this body vehemently protested the neglect of the people of the states in all discussions on federation and political reform. The RTC in London was an obvious place to demand a more responsible form of government for all units composing the projected federation in order to

[29] Ashton 1982: 150.

[30] Ramesan IV 1966: 20–1.

[31] The Hyderabad State Congress claimed that a considerable number of volunteers from Hyderabad had offered services to the INC during the Civil Disobedience campaign in British India, see SFHS 1938: 4.

[32] Comments and information on Congress' attitudes versus Indian States from *Servant of India* and *United India and Indian States*, 1934 and 1935, in L/P&S/13/554.

prevent 'the yoke of autocracy getting fixed more firmly than ever on the necks of the States' people'.[33] However, no room was made for AISPC representatives at the conference table. The princes had made it clear that they would never tolerate sitting in a conference with their own subjects. Both the Secretary of State and the Viceroy were intent upon the success of the RTC and agreed that it would be a tactical blunder to alienate the princes.[34] Therefore, the British complied and acknowledged that rulers of states were the only persons who could speak with authority on questions of constitutional policy. They also agreed that the internal government of the states was not on the agenda.

AISPC representatives were thus not allowed at the RTC, and its secretary complained to the government in London (1931) that the people of the states were treated as political untouchables. 'Even women and Depressed Classes are represented on the RTC while 70 millions of the States are not at all represented.'[35] A weak point however, acknowledged by its leaders but neglected by historians like Handa and Phadnis, was the poor response the AISPC received in the same states. At the fourth session at Bombay in 1933, the president, N.C. Kelkar, regretted that the movement had not been successful in rousing the large mass of subjects in the states to take interest and give support to it. He wondered 'whether the States' people deserve the friendliness they get from public spirited men in British territory, if they . . . are not ready to take even their due share of the work of organization'.[36]

That lukewarm attitude was attributed, among other things, to a loyalty to the rulers that was said to be still very strong in the states.[37]

Although the AISPC may have held a marginal position, the Political Department followed its reforming zeal with a great deal of interest and not without some appreciation. Referring to the 1933 AISPC session where the usual political demands were formulated,

[33] Letter from G.R. Abhyankar and Amritlal D. Sheth (AISPC) to Lord Sankey, Lord Chancellor, London 31.10.1931; *To the Nations of the World: a manifesto on behalf of the people of the states*, n.d., printed pamphlet AISPC, L/P&S/13/554.

[34] Exchange of letters and telegrams between Wedgewood Benn, Secretary of State for India, and Lord Irwin, Viceroy, 1929–30, L/P&S/13/887.

[35] Letter from G.R. Abhyankar (AISPC) to Sir Henry Snell, Under Secretary of State for India, 19.3.1931, L/P&S/13/554.

[36] N.C. Kelkar, Presidential Address to AISPC, Bombay 1933, L/P&S/13/554.

[37] Note on the Position of the Subjects of Indian States by Dewan Bahadur Ramachandra Rao, 19.11.1931, circulated at the second RTC, L/P&S/13/554.

P.J. Patrick, Secretary to the Political Department in London, commented in a personal note, 'There is a good deal of common sense in much of Mr. Kelkar's [Presidential] address and some of the resolutions should be good reading for certain princes.'[38]

The main factor threatening a continuation of Hyderabad's political existence was the very power that had pledged itself by treaty to safeguard the state's semi-autonomous status: the British government. Of crucial importance, in this respect, was the Government of India Act (August 1935) which provided for the integration of Hyderabad and other princely states with the British provinces in an all-India federation. The federal part of that Act, however, could be implemented, if and only when a sufficient number of states proved willing to accede. From many sides the princes were strongly encouraged to enter the federation and to prepare their people for that purpose as the best safeguard for the preservation of their internal autonomy. The Viceroy was the most prominent among them. At the opening session of the Chamber of Princes in 1935, with galleries crowded by ministers and other prominent visitors, the Viceroy strongly advised the princes that it was in their own interest to join the federal scheme.[39] To accede or not to accede thus became the dominant political question after 1935.

Under different treaties, the states had already given up control over their external and military affairs. Under the federation as projected by the 1935 Act they had to surrender also a great part of their powers in revenue, finance, communications and the administration of justice. Individual princes were allowed to make certain limitations on the extent to which they agreed to the transfer of any particular subject, but it would fall to the British government to decide whether or not these limitations were compatible with the principle of federation.[40]

The transfer of these powers was to an all-India executive and legislature. The Federal Assembly, the most important part of this bicameral legislature, numbered 375 members; 250 of these members were popularly elected from the British Indian provinces and had to take seat next to 125 delegates from the princely states. There was also a Council of States, or Upper House, which numbered 156 members

[38] Handwritten note by P.J. Patrick, 7.11.1933, referring to the fourth AISPC session in Bombay (1933), presided by N.C. Kelkar, L/P&S/13/554.

[39] Text of the opening address 22.1.1935 in Collection of English newspaper cuttings in APSA Hyderabad, the names of the newspapers not given.

[40] Ashton 1982: 147.

from British India and 104 from the states.[41] This distribution of seats gave much weightage to the states which were allotted more seats than their population percentage would have warranted.

Only 105 of the 250 British Indian representatives in the assembly were to be elected from general constituencies. The remainder (82) was reserved for Muslims and other special communities and interests. As it had become virtually impossible for the Indian National Congress to win a substantial number of Muslim seats, the composition of the assembly was such as to prevent the Congress from securing an absolute majority. And that intentionally so. In the House of Commons Attlee, speaking for the Labour opposition, had rightly protested that the Bill was 'deliberately framed so as to exclude as far as possible the Congress party from effective power'.[42] The only other way for Congress to gain a majority was by capturing a large number of the 125 seats reserved for the states. Hyderabad had received no less than 16 seats, Travancore 5 and Baroda 3. Groups of smaller states were to be formed with one representative for each group.

Congress—supporting the AISPC in this matter—had tried to bring pressure upon the rulers to agree that representatives from the states should be elected instead of nominated, but in vain. The British were also not likely to press for elected representatives and on the vexed question of election versus nomination the 1935 Act (first schedule) had used the evasive term 'appointment' which let the rulers ample latitude. Earlier, Lord Irwin had commented that the princes were sufficiently informed of government opinion on the need for progressive reforms and that no more could safely be done. The princes justified their reluctance by stating that first they wished to see what the constitutional experiment in British India would lead up to, and government concluded that reform had to be left to a growing public opinion inside and outside the states.[43]

In consequence, Congress rejected the federal provisions as embodied in the Act. In the following years, however, the vital importance of the 125 state representatives for gaining a dominant position in the projected assembly was to become a major reason for Congress to take

[41] Full text Sever II 1985.

[42] Quoted in Burke and Quraishi 1995: 300. In a Secret Cabinet Paper, London, February 1939, that intention was made very explicit, L/PO/5/20.

[43] Note 1927 and letter 18.1.1930 by Lord Irwin in L/P&S/13/887. See also India Office Note (London) on Representative Institutions of Government in Indian States by P.J. Patrick, 1929, L/P&S/13/886.

a growing interest in state affairs. Another reason to concentrate more upon the states was the wish not to leave this important field to the more radical wing within the Congress (Subhas Chandra Bose) or to Hindu extremist groups in Maharashtra (N.C. Kelkar and others).

EMERGING MOVEMENTS FROM BELOW

The independent kingdom which the ancestors of the last Nizam had carved out from the crumbling Mughal Empire covered some very important but divergent regions. The most important were Telengana (Medak, Warangal) and Marathwada (Aurangabad, Gulbarga), whose inhabitants shared language and culture with people of neighbouring provinces like Madras and Bombay. In Hyderabad, about one half of the population spoke Telugu and one quarter Marathi, the remainder speaking minority languages like Kannada, Urdu or Hindustani. In 1922 the medium of instruction at secondary school stage was changed from English to Urdu. This measure, intended to feed Osmania University and the state services, strengthened existing feelings of exclusion among the large majority of non-Urdu speaking Hindus. Local movements, like a Hyderabad State Subjects and Sympathizers Conference, held in Bombay 1926, demanded education in the vernaculars.[44]

The HSPC, discussed above as fighting for the state's preservation, also contained forces that were greatly subversive to its survival. At its third conference (Poona 1928), the artificiality of state borders criss-crossing cultural and linguistic regions became the dominant theme. One of the speakers referred to the Hyderabad population as falling apart in different cultural groups like Andhras (Telugu), Maharashtrians (Marathi) and others, separated from their close relatives in British India by artificial boundaries.

The same theme was harped upon by the president of the session, N.C. Kelkar, who was also active in the AISPC and earlier served as president of the Hindu Mahasabha—merely a coincidence, in his own words. In clear defiance of Hyderabad sovereignty Kelkar told the conference: 'We are not going to be mindful of the artificial borders when we do not feel them.' He also severely criticised the Hyderabad government where none was strong enough 'to put some sense in the

[44] Yazdani 1985: 90.

head of the Nizam'[45] as well as the people of the state who should be more eager to suffer for their cause. The guest speaker, Subhas Chandra Bose, also called the division between the states and British India an artificial one, but we may doubt whether the natural unity Bose had in mind coincided with the one that the other speakers stood for.

The first party to champion regional culture was established in Telengana. The *Andhra Jana Sangham*, following a much earlier political awakening of Telugu people in Madras Presidency,[46] started to work for the protection and encouragement of the Andhra language and culture in the Telengana region of the Nizam's territory. Sponsored by wealthy Telugu landlords, it was soon engaged in a much wider range of activities, from land revenue and prohibition to democratic elections. It expanded into a large body, the Andhra Mahasabha, which was formed in 1930 and led by people like Hanumantha Rao, Narasingh Rao and Keshav Rao Koratkar. As its annual conferences were held in Hyderabad, it was rather moderate in tone. Similar organizations, propagating Marathi or Kannada language and culture, emerged in Marathwada and the Karnataka region of Hyderabad.[47] The agitation for greater linguistic unification was also stimulated by Congress policy to set up linguistic units for party organization.

The British, led by their own reading of history, reacted rather nervously to what they saw as a return to the chaos of pre-British inter-state hostility.[48] They did not stand alone in this. The Hyderabad establishment, the Resident reported, also perceived the vigorously propagated Maratha revival and the more subtle Andhra movement as great dangers to the state's integrity and security. The Nizam, for instance, was convinced that this Maratha revival had its roots beyond the border, among the Brahmins in Poona, and was, in fact, a recurrence of the old pressure of the Peshwas' Maratha Empire.[49] The disturbing fact that there were more Marathas living in Hyderabad than in the three larger Maratha states (including Kolhapur) put together did not serve to set these anxieties at ease.

[45] Quotations from Ramesan IV, 1966: 70, 67.

[46] Raghunadha Rao 1988.

[47] Reddy 1987: 73; Bawa 1992: 99, 149, 153; Pernau-Reifeld 1992: 250 ff.

[48] Pernau-Reifeld 1992: 249.

[49] Letter by Terence Keyes, Resident of Hyderabad, to Foreign and Political Department, 15.4.1930, L/P&S/13/548.

Finally, among the movements that appealed to shared cultural symbols and assets reference should also be made to the Arya Samaj and the Hindu Mahasabha. The former started as a movement for the inner reform of Hinduism. A Hyderabad branch was established in 1893 and its border-crossing literary activities drew much support from local Kayasthas who became leading participants.[50] Later, popular resistance against government repression in Hyderabad increasingly took a religious turn and the Arya Samaj became the vanguard in championing the cause of the people. 'Hindus raised their head against the suppressor but unfortunately this protest took a religious shape,' Tirtha[51] was to write later.

Pandit Keshav Rao Koratkar, a judge of the Hyderabad High Court and earlier Congress activist, functioned as the main leader of the Arya Samaj. At the time of his death (1932), this body was actively engaged in improving its organization in Hyderabad. The *Pratinidhi Sabha* was established as a central body in the capital with several district branches. There was also a Standing Committee for the removal of the disabilities of Arya Samajists not only in the field of religion but also in that of language, politics and employment.[52]

In 1934 the Samaj held objectionable lantern lectures showing pictures of His Majesty the King shaking hands with Gandhi, who was seated. The Resident thought these lectures serious enough to take the matter up with the state authorities.[53] Also, in direct challenge to the state government, the Arya Samaj held processions and meetings without previous permission. Even more explosive were the reconversion movements. The Samaj aimed not only at religious reform but also at winning back Hindus that had gone over to other religions (*shuddhi*). This reconversion drive alarmed the local Muslims who in their turn launched a *tabligh* movement to spread Islam among the untouchable and low caste Hindus. Records in the Hyderabad Home Department show interesting cases of Dhers (untouchables) changing religion back and forth, and a case of temple pujaris complaining of Arya Samajists who brought Dhers to the temple compound and had

[50] Leonard 1978b: 199, 207.

[51] Tirtha 1967: 76.

[52] *The Arya Samaj in Hyderabad*, Whitebook published by Order of His Exalted Highness the Nizam's Government, n.d. (1939), L/P&S/13/1231.

[53] For this and other Arya Samaj activities, see Resumé of Events in Indian States, 1934–7, L/P&S/13/1200; also Ramesan IV, 1966: 88 ff.

tea with them. This was all not just a religious rivalry for converts. A constitutional reform, which sooner or later was bound to come, would surely dispense political privilege like seats and appointments along lines of caste and religion, and thus numerical proportions assumed political importance.

After 1935 the activities of the Arya Samaj increased. Resident Mackenzie reported that it had made 'deep inroads' in Hyderabad[54] and the government of the state watched the organization with growing distrust. In 1937 its Home Department considered proscription of *Satyarth Prakash*, a Vedic commentary by Swami Dayanand, held in great esteem by the Arya Samajists but resented by Muslims on account of its unrestrained criticism of the Koran. No action was taken, however, as proscription would present activists all over India with a welcome issue for agitation against Hyderabad. Moreover, even Urdu and Marathi translations of the book do not seem to have aroused much attention in the state.[55]

The Hindu Mahasabha, invited to Travancore by Sir C.P. Ramaswamy Aiyar was a political rather than a religious association. Its president, V.D. Savarkar, once explained that his organization was pledged 'to protect and promote all that contributes to the freedom, strength and glory of the Hindu Nation',[56] leaving the Muslims a marginal place within that nation, if any place at all. In 1932 the local branch of the HM, the Hindu Civil Liberties Union, started investigations into Hyderabad conditions with the express purpose of protecting the Hindus against their own government. Like the AS, the HM in Hyderabad counted only a few members but it had a great potential because of its connections with a parent-organization operating beyond the state frontiers.

Mention should also be made of the Majlis-i-Ittihad-ul-Muslimin (Council of the Union of Muslims), a socio-religious organization of local Muslims (1929) intended to bring together all Muslims without regard to sect. It became increasingly militant under the leadership of Bahadur Yar Jung, a small jagirdar whose ancestors had come from Jaipur. Though an ardent supporter of the Nizam, Bahadur Yar Jung

[54] Secret Note on Hyderabad Affairs, D.G. Mackenzie Resident, covering letter 14.1.1937, L/P&S/13/1200.

[55] See correspondence on this subject in Home Department, Confidential Records, 1928–40, APSA Hyderabad.

[56] Quoted from Burke and Quraishi 1995: 165.

widely propagated the view that power resided not in the person of the ruler but in the community of Muslim believers who allowed him to rule.[57]

Till far into the twentieth century Hyderabad enjoyed a fair amount of communal harmony. Riots between Hindus and Muslims remained local in character and the first large and violent conflict took place in 1924 (Gulbarga). After 1924 the number of officially registered communal riots showed a distinct increase.[58] In 1937 the concurrence of Moharrum processions with the Holi festival led to a considerable number of communal incidents including loss of life. District officers declared they had no knowledge that troubles were brewing, as the riots arose suddenly out of petty trifles. Tension was most marked in the western districts of Bhir and Osmanabad. In some cases Muslims were the aggressors, but the Director-General of Police pointed out that the affected districts were precisely the places where for some time Arya Samaj efforts had been concentrated. Previous Samaj activity and Muslim reaction, in his words, 'had created an atmosphere unfavourable to good feelings'.[59]

As speakers at public meetings of the Arya Samaj deliberately spread communal disaffection and openly instigated disturbances, government responded by restricting the freedom of religious expression, requiring prior sanction for all meetings and processions. Incoming speakers only increased existing tensions by exhorting Hindus to fight their oppression under the Arya flag and teach the Muslims a sense of equality from the Vedas.[60] For that reason religious preachers from outside were forbidden to enter the state. It was of no use and only reinforced accusations that religious activities in Hyderabad were suppressed. The political future seemed gloomy and uncertain, resulting in uneasiness that made people look for safety behind communal boundaries.[61]

[57] Bawa 1992: 148.

[58] Pernau-Reifeld 1992: 244 ff., 264 ff.; a detailed list of major communal disturbances in Hyderabad 1937–40, in Copland 1988: 784.

[59] Confidential note on communal troubles from officiating Director-General of Police and Jails, Mr G.A. Anderson, 25.4.1937, in Home Department, Confidential Records, APSA Hyderabad.

[60] Police extracts of speeches made at AS meetings in Hyderabad City for the year 1937, in Home Department, Confidential Records, APSA Hyderabad.

[61] This hardening of communal lines is clear from the AS endeavour to keep Hindus away from Muslims rituals and festivals. The Resident reported that a tract

REFORM AND FEDERATION IMMINENT (1937–1938)

True political life started at the end of the 1930s, so we quoted Tirtha in the second section of this chapter. By that time the movements for constitutional reform and political federation were reaching a critical stage. In April 1937 the provincial part of the 1935 Government of India Act went into operation with responsible ministries assuming power in all British-Indian provinces. In the provinces immediately bordering on Hyderabad, i.e. Bombay, Madras and Central Provinces, these ministries were formed or at least were dominated by the Congress. This achievement of provincial autonomy could not fail to make an impression on Hyderabad where political reforms were felt to be long overdue. However, reform meant the sharing of power and in Hyderabad the question as to who should share it and in what proportion was an extremely delicate one.

In September 1937, Sir Akbar Hydari, as 'the bearer of a Message from our August Sovereign', informed the Legislative Council that a Constitutional Reforms Committee had been appointed under the chairmanship of Diwan Bahadur Aiyangar, legal adviser for the Residency, '. . . to investigate and report on all suitable alternatives for the more effective association of the different interests in the State with the Government whereby the latter may be placed in continuous possession of their needs and desires'.[62]

The committee had five members, three non-officials and two Hindus, and was asked to submit its report within six months. Its appointment failed to arouse much public enthusiasm in Hyderabad. Those who felt that Muslims had lost the moral right to rule were disappointed that the terms of reference did not include any promise of a government responsible to elected people's representatives. The Muslim elite, on the other hand, had so long monopolized the administration that any change that might affect a continuation of their power was viewed with alarm. An appeal was made to Deccani culture and tradition to keep a tottering administrative system from falling apart. But what Hyderabad really needed was time to face the coming

entitled *Angles of the Grave*, condemning the practice of Hindu women visiting Muslim graves, had a large sale at AS meetings, Resumé of Events in Indian States, Hyderabad, for fortnight ending 15.7.1935, L/P&S/13/1200.

[62] RRC 1938: vii.

political change and qualified men to give the necessary lead. According to British officers, both were painfully lacking.[63]

The Reforms Committee evoked no enthusiasm, but stimulated a great deal of political activity. In anticipation of its report, representatives of different sections of the public met from November 1937 under the name of the Hyderabad People's Convention. They submitted a scheme of responsible government under the aegis of the ruling dynasty, consisting of a bicameral legislature with an elected majority and power to appoint half the members of the Executive Council. However, a significant cleavage surfaced when the six Muslim members of the Convention refused to sign the scheme. Their main objection was that the percentage of Muslim representation in the legislative was not agreed upon.[64]

While government and people in Hyderabad were waiting for the Reform Committee's proposals, the British government stated in Parliament that it would certainly not obstruct any proposals for constitutional reform that Indian states might have in mind.[65] Yet the main constitutional advance the Reforms Committee had in mind was an extension of the legislature. How political representation in that legislature had to be organized was one of the most difficult problems to solve. After much deliberation, the majority of the committee suggested the introduction of a system of representation on the basis of economic and other interests through organizations representing such interests.[66] By that way the Committee hoped to dispense with all forms of communal representation and to prevent any single section of the population from securing a predominant majority for itself. A dissenting voice came from Kashinath Rao Vaidya, who preferred the adoption of territorial constituencies as elsewhere in India but without any form of communal reservation to safeguard minority interests. He stood alone in his wish to give the new legislature more powers than just a right to discuss the budget. The committee's

[63] Secret Notes by D.G. Mackenzie, Resident Hyderabad (covering letter dated 14.1.1937), L/P&S/13/1200, and by Th.Tasker, Head Revenue Department, December 1937, R/1/1/3222.

[64] Resumé of Events in Indian States, Hyderabad, fortnight ending 15.1.1938, L/P&S/13/667; note by Kashinath Rao Vaidya, no date, L/P&S/13/1231; SFHS 1938: 5 ff.; Ramesan IV, 1966: 146–7; Bawa 1992: 168 ff.

[65] Statement in the House of Commons in answer to question by Captain Heligers, 21.2.1938, in R/1/1/3060, also discussed in Chapter 3.

[66] RRC 1938: 129.

report was finally submitted on 31 August 1938, but remained unpublished.

What is important to note is the gradual transformation that in the 1930s was taking place in the conception of kingship. So long as the Nizam himself was the fountainhead of all power, nothing else was needed to sanction his position. The report of the Reforms Committee however, called the Nizam not only the source of all authority and justice, but also the embodiment of the sovereignty of his people. Political associations were not slow to follow and called the ruler the personification of Deccani nationalism or—as we have seen above—the embodiment of Muslim sovereignty.[67] What all these statements had in common is that the power of the Ruler was derived from his people and not the other way round.

In the meantime the government of Hyderabad was seeking to determine its attitude towards federation. In 1936 the draft Instruments of Accession were issued and Sir Arthur Lothian was appointed the Viceroy's special representative to explain the federal proposals to the southern rulers.[68] In Hyderabad Lothian found to his great dismay that Sir Akbar Hydari had become very critical of the federal scheme. He fiercely resisted the surrender of Hyderabad's own coinage, post and telegraph and argued for wide reservations in respect of railways in what Lothian called an endeavour to ride out on side issues. The point was, Lothian informed the Political Department, that the position of Hydari in Hyderabad was not very strong. With all his abilities Hydari remained a non-*mulki* without local following who on the issue of federation lacked the vital support of the Nizam.[69]

In answer to the draft Instrument of Accession the government of Hyderabad published a bulky printed Memorandum elaborating the state's requirements for accession (1937). Preservation of the status quo was the guiding principle in which the many detailed reservations were framed.[70] Along with the usual reference to the state's wealth of history and tradition Hydari informed the Political Department that Hyderabad had made these reservations 'with a view to securing protection against attempts at enforcing a drab uniformity in certain

[67] RRC 1938: 7–8; SFHS 1938: 12; Leonard 1978a: 88; Ramesan IV 1966: 137.

[68] Lothian 1951: 147–9.

[69] Letter from A.C. Lothian to Sir Bertrand Glancy, Political Department, 21.11.1936, L/P&S/13/667. See also Lothian 1951: 149 and Copland 1997: 155.

[70] See comment in Gibson's Minute Paper, London 28.9.1937, in Hyderabad's Attitude towards Federation, L/P&S/13/667.

fields best left, even in the interests of all India, to the local genius of the people and to the Government of the State. Some others [i.e. reservations] . . . were conceived with a view to preventing a possible loosening of the bonds that hold together its different peoples under one sway.'[71]

On official occasions the Nizam expressed his willingness to earnestly consider all federal proposals, while the Viceroy assured him that Indian rulers would be given unfettered authority to decide whether to accept or reject the federal offer.[72] But in fact, the Hyderabad government wanted decisive action deferred as long as practicable. In his discussions with Sir Bertrand Glancy of the Political Department, Hydari tried again and again to exclude more subjects from transfer to federal jurisdiction. Glancy argued that by cautious negotiations they had managed to meet Hyderabad's demands to an extent previously thought impossible and that the states would never get such an offer again. However, Hydari and the Hyderabad officials could not get rid of their deep suspicions of the motives which would inspire the future federal legislature and ministry as far as the states were concerned.[73]

A recurring problem in all deliberations about federation was the system of government in the acceding states. Congress spokesmen, full of self-confidence after their sweeping victory at the 1937 polls, reiterated again and again that federation implied the Indian states sending their representatives to the federal assembly by means of election. This was strongly resisted by Hyderabad as well as the other states. Hydari told the Resident that responsible government could never be a condition for accession to the federation. In this he was supported by Lord Zetland, the Secretary of State for India. In a cautious speech Lord Zetland had answered the question of popular election of states' representatives in federation, with the comment: 'Well, that is for the Princes to decide. There is nothing in the Act to prevent it. . . .'[74]

[71] Letter from Hydari to B. Glancy, Secretary Political Department, January 1938, and other relevant documents in L/P&S/13/667.

[72] *Hyderabad Political Notebook*, Vol. II (1919–45), 1945: 69, in Lothian Collection, Lothian Collection Nr. 63.

[73] Correspondence on Hyderabad's Attitude towards Federation 1937–8, L/P&S/13/667.

[74] Speech Secretary of State for India, 27.5.1938, in L/PO/5/20. See also letter from Hydari to British Resident, 23.11.1938, L/P&S/13/1231 and speech by S. Satyamurthi MLA, in *Madras Mail* 2.11.1938.

GROWING TENSION AND SATYAGRAHA (1938)

In February 1938 at the INC annual session in Haripura, it was resolved that for the internal political struggle in the states independent organizations should be started, not using the name of Congress and without committing local Congress Committees. Individual Congressmen, however, were allowed to take part in that struggle in their personal capacities. Though not in words, in practice Haripura heralded a change of policy, Gandhi and other Congress leaders favouring a more active interest in state affairs.

This Haripura session is said to have been attended by no less than 500 people from Hyderabad. They returned convinced that the formation of a political and non-communal organization for the attainment of responsible government was the need of the day. A few months later, the first major communal riot in Hyderabad City (Dhulpet) took place. A Muslim procession through a predominantly Hindu locality that was held for years without any objection being taken resulted in a violent clash, leaving several dead among whom were two cousins of Bahadur Yar Jung, the leader of the Ittihad. The Deputy Director-General of Police, Mr Anderson, attributed the outbreak of violence to the vehement propaganda carried on by Hindu and Muslim communal leaders and the tension created by the *tabligh* and *shuddhi* movements. Hydari, suspecting a foreign hand in it, declared that the disturbance was 'not entirely, nor mainly of local make', but also prohibited the state services from participation in any communal activity.[75]

A first start in the formation of a new political organization had been made by the People's Convention in January 1938 under the presidentship of M. Hanumantha Rao. From that platform a provisional committee of the Hyderabad State Congress (HSC) was launched in July. It formulated as its main object the attainment by the people of responsible government under the aegis of the Nizam to be achieved by all peaceful and legitimate means.[76] Another stream that joined in the formation of the HSC were the regional movements, the Andhra, Maharashtra and Karnataka conferences. In the view of Tirtha, who took an active part in its formation, the HSC was a movement from

[75] Report by G.A. Anderson, Deputy Director-General of Police Hyderabad, 14.4.1938, R/1/1/3089; speech by Hydari before Legislative Council, Summer 1938, in Home Department, Confidential Records, APSA Hyderabad.

[76] SFHS 1938: 19; Bawa 1992: 180.

the regions that converged in the capital.[77] The first HSC president, Govind Rao Nanal, had also presided over the Maharashtra Conference (1937) which led to the formation of the Maharashtra Parishad.[78] Leonard (1978a) is more inclined to view the HSC as a continuation of the *Mulki* League.

One might say that in the HSC several local traditions and organizations came together, from Deccani protagonists to cultural nationalists. This many-stranded character explains the state Congress' wide attraction but also its high vulnerability. As the provisional committee was still preparing the founding meeting, a government notification declared it to be an unlawful association under the Public Safety Regulation. Government said they would have no objections to the establishment of political organizations, provided that they were on a strictly non-communal basis and had no affiliations with bodies outside the state. However, the participation of persons predominantly communal in outlook was said to disqualify the HSC from official recognition: 'the movement, ostensibly political, is in fact a cloak for subversive, communal activities to which the prestige of the name "Congress" has been deliberately attached for misleading the public'.[79]

The HSC rejected both allegations. In a public statement it referred to its draft constitution which excluded persons belonging to a communal organization from holding office. Also, membership was open to anyone and the provisional committee pleaded helplessness for the Muslims staying away.[80] Nevertheless, the simultaneous involvement of leaders like Govind Rao Nanal, Kashinath Rao Vaidya and others in the AISPC, the Maharashtra regional conferences and the defence of Hindu communal rioters could not but make the new organization suspect in government eyes.[81]

Affiliations with bodies outside the state were also emphatically denied by the HSC. A party statement declared all connections, official or non-official, with the INC non-existent: 'no outside agency, either political or religious, has anything to do with this indigenous institution'. The name 'Congress', the statement explained, had been adopted merely to emphasize the nationalist basis underlying the party

[77] Tirtha 1967: 75.

[78] Razvi 1985: 8.

[79] Text in SFHS 1938: 29–30.

[80] Text in SFHS 1938: 31–4.

[81] Pernau-Reifeld 1992: 292 note 179. In 1937 Hanumanth Rao, HSC leader, had sent letters of greetings to the AS Youth Conference held in Hyderabad City.

as distinguished from that of a communal or provincial movement. But reference, even if in name alone, to an organization moving beyond and across state borders was already disturbing enough for the Hyderabad government, in spite of the HSC's loud professions of loyalty to the King as 'the embodiment of the glory and the power of his State'.[82]

In view of the government ban, the general meeting to found the Hyderabad Congress was postponed *sine die*. During prolonged discussions about a possible uplift of the ban, the HSC became increasingly frustrated by new and additional conditions laid down by government. One of these conditions, formulated by Nawab Ali Yavar Jung, Secretary to the Hyderabad government, was that the word 'Congress' should be deleted from the name Hyderabad State Congress, as this name 'was said to bear a strange resemblance to a dangerously non-violent organization in British India'.[83]

Discussions about official recognition of the HSC proved futile. Government was not prepared to lift the ban. Therefore, in October 1938 the HSC decided to launch a satyagraha campaign for the attainment of fundamental civil rights for the people including the right to political association. The provisional committee dissolved into a Working Committee which in an open challenge to government orders declared the formation of the HSC. Tirtha in his memoirs wrote that 'the feudal-cum-communal hierarchy' would not tolerate the emergence of a party working for civil rights and responsible government.[84] As the first Congress 'dictator' he informed the Police Commissioner of his intentions to defy the law and was duly arrested. The satyagraha meant that small groups of persons gathered daily in public streets, read out a statement and were arrested. The proceedings, the Resident reported, were good-tempered and the leaders kept in the background.[85] Tirtha described the HSC campaign as a move-

[82] Statement of Aims, 5.9.1938, in Ramesan IV, 1966: 137. Similar statements in ibidem 153 and SFHS 1938: 12.

[83] Ex-official, *Hyderabad in Retrospect*, 1949: 8. Among the Lothian Papers in the OIOC I found a copy of this book with marginal comments by Arthur Cunningham Lothian, Resident of Hyderabad 1942–6. On the title-page Lothian had scribbled that the ex-official was this same Ali Yavar Jung. He further comments that Ali Yavar Jung wrote this book after Independence 'to curry favour with Congress as a result of which he secured an Ambassadorship'. Lothian Collection Nr. 44.

[84] Tirtha 1967: 84.

[85] Resumé of Events in Indian States, Hyderabad, fortnight ending 15.11.1938, L/P&S/13/1200.

ment from within, but had to acknowledge that it was seriously hampered by a poor turn-out, especially in Hyderabad city.

About the same time a student satyagraha broke out at Osmania University. This university had three hostels, each with two prayer halls, one for Hindus and one for Muslims. When Hindu students started the recitation of *Vande Mataram* in their prayer hall, the authorities of Osmania University prohibited them from doing so, but the students refused to listen. Tirtha and Razvi have tried to subdue the communal character of this action by representing it as part of a larger anti-Nizam struggle.[86] In any case, this open association of a national song with a place of Hindu worship—supported from outside by nationalist Hindus from Gandhi to Savarkar—could not but evoke harsh measures from a university that was tightly controlled by government. The defiant students were removed from the hostel and their attendance at college was suspended. A large number of students, among whom was P.V. Narasimha Rao (later to become the Prime Minister), went on a strike and their protest lingered on for months.[87]

The satyagraha in Hyderabad was followed with close interest by the INC. The federal structure was drawing near and the burning question of state representation still remained unresolved. The INC, insisting on elected representation, warmly welcomed local movements for responsible government, especially in states like Hyderabad, Mysore, Jaipur and Travancore, which enjoyed a substantial number of seats in the proposed federal legislature. In December the (CWC) called for an increasing identification with the great awakening that was taking place among the people of the states. Gandhi, suggesting a connection between this awakening and the Haripura session, warned the Indian princes that there was no half-way house between total extinction of their states and the sharing of power with their people. Congress still advised people from outside the states to abstain from participation in local politics, as it would bring no real strength to the movement and might embarrass the local people.[88] Nevertheless, though less in words, Congress attitude towards the states was changing. It abandoned its former policy of non-interference and national leaders

[86] Tirtha 1967: 97; Razvi 1985: 5–7.

[87] Raghunadha Rao 1988: 138; Bawa 1992: x, 181–2.

[88] Resolution Congress Working Committee, Wardha 14.12.1938, L/P&S/13/887. See also *The Times of India* 15.12.1938 and M.K. Gandhi in *Harijan*, 1-10-1938 and 3.12.1938.

began to direct and support local groups advocating responsible government.

As far as Hyderabad was concerned, British-Indian Intelligence reported that at Poona people of divergent political convictions assembled for the purpose of rendering support to the satyagraha in Hyderabad. Among them was at least one committee of INC-minded and non-communal sympathizers. Similar committees under the aegis of INC had been formed at Nagpur and Akola, and plans were made to send *jatthas* (processions of volunteers) into Hyderabad territory. The same intelligence sources, strongly influenced by the Hyderabad government, considered the establishment of the HSC an attempt of the INC to make an inroad into Hyderabad.[89] Gandhi admitted in *Harijan* (4.12.1938) that the states' people not only looked up to Congress for leadership but were in many cases also guided by it.

Simultaneous with the HSC campaign a satyagraha was conducted by the Hyderabad Arya Samaj and Hindu Mahasabha. The former fought for the principle of religious freedom which was said to be denied to Hindus under Muslim tyranny, while the latter aimed at a more general improvement of the position of Hindus in Hyderabad society. Till the end of 1938 the three movements remained largely confined to Hyderabad state but their synchronous action was quite confusing. Most serious from the Congress point of view was that through the HSC it became associated with movements that made no secret of their distinctly communal character. Hyderabad's Prime Minister Hydari, for one, was absolutely convinced that the persons who inspired the HSC satyagraha were at the same time guiding the parallel activities of the Samaj and the Mahasabha. British officers agreed. The Resident maintained that the two organizations were operating separately for tactical reasons and Crofton, a British member of the Hyderabad Council, observed that Congress, whatever its professions, was in close touch with the communally minded Hindu politicians in the state, urging them to exploit the existing situation.[90] Hydari greatly

[89] Review compiled in the Intelligence Bureau, Home Department, no date, in R/1/1/3289. This review was largely based on reports by the Hyderabad Resident who got his information mainly from the Hyderabad government. See also the file Congress Activities in the Hyderabad State, R/1/1/3173.

[90] Letter from Sir Akbar Hydari to Congress leader Jamnalal Bajaj, 16.11.1938, L/P&S/13/1231. Secret note R.M. Crofton, Revenue and Police Member Hyderabad Executive Council, 20.10.1938, R/1/1/3222. Resumé of Events in Indian States for the fortnight ending 15.11.38, Hyderabad, L/P&S/13/1200.

resented this outside interference and wondered how Hyderabadi intervention in a Bombay textile strike would be received in British India.[91]

Soon after the commencement of the campaigns, Prime Minister Hydari had told the British Resident that if the paramount power would declare that the election of delegates was no condition to federation, outside intervention in the state would come to an end. Hydari also asked the Bombay government to prevent the sending of *jatthas* from Maharashtra in Hyderabad. The state had no jurisdiction over British-Indian railways traversing its territory and was thus debarred from taking action to prevent the ingress of *jatthas* by rail.[92] But no help was forthcoming from the provincial governments dominated by a Congress party that had just passed its Haripura resolution.

The Bombay government was not prepared to stop satyagrahis going to Hyderabad. It admitted that *jatthas* of satyagrahis were organized on its territory for the purpose of going into Hyderabad and to cause obstruction to the administration of that state. Yet the Bombay government did not consider themselves under any obligation to take action in order to prevent these incursions into Hyderabad or any other Indian state, so long as the intentions of the satyagrahis were non-violent and their activities in the province did not create hostility between the communities. 'The odium of dealing with those who protest against what they allege to be repression and injustice in Hyderabad State must fall upon the State authorities.'[93]

The Governors of Bombay and the Central Provinces also pleaded unable to prevent political agitation from spreading into Hyderabad territory. They possessed special powers to overrule their Indian ministers, but refrained from exercising them to avoid any conflict with the ministries recently constituted under the Government of India Act. Only Madras seems to have been a bit more accommodating.[94]

[91] The Montford Report had called non-interference a mutual obligation (ICR 1918: 191).

[92] Correspondence Hydari and Resident Hyderabad, 1938, and letter from Gidney, Resident Hyderabad, to Secretary to Crown Representative, 9.11.1938, L/P&S/13/1231.

[93] Letter from Government of Bombay, Home Department, to Government of India, Home Department, 9.12.1938, and related correspondence L/P&S/13/1231.

[94] Letter from Governor of Bombay, 14-10-1938, L/P&S/13/887 and from

The satyagraha campaigns in Hyderabad continued, but at a low pitch. At the end of December 1938 Kashinath Rao Vaidya announced that his organization had decided to suspend satyagraha, awaiting 'the necessary moral reaction' from the government. Advice from Congress leaders like Mahatma Gandhi and Maulana Azad had a strong bearing on this decision, indicating the extent to which actual control over the HSC had shifted to the INC. The satyagraha had assumed a communal character and in view of the precarious communal balance in British India, the INC could not afford to get mixed up with a movement that might be dubbed as an anti-Muslim movement in a Muslim princely state.[95] In spite of all its sympathy for the states' people, Congress was not enamoured by the state-based organizations, many of which were weak, left-wing dominated or, as in the case of Hyderabad, had strong communal overtones.[96] Therefore, a growing INC control over the HSC was also meant to prevent it from getting too much entangled in communal activities. At the moment of suspension a few hundreds of HSC satyagrahis were in jail.[97]

The All India States' People Conference in Ludhiana praised the self-constraint shown by the HSC. In one of its resolutions the AISPC stated that a satyagraha with the object of getting religious disabilities removed was not communal. However, it was also not opportune, as it gave a pretext to state authorities to oppose the larger movement for responsible government and religious freedom (*The Hindustan Times* 9.2.1938). According to the same paper (26.2.1939) the suspension

---

Governor of Central Provinces and Berar, 8-12-1938, L/P&S/13/1231. In fact, the Indian Legislative had passed an Act (XI of 1934) meant to protect the administrations of Indian states from activities which tended to subvert such administration. Under this Indian States Protection Act it was enacted that magistrates in British India might prohibit attempts to promote assemblies of persons for the purpose of proceeding from British India into the territory of an Indian state, if in their opinion the entry of such persons was likely to cause obstruction to the administration of such a state. See Political General Correspondence in Confidential File No. 34 3C, HPO Baroda.

[95] Resumé of Events in Indian States for the fortnight ending 31.12.1938, Hyderabad, L/P&S/13/1231; *Servant of India* 19.1.1939; Pernau-Reifeld 1992: 296.

[96] Copland 1985: 125–6.

[97] According to Tirtha 1967: 106, there were 400 HSC satyagrahis in jail when the movement was suspended; Hydari in a letter to the Resident, 19.6.1939, mentioned a number of 223 (L/P&S/13/1232), whereas a Review compiled by the Intelligence Bureau, Home Department, no date, came to 535 HSC arrests, not one of them Muslim, R/1/1/3289.

decision had the desired effect in removing the ideological confusion created by the coexistence of a HSC with an Arya Samaj and Hindu Mahasabha satyagraha. The INC tried to keep its distance from Hyderabadi communalism by openly condemning the continuing agitation by the Arya Samaj and Hindu Mahasabha. However, many Hindus looked for guidance in matters of religion to these bodies, and thus were susceptible to calls to continue the struggle. British Intelligence also reported that some INC leaders individually supported the communal agitation after December 1938.[98]

INCREASING INVOLVEMENT OF HINDU COMMUNAL ORGANIZATIONS (1939)

An important consideration in the decision of Congress to exert a moderating influence on the HSC was the increasing involvement in Hyderabad affairs of communal organizations outside. Both the All-India Arya Samaj and the Hindu Mahasabha had been preparing conferences on Hyderabad which finally took place in the last week of December 1938. The Arya Samaj conference at Sholapur, close to Hyderabad's borders in Maharashtra, levelled a bitter attack at the state government for depriving Hindus of the elementary rights of public worship, public preaching, the building of temples and the opening of schools. It demanded that the Nizam's government immediately change this state of affairs, if it did not want to be swamped with a sea of satyagrahis.

The simultaneous Mahasabha meeting at Nagpur also referred to what it considered to be 'the most fanatical and outrageous treatment to which the Hindus have been for years subjected in the Nizam state'. President Savarkar accused Syrian Christians of craving for power in Travancore and denounced what he called Hyderabad's policy of extirpating all Hindus in order to turn the state entirely into a Muslim one. In a move to adapt its communalism to a democratic idiom the Mahasabha urged a fight against the state government 'until all the rights are conceded to the Hindus in accordance with their numerical strength'.[99]

[98] Residency correspondence in L/P&S/13/1200 and L/P&S/13/1232. Review Intelligence Bureau, Home Department, n.d., R/1/1/3289.

[99] Quoted in *The Times of India* 30.12.38. See also files in L/P&S/13/1232 and correspondence V.D. Savarkar, President All-India Mahasabha, in L/P&S/13/1231, and his contribution to *The Hindu Outlook* 30.11.1938.

These December conferences mark the final taking over of the local satyagraha movement by the two organizations, strengthening their claims to speak for the entire Hindu population. But it also enabled the local movements in Hyderabad to make use of what Kloos calls 'global forces' to attain their ends. This meant, first of all, material support, as secretaries in British India were called upon to collect money for the cause. Next, the international Aryan League in Delhi started a vehement publicity campaign, accusing the Nizam's government of molestation of Hindu women, forced conversion in jails and official support to Islamic proselytization. Local Arya Samaj branches, especially in the Punjab, Bombay and Central Provinces, joined the chorus and appealed to the British paramount power to stop the barbarous and reprehensible methods of ruthless repression of satyagrahis in Hyderabad.[100] The mobilization of forces in support of Hyderabad Hindus increased communal tension in British India and in some places resulted in communal rioting.

The support from British India that hurt most was the sending of *jaťthas*. In a spate of letters Hydari complained about these annoying intrusions and the dubious quality of the people involved. Also, he still felt at war with the HSC which in his view had not suspended satyagraha unconditionally but with a veiled threat that not suited the professed spirit of appeasement. Emphasizing that the HSC had not purified its ranks and still numbered many communal elements, Hydari tried to convince Gandhi and other INC leaders that the HSC in no way deserved Congress' sympathy and support.[101]

Writing to the British Resident, Hydari called the HSC satyagraha a movement 'ostensibly operating from within the boundaries of the State'. The HSC might pretend independence from the INC, but Hydari contended that inspiration and guidance came directly from Congress headquarters in Wardha. Amongst the arrested HSC satyagrahis there was not a single Muslim, and Hydari concluded that this was sufficient comment on the state Congress' claim to be a

[100] Hyderabad men like Y.D. Joshi, Bhaskar Rao Keskar and Shamlal were very active in establishing links between their local organization and the All-India Arya Samaj. See Home Department, Confidential Reports in APSA Hyderabad, and Hyderabad: Arya Samaj Agitation 1939, L/P&S/13/1231 and L/P&S/13/1232. One letter to AS secretaries, dated 3.11.1938, expressly stated: 'You should also try your utmost to participate in the Congress.'

[101] Letters from Hydari to Gandhi, 5.1.1939 and 16.2.1939, and to Maulana Abul Kalam Azad, 17-2-1939, L/P&S/13/1231.

non-communal body working for political reform: 'The real objective of the State Congress, and of the men in British India under whose guidance it works, is and has always been Hindu political dominance.'[102]

Even more caustic were Hydari's comments on the Arya Samaj and Hindu Mahasabha. They were openly operating from British India and Hydari was convinced that, if the influx of *jatthas* from outside could be stopped, there would be practically no Hindu satyagraha in Hyderabad. Yet, the Viceroy went no further than sending a cautious instruction to his governors to impress on their ministries 'the gravity of the present situation', if they saw no objection to that course.[103] When in May 1939 Gandhi asked the Hyderabad government to concede the demand of freedom of religion as a gesture of peace,[104] Hydari was seriously offended. He explained to the Mahatma that the sending of *jatthas*, mainly composed of strangers to the Deccan, to remote and weakly controlled points of the countryside was intended only to embarass the administration and to disturb the minds of the local people: 'the true spirit of satyagraha which we can respect, has been travestied by methods not unlike those favoured in Berlin . . . fostering . . . a spirit of aggression by the paraphernalia of flags, "dictators" in special trains proceeding to the "front" and a "war council" '.

Those responsible for this travesty, Hydari wrote, remained in the background, in Wardha and Sholapur.[105]

Hydari and his colleagues left no opportunity unused to emphasize that the control by his government was not meant to restrict religious freedom but to maintain law and order. These were continually threatened by incoming *jatthas* shouting: 'Hyderabad belongs to Hindus' and 'We will destroy mosques and build temples'. In one of his letters to the Resident, Hydari described a large *jattha* that tried to cross the border into Hyderabad. Far from being non-violent, the crowd was

[102] Letter from Hydari to Gidney, Resident Hyderabad, 3.4.1939, L/P&S/13/1231.

[103] Telegram from Viceroy to Governors of Bombay, Central Provinces and Madras, 23.4.1939, L/P&S/13/1231 and R/1/1/3289.

[104] Letter from Gandhi to Hydari, 15.5.39, L/P&S/13/1232; also in Ramesan IV, 1967: 163–4.

[105] Letter from Hydari to Gandhi 30.5.1939 Hyderabad, L/P&S/13/1232. At an AS meeting in Hyderabad City on 18.3.1938, N.P. Saxena had praised Hitler for taking over Austria without causing any bloodshed: 'Hitler was an Arya and had done the work of Aryas', see police extract of speeches made at weekly AS meetings in Hyderabad, Sultan Bazaar, in Home Department, Confidential records, APSA Hyderabad.

pelting stones at the Hyderabad Police, shouting a song to the effect that, whereas in the past temples had been dismantled to construct mosques, now they were going to enter the state to dismantle mosques and construct temples.[106]

In the meantime the All-India Arya Samaj had started a press-campaign all over India, the main thrust of which was that more than 10,000 satyagrahis, the large majority originating from Hyderabad state, were suffering from severe maltreatment in local jails. As far as numbers were concerned, the Resident's reports, based on official information, contained detailed figures for every fortnight but these were, as could be expected, considerably lower. In May 1939 the total number of arrests had come to about 5,000.[107] Questions were asked in the House of Commons about the number of prisoners in Hyderabad. The answer was something over 5,000 prisoners till the end of May and reflected the information received from the Residency.[108] Later, in its review of the year 1938–9, the Hyderabad Administration Report mentioned a total number of 9,525 prisoners which came close to the Arya Samaj claims but was taken at a much later date.[109]

The official information from Hyderabad held that about 80 per cent of the satyagraha prisoners were outsiders, completely ignorant of conditions actually obtaining in the state. The administration stated that of the 9,525 prisoners admitted to the jails 1,710 were residents and no less than 7,815 came from outside. Many of these outsiders made no secret of the fact that they had been hired, whereas several Hyderabadi prisoners had visited the conferences in Sholapur and Nagpur and were considered victims of virulent propaganda.[110]

British officers in Hyderabad denounced not only the aggressive behaviour but also the poor quality of the volunteers sent from British India. Hollins, Director-General of Police and in charge of jail admin-

[106] Letters from Hydari to Resident Hyderabad, 26.5.1939 and 19-6-1939, L/P&S/13/1232.

[107] Resumé of Events in Indian States, Hyderabad, fortnightly reports for April, May and June 1939, L/P&S/13/1200 and L/P&S/13/1231.

[108] Question by Col. Wedgwood in the Commons, 19.6.1939, L/P&S/13/1231. Wedgwood seems to have been in personal correspondence with the AS in Delhi, see L/P&S/13/1232. On 10.7.1939 new questions on this subject were raised by Col. Wedgwood together with Mr Grenfell.

[109] RAND 1941: vii.

[110] Resumé of Events in Indian States, fortnightly reports from Hyderabad, first months of 1939, L/P&S/13/1200.

istration, observed among the *jatthas* many children under 15 and old men of over 60, in addition to sick, blind and maimed persons. He was convinced that the Arya Samaj had deliberately sent sick and infirm persons to court arrest, hoping in case of death to make capital out of so-called ill-treatment.[111] Tasker, Member of the Hyderabad Council, concurred that the AS wanted to disorganize the administration by swamping the jails. He considered the presence of aged men, sick people and even a lunatic among the *jatthas* evidence of the want of care exercised by those who sent them.[112]

In spite of all Hydari's protestations, many of them shared by British officers, the Arya Samaj could count on a certain sympathy in Congress circles. K.M. Munshi, Bombay Home Minister, took over many of the Samaj grievances. He complained to the Viceroy that no primary and secondary schools were permitted without Urdu as the medium of instruction and that the Hyderabad Ecclesiastical Department was run by Muslims solely out to control Hindu religious observances. Therefore, he stated that if the people of Bombay wanted 'to utilize the freedom that they possess for purposes of ending slavery elsewhere', they should be completely at liberty to do so. The Congress Ministry in the Central Provinces joined with Bombay in this stand. It decided not to sympathize with the Hindu Mahasabha agitation which was political, but to be gravely perturbed about the Arya Samaj which aimed for religious liberty for the Hindu majority. 'The contrast between British India and Hyderabad in the matter of religious and cultural liberty is so glaring as to call for speedy action by the Paramount Power.'[113]

The allegations of the Arya Samaj and its Congress sympathizers led to a sharp rejoinder from the Hyderabad government and the British Resident. They stressed the religious freedom that had existed in Hyderabad from time immemorial. There was no objection to the opening of private schools following any curriculum and using any

[111] Hollins quoted in letter from Lord Linlithgow, Viceroy, to Lord Zetland, Secretary of State for India, 30.7.39, L/P&S/13/1232.

[112] Note by Tasker, Revenue and Police Member Hyderabad Executive Council, 15.7.1939 and his reply to Representation by Council of Ministers, CP and Berar, n.d. (June 1939), L/P&S/13/1232.

[113] Letter from K.M. Munshi to Viceroy, Simla, 27.5.39; declaration by K.M. Munshi in Bombay Legislative Assembly, 24.3.1939, quoted in secret letter Hydari to Gidney, Resident, 19.6.1939; representation by Council of Ministers, Central Provinces and Berar, n.d. (June 1939), L/P&S/13/1232.

language, provided that schools with less than 15 pupils were no longer registered with the educational authorities. The ban on the entry of religious preachers, they contended, was solely to prevent communal riots; it applied to preachers of all denominations without distinction, but not to local ones. Government permission for religious ceremonies and processions was indeed required, but only in case of new ceremonies. Further, Hydari's government argued that its Ecclesiastical Department was not out to control Hindu religious activities: with the department's permission 150 new temples had been built over the last eleven years, and 825 temples had been repaired.[114]

The British Resident did not challenge this account of the state of affairs, but commented that implementation of existing regulations by petty Muslim officials was not always fair and free of communal bias.[115] The Hyderabad Home Department indirectly acknowledged this bias by drafting fresh instructions for taluqdars to dispose of applications for licensing places of worship without delay. These instructions however were not issued and Samaj leaders admitted in a conversation with Hollins that the opening of more than 100 Samaj centres in Hyderabad disproved their own propaganda that the Aryas were being oppressed.[116] Nonetheless, the Home Department of the Government of India observed that there was ground for thinking that Hindus in the state suffered from 'certain difficulties, if not disabilities', and that the Samaj made use of them as a good cause for complaint.[117]

In Bichkonda, Aryasamajists infuriated local Muslims by establishing a *mandir* without government permission and hoisting their flag

[114] Munshi's critical views were contested and refuted by the Hyderabad Information Bureau, 17.7.1939 and by Gidney, Resident, letter to Viceroy, Hyderabad 6.7.1939; see also Sir Amin Jung Bahadur in *The Indian Review*, December issue 1936; the Representation by the Council of Ministers of Central Provinces was contradicted by Hydari, 14.7.1939, Gidney, 12.7.1939, and Tasker. See L/P&S/13/1232.

[115] Letter from Gidney, Resident, to Political Department, Delhi, 7.7.1939, L/P&S/13/1232.

[116] For Hollins' discussion with Arya Samaj leaders and correspondence on the draft instructions to taluqdars, see Home Department, Confidential Records, APSA Hyderabad.

[117] Note from Home Department Government of India to Under Secretary of State for India, 5.7.39. An internal note of the Political Department, London, 20.7.1939, stated condescendingly that no application for permission to build a place of worship was considered without a blue-print and that no-one in the districts knew what a blue-print was, L/P&S/13/1232.

on it. They told the District Superintendent of Police that flying an OM flag was not illegal—which was true—but refrained from asking permission for the opening of the *mandir* which adjoined a slaughter-house. Their unwillingness to petition government may have to do with the above mentioned bias of petty Muslim officials, but the police officer, a Reddy by caste, was convinced that the Arya Samajists were primarily out to defy government orders and looked for a case to rouse public indignation.[118]

Most important to our purpose is the impact the sending of *jatthas* might have had on the internal situation in Hyderabad. Here again, we have to cope with contradictory evidence, this time originating in the same source. Whereas we have so far heard Hyderabad complain of the harmful effects of outside intrusions, there are also many official references to the inefficacy of the *jatthas* and the lack of interest among local Hindus. In one of his letters to the Resident Hydari comments that the arrival of satyagrahis was greeted by a few idle onlookers with boredom. Usually, they were incarcerated before the general public was aware of their arrival. In another letter, he writes that, if outside satyagrahis managed to drive into Hyderabad city and were not promptly arrested, 'they would be given short shrift by the Muslim public'.[119]

Another unintended result of the interference by Hindu volunteers was that the Ittihad (Unity), the local Muslim association, was gathering strength in proportion as Muslims felt threatened. Moreover, the inability of the Government of India to check the *jatthas* made Muslims suspect that government of supporting the INC in its resolve to destroy the state of Hyderabad.[120] Feeble attempts to unite the state's Hindus and Muslims were frustrated, as the external threat enabled a more extremist leadership to gain command of the Ittihad. So the influence of global forces strengthened hostile movements at the local level, thus hardening communal boundaries.

Finally, the satyagraha against Hyderabad state, which was to peter out in the summer of 1939,[121] brought home to the government and

[118] Confidential diary of District Superintendent of Police, Nander, 21.4.1939, in L/P&S/13/1232.

[119] Letter by Hydari to Gidney, Resident, 3.4.1939, L/P&S/13/1231; letter 19.6.1939 L/P&S/13/1232.

[120] See Congress Agitation in Indian States, L/P&S/13/887.

[121] In spite of repeated calls to sacrifice their lives for the sake of their religion, their nation and their honour, very few Arya Samajists were ready to offer satyagraha. So, the Arya Samaj cultivated Dharam Prakash, a local labourer killed in a street row, as its martyr of the faith. See Khodwe 1947 and Ramesan IV 1966: 91.

large sections of the public that their state had few friends in the larger India; that the surrounding Congress governments, the prospective partners in federation, had done next to nothing to alleviate its predicament; and that it was absolutely necessary to secure in any constitutional change that no one community should numerically dominate another. As a Political Department note put it succinctly: 'The federal offer has reached Hyderabad in circumstances most unpropitious for its sympathetic consideration.'[122] One may add that it also provided those who cherished the status quo with a most welcome argument to reject the whole federal scheme.

THE FEDERAL OFFER TURNED DOWN (1938–1939)

With final decisions on federation drawing near, Hyderabad and a few other large states on the initiative of Travancore's Sir C.P. asked the paramount power for a statement of policy regarding the selection of state representatives to the federal legislature. Their request was partly met by arranging for a question in the House of Commons, asking in what way the attitude of His Majesty's Government towards constitutional reform in Indian states had been modified. The Under Secretary of State answered that there was no change in policy: the paramount power would not obstruct proposals for constitutional reform initiated by rulers nor bring any form of pressure to bear upon them to initiate such reform.

A few days later, the Viceroy, Lord Linlithgow, seemed to go one step further. In a public speech he acknowledged that it would be difficult to secure constituencies for the selection of state representatives in the federal legislature unless there were some representative institutions in the state itself.[123] However, because of its ambiguity this statement failed to satisfy either the champions or the opponents of more responsible forms of government.

At the end of 1938 new draft instruments of accession were submitted to the Indian rulers. After careful study of all its clauses Hydari warned the Political Department in Delhi that the Nizam's govern-

[122] Secret Internal Note, Political Department, London, 8.2.1939, L/P&S/13/667. Copland 1997: 170–1.

[123] Reply to Sir J.Wardlaw Milne's question in the House of Commons, 16.12.1938, and public speech by Viceroy, 19.12.1938, L/P&S/13/887; L/PO/5/20; L/P&S/13/1231.

ment had major objections to the scheme which would make accession impossible in any event. He presented a long list of subjects that should be preserved from federal interference, from treaty rights and defence to broadcasting and industries. But the main plank of his opposition became the clause dealing with the administration of federal subjects. Hyderabad demanded that the local administration of federal subjects should remain entirely in the hands of the state and its officers and that no federal officer should enter the state for administrative purposes. In this he was strongly supported by Tasker who seemed nervous about the possible influx of Hindu federal officers.[124] It would not only weaken the Nizam's hold on his own administration, but might also disturb the precarious communal balance. At a meeting of princes and state ministers in Bombay, Hyderabad, represented by Ali Yavar Jung, turned out to have become the main opponent of federation.[125]

In view of Hyderabad's opposition, the Viceroy suggested a policy of isolating the state. In his reply, the Secretary of State, Lord Zetland, suspected a considerable element of bluff in Hydari's position. He also believed that Hydari's attitude was largely affected by the onset of Congress pressure through *jatthas* and otherwise which had alarmed the *mulki* party and proportionately discredited Hydari as an earlier champion of the federal scheme.[126] Zetland described himself as 'on the horns of a painful dilemma'. Any pressure upon the states with the object of bringing about some constitutional reform would be bitterly resented by the princes, and federation could come into existence only if a sufficient number of them agreed to accede. He also realized that, if the present chance was lost, it would never return.[127]

Although comparatively few problems remained to be solved between the Government of India and the Secretary of State, it was not until January 1939 that the Viceroy was able to make his federal offer known to the princes. In a circular letter he communicated to them the final terms on which they were expected to execute their

[124] Letter by Hydari to Glancy, 25.11.38, and Tasker in interview with Patrick, Political Secretary at the India Office, 10.2.1939, L/P&S/13/667.

[125] For a short report of the meeting see letter by Glancy, New Delhi, 2.12.1938, L/P&S/13/667.

[126] Correspondence between Viceroy and Secretary of State for India, 1938–9, especially letter by Zetland, 20.12.1938, L/P&S/13/667.

[127] Letter from Lord Zetland to Carl Heath, 19.12.1938, L/PO/5/20.

instruments of accession. He asked them to reply within six months.[128] That meant that the Hyderabad government had to make up its mind about the surrender of powers to a new federal structure during the same months that it had to face fierce attacks by communal movements operating within and outside its territory.

At this critical juncture Hydari felt greatly disturbed by any doubt about his anxiety to secure early federation. Yet at the same time he was raising new, and for the British unacceptable, propositions. Though there was no ground left to him to hope for a material modification of the federal offer, Linlithgow said in a private letter: 'it is tiresome that the old man should be so difficult to pin down'.[129] The key to the problem, however, was the Nizam himself. The British assumed that Hydari was convinced of the vital importance of federation to the states, as he had made clear at the Round Table Conference. But they also believed that the Prime Minister had great difficulty in carrying his ruler with him, as was confirmed in a letter by Hydari's son. Hydari's position was so uncertain, the argument ran, that if he wanted to remain Prime Minister, he must be prepared to join the ranks of federal opposition.[130]

The India Office grew increasingly worried about Hyderabad's final stand, especially after a committee of the Chamber of Princes under the chairmanship of Hydari had decided that the revised instruments of accession were still unsatisfactory and could not be accepted in their present form. It was realized that without Hyderabad's accession it would be unlikely that a sufficient number of states would secure the desired federation. On the other hand, any weakening of the proposals was no guarantee of acceptance as new objections would certainly crop up. In their private correspondence Zetland and Linlithgow began to reckon with the possibility that the states, in particular Hyderabad, were not prepared to part with their old power and independence.

Lord Zetland, making up the balance, thought that the decisive factor lay in the states' recent experience with outside interference which had shown that little reliance could be placed upon the protection to be derived from the provincial governors' special powers. Apart

[128] Lothian 1951: 147 ff.

[129] Private Letter from Lord Linlithgow to Lord Zetland, 7.2.1939, L/P&S/13/667.

[130] Letter from Linlithgow to Zetland, 27.4.1939, L/P&S/13/667. Letter from young Hydari to Gilbert, Private Secretariat's Office, 28.4.1939, L/PO/5/20.

from that, the INC attack on nominated representatives in the federal assembly confronted the rulers with implications of federation which they had hitherto steadfastly declined to entertain. Muslim states, in particular Hyderabad, were also influenced by a general antipathy to federation, because of the dreaded prospect of a democratic centre which must be preponderantly Hindu. Nevertheless, Zetland refused to re-open the negotiations. In case of rejection of the federal offer, he preferred to conduct the central government upon the existing statutory basis until different counsels prevailed.[131]

British assumptions proved right. In June 1939 the Nizam informed the Viceroy with great regret that he was not willing to execute an instrument of accession within the terms indicated by the latter. He submitted a long list of objections, not inconsistent with earlier statements, ranging from railways and industries to customs and the recent *jatthas*, which had evinced no federal spirit. More in particular the Nizam objected to the federal legislative's power to extinguish a treaty right. His Highness thought it to be fundamental that such treaty rights as he possessed should continue under federation, military protection included. He could also not agree with any transfer of administration to federal officers who were not his servants and owed him no allegiance.[132] The Indian government decided to extend the final date for acceptance of the federal proposal to 1 September, but by that time other events took up all their attention.

THE END OF THE REFORMS (1938–1939)

As we have seen, the report of the Hyderabad Constitutional Reforms Committee was submitted in August 1938 but remained unpublished. About the same time Narasingh Rao (HSC) and Bahadur Yar Jung (Ittihad) started their so-called Unity Talks about the delicate issue of communal reservation in the legislative and administrative services. An agreement was eagerly sought in order to get the ban on the HSC lifted and to give the reform proposals a more promising start. At several moments an agreement seemed close, including a detailed

[131] See the successive draft letters from Zetland to Linlithgow, final version 30.5.1939, L/P&S/13/667. Barton agreed with the first argument when he wrote that 'But for outside interference Hyderabad would by this time in all likelihood have led the way into federation . . .', *Western Morning News*, 28.8.1939.

[132] Letter by the Nizam, Mir Osman Ali Khan, to Linlithgow, Hyderabad, 9.6.1939, L/P&S/13/667. Copland 1997: 174 ff.

distribution of the communities in the legislative and the services. Yet in March 1939 the talks finally broke down on the question of responsible versus responsive government.[133]

At the end of the same month a memorial of the Ittihad emphatically declared that the Muslims of the Deccan would accept no constitutional change which would adversely affect their traditional supremacy. It demanded that Muslims should be in a statutory majority in all legislative bodies, that there should be separate electorates and no proportional communal representation in the public services, and that special programmes should be started for the economic uplift of the Muslims.[134] Other demands raised by Bahadur Yar Jung—supported behind the scenes by the Nizam himself—were a reference in the reforms to Hyderabad as a Muslim state and the reservation of the three *Sarf-i-Khas* seats in the proposed legislative assembly to Muslims.[135]

The uncompromising attitude and growing communalism of the parties involved had a retarding influence on constitutional reform. Time and again, the British Resident urged the Nizam and his Prime Minister to publicly give their opinion on the Reform Committee's proposals, also as a means to combat the satyagraha, but as many times the Hyderabad government shrunk from taking the final step. In the meantime, the Resident had been able to peruse the intended reforms. In April 1939 he reported that the reforms proposed a legislature with a strong body of experts, a kind of corporate state, to avoid a Hindu majority and the almost inevitable communal representation. But Sir V. Dawson, the legal expert at the India Office, thought it an undeserved tribute to regard the proposals as a conscious adoption of the principles underlying the structure of the Italian state. In his view the reform scheme was 'a hotch-potch based on little or no appreciation of its probable results'.[136]

In July 1939 the Executive Council, with the consent of the Nizam, finally announced its decisions on the Reforms Committee's recom-

[133] See Resumé of Events in Indian States, Hyderabad, for November 1938–March 1939, and letter from A. Kamal Azad to Hydari, January 1939, L/P&S/13/1231; see also R/1/1/3173.

[134] *The Hindustan Times* 27.3.1939.

[135] Ex-Official 1949: 6; *Hyderabad Political Notebook*, Vol. II, 1945: 73, in Lothian Collection, Nr. 63.

[136] Letter from Gidney to Glancy, Hyderabad, 24.4.1939, and comment by V. Dawson, 26.6.1939, L/P&S/13/1200.

mendations. The recommendations were accepted but with a few important modifications. To achieve an elected majority, the council increased membership of the new legislative assembly to 42 elected members and 33 members nominated by government and large estate-holders. Three representatives appointed by the Nizam from the *Sarf-i-Khas* and the members of the Executive Council also received seats.

The council was impressed by the wide gap separating on the one hand Muslims demanding separate electorates and statutory majority in all the representative bodies and on the other Hindus who wanted exactly the opposite. It observed that it was impossible to bridge this gap by an appeal to Deccani nationalism or a united state consciousness. Besides, the council thought the historical and political importance of the Muslim community to be so obvious as to preclude its reduction to the status of a minority in the assembly. Therefore, contrary to the Reform Committee's recommendations, the council decided not to abandon communal representation altogether, but to accept the ratio of 50:50 as between Hindus and Muslims in all representative bodies, both in case of election and nomination.

In view of this equality in number between Hindus and Muslims, two Christians and a Parsi held a decisive position in the proposed Hyderabad assembly and for that reason were given nominated seats. No recommendation of separate electorates was made. The reservation of seats must in the council's opinion be realized within the different interest groups on the basis of joint electorates, conditional on a candidate obtaining at least 40 per cent of the votes of his community as cast in each interest. For that reason all interest groups (jagirdars, agriculturists, labour, commerce, professions, etc.) were entitled to an even number of seats (2, 4 or 8). The council concluded that the gradual evolution of the constitution to its full stature must ultimately depend on 'the successful working . . . of the different communities within the interests. . . '. Also, a formula was found for reference to Hyderabad as a Muslim state in a context which asserted at the same time that it was the 'indivisible asset' of all its people.[137]

Satyagraha by Hindu organizations was dragging on, though with reduced vigour, and Muslims were beginning to hit back. Therefore, the publication of these reform proposals offered the Arya Samaj and Hindu Mahasabha a welcome opportunity to stop the struggle without

[137] Text of the council's *Arzdasht*, 15.7.1939, submitting the opinion of the Executive Council with the consent of the Nizam, L/P&S/13/1234. Ex-Official 1949: 6.

undue loss of face. Satisfied with the acknowledgement of joint electorates in principle, they decided on a temporary and later unconditional suspension of their campaigns.[138] Dr. Moonje, vice-president of the HM, heartily congratulated the HM and AS on the achievements and called their sufferings and sacrifices a clear demonstration of their 'grievances in respect of their nationalism, observances of their religion and their cultural progress'.[139]

The decisions on reform were in fact a clear compromise. Even though the lion's share of the advantage went to the Muslims, the Muslim reaction was generally more disapproving than the Hindu one. The executive of the Ittihad called the decisions unsatisfactory, even prejudicial to Muslims, and demanded a revision of the whole scheme, if government did not want to lose Muslim cooperation. Protest demonstrations led to communal rioting, leaving many wounded and several killed.[140] At a mass meeting on the occasion of the Nizam's birthday (August 1939), Bahadur Yar Jung reiterated that the Muslims would not be satisfied with anything that did not in their opinion preserve Muslim supremacy within the last remnant of the Mughal Empire. On that day, the Nizam released all political prisoners of the Samaj and Mahasabha, and even paid the fares home of the thousands who had come from northern India.[141] Characteristic of the growing importance of global forces was that the preliminary discussions on the release of these prisoners had taken place in Delhi between the President of the Arya Samaj and Glancy, the Political Adviser.[142]

Mohammad Ali Jinnah, leader of the All-India Muslim League, could not attend the Nizam's birthday. He visited Hyderabad a month later, to strengthen the bond between his Muslim League (ML) and the Ittihad and was to a large extent successful. Whereas a year earlier Jinnah had tried in vain to induce Bahadur Yar Jung to join the ML, he now succeeded in incorporating the Ittihad in his own political scheme. This gave the Hyderabad organization the heightened status of being part of a larger body and at the same time reinforced Jinnah's claim to be the spokesman of all Indian Muslims.[143] Jinnah and Bahadur Yar

[138] Resumé of Events in Indian States for the fortnight ending 31.7.1939, Hyderabad, L/P&S/13/1232; Pernau-Reifeld 1992: 300.

[139] *The Hindustan Times* 21.7.1939.

[140] Ibid., *Hyderabad Political Notebook*, Vol. II, 1945: 75.

[141] Resumé of Events in Indian States, Hyderabad, for the forthnight ending 31.8.1939, L/P&S/13/1200.

[142] Pernau-Reifeld 1992: 297.

[143] Yazdani 1985: 195; Pernau-Reifeld 1992: 301.

Jung also discussed the establishment of an All-India States Muslim League (AISML) to safeguard Muslim interests in a larger India as a counterpart to the AISPC. It was established in the autumn of 1939, with Bahadur Yar Jung as President. In these endeavours Yar Jung was moved by a strong belief that Hyderabad's Muslims as the rightful heirs to the past glory of the Mughals should lead the Muslims of all India.[144] In the long run, the ambitions of Jinnah and Yar Jung would have been difficult to combine.

During his visit Jinnah had two long meetings with the Nizam. There can be no doubt that the improved relationship between the Muslim League and the Ittihad was largely due to the fact that Jinnah was of great use in influencing the Nizam on Muslim demands regarding the local reforms.[145] The meetings resulted in an assurance to the Ittihad in writing that the Nizam would appoint only Muslims to represent the *Sarf-i-Khas* and that no candidate would be declared elected unless he had obtained, within the framework of joint electorates, at least 51 per cent of the votes cast by his own community. In practice, that assurance meant the introduction of separate electorates for the Muslims, as they became entirely independent of the Hindu vote. They were thus to receive half the number of seats in the new assembly while the remaining seats would be divided between Hindus, Christians and Parsis. In return for this grant of concessions, the Ittihad would refrain from all action against the government.[146]

The understanding between the Nizam and Bahadur Yar Jung's party repudiated the official announcement of political reforms and rendered them absolutely unworkable. Documents from the Residency suggest that neither the Nizam, nor his government at that time realized that their concession to the Muslims completely stultified the joint electorate scheme.[147] One of Hyderabad's highest officials, however, Ali Yavar Jung, was of the opinion that the concessions to the Ittihad were a deliberate betrayal of trust and therefore, had to be kept secret.[148] In any case, when the real implications of this political move dawned

[144] All India States Muslim League, R/1/1/3706; Activities Nawab Bahadur Yar Jung, R/1/1/3231; speech by Yar Jung at annual session Ittihad January 1940, L/P&S/13/1201.

[145] Telegram-letter from Resident Hyderabad, 2.10.1939 to Political Adviser, in Activities of Mr. Jinnah in Hyderabad, R/1/1/3229.

[146] Report on the Internal Situation in Hyderabad for the second part of September 1939, L/P&S/13/1200.

[147] *Hyderabad Political Notebook*, Vol. II, 1945: 76, in Lothian Collection, Nr. 63.

[148] Ex-Official 1949: 7.

on the government, it had to face the awkward dilemma of 'either exposing to the world their Ruler's folly. . . or abandoning in effect their announced policy'.[149] Caught in this dilemma, the Government of Hyderabad was more or less saved by the timely outbreak of World War II, which for the next few years came to dominate all other political issues.

Already on the eve of World War II the Nizam had assured the Viceroy of his wholehearted support and cooperation to the British Empire in the event of War. When War was actually declared he issued a State Gazette Extraordinary, appealing to the people of India and the Muslims in particular 'to lay their differences and rally to the assistance of the British government in the war against aggression'. He personally offered His Majesty the King all his resources for the successful prosecution of the war.[150] Whereas local Hindus demanded a merger of the Marathi-speaking districts in a larger Maharashtra and Muslims insisted on the return of ceded territories, the Nizam refused to make his support to the War effort conditional on any concession on the part of the paramount power. He counted on his friendship with the British to secure an independent survival of his state.

In another way the Nizam did make capital out of the new conditions created by the War. In September 1939 the Resident reported that the ruler and his council were contemplating the possibility of keeping political reform in abeyance by an appeal to the critical War situation. The Nizam sent a letter to the Viceroy, Lord Linlithgow, explaining that he was not in a position to support the British War effort in the same unrestricted way as during 1914–18, in view of the growing influence of the people on his administration.[151] The War situation thus was a suitable excuse for leaving the political status quo unchanged. In spite of announcements that the reforms would be introduced in gradual stages, they were postponed *sine die*.

In case the British might have doubted his interest in constitutional

[149] Lothian, Resident Hyderabad, to Political Department, 28.10.1944, R/1/1/4908 and to Sir Francis Wylie, Political Adviser, 29.10.1944 in *Hyderabad Political Notebook*, Vol. II, 1945: 75–6 in Lothian Collection Nr. 63. Pernau-Reifeld 1992: 301, 304. Here I differ from Bawa 1992: 172.

[150] Quotation from Ex-Official of Hyderabad 1949: 76. Report on the Internal Situation of Hyderabad for the first part of June 1940, L/P&S/13/1201.

[151] Report on the Internal Situation in Hyderabad for the second part of September 1939 and letter Mir Osman Ali Khan, Nizam, to Linlithgow, Viceroy, 28.9.1939, L/P&S/13/1200.

reform, the Nizam sent them another letter in which he assured the Viceroy of the great importance 'that attaches to the voice of the people in these democratic times'. Yet that letter served a completely different purpose and was meant to silence all remaining discussions about federal schemes. He informed the Viceroy that 'So far as I know, my beloved subjects and people are not in favour of "Federation", however attractive or otherwise may be the terms offered.'[152]

Therefore, the main thrust of the Nizam's argument was that, the more Hyderabad took its stand on its old established traditions, the more it would be in a position to come to the assistance of the British government in its hour of need. As earlier the infiltration of *jatthas*, now the conditions of War could be seized upon as an argument to frustrate all attempts to introduce more responsible forms of government and to bring Hyderabad into a larger Indian union. Whereas Indian political movements worked for constitutional change and the British-Indian government strove after political federation, the ruler of Hyderabad rejected both. And for the moment he was able to hold his own.

CONCLUDING OBSERVATIONS

The Nizam's was however a pyrrhic victory. The state was seriously weakened by attacks from above and below. Regional conferences since the early 1930s promoted the Telugu and Marathi languages and culture. They looked for support among fellow-speakers in the neighbouring British provinces. The wider solidarity they envisaged did not extend beyond the cultural region, but even so they exposed the artificiality of the existing state boundaries. The most dangerous threat to Hyderabad's independent existence were the links established between local political movements and forces at the all-India level that together came to hold the state in a deadly embrace. The forces of Deccani nationalism, never very strong, were strangled by this pincer movement.

The Hyderabad State Congress contained strong regional undercurrents but it was more than that. Its main objective was to part with the old feudal-autocratic regime and to establish a constitutional monarchy with the Nizam as the embodiment of his people's sovereignty. During the Second World War frequent consultations took place

[152] Letter from Nizam to Viceroy, 25.8.1939, L/P&S/13/667.

between the INC and the HSC that still suffered under an official ban. There was an increasing association between the two organizations and although the existence of formal linkages was still denied, the nationalists had been able to build a bridge crossing the borders of the old princely state.

Several globalization theorists have drawn attention to the emergence of a strange paradox: in a world that is becoming more unified, local (often ethnic) identities are growing more important too, and these two processes are interrelated. According to Kloos (1995, 1996), the globalization process calls forth movements in search of sub-state identities, and these local movements make use of global forces to attain their ends. The same processes can be seen at work in the state of Hyderabad, albeit with some important qualifications.

The Arya Samaj and Hindu Mahasabha already had their own branches within the state. After their conferences in December 1938, however, they were able to incorporate these branches more firmly into their own organizations and to take over the local satyagraha movements. Local Hindus, in search of a greater share of power through constitutional reform, could make use of the parent-organizations and did benefit from the associated publicity, material resources and volunteers. The origin of the incoming volunteers is heavily disputed, but the available evidence suggests a clear majority from outside. The small local branches of these organizations were considerably strengthened in this process, and the opposite is equally true. That the Hindu religion was not just a sub-state identity, restricted to Hyderabad, but a cultural symbol shared at the all-India level, made things only more ominous for the future of Hyderabad state.

The Muslims of Hyderabad represent a clear case of a more local identity movement called forth by a process towards larger political unity. The Muslims ruled the state and Hindus worked the land, and till far into the twentieth century this arrangement worked relatively well. In 1918 Resident Fraser could still call Hyderabad 'the greatest Mahomedan State in India' without creating a stir.[153] But things were changing rapidly. The call for constitutional change that was raised after the First World War greatly alarmed the Muslim minority who, like earlier in British India, reacted to reform by a demand for separate electorates. Prospective entry into a larger India and attacks from

[153] Speech by Stuart Fraser, Resident, at banquet given by the Nizam, Hyderabad, R/1/1/842.

outside by hostile Hindus created even more uneasiness and made Muslims in Hyderabad seize upon religion as a shared symbol to mark their communal boundaries and defend their interests. In these strained circumstances leaders of the Ittihad (that was never banned) came to identify the state with Islam and raised the demand that Muslim supremacy should be preserved within the last remnant of the Mughal Empire.

The Muslim communal identity created by the subcontinental process of globalization was not out to destroy the state, but to defend its independent existence. By that very defence, however, the state was seriously undermined, as Muslims and Hindus became involved in a mutual struggle for power. With its two main communities ('the two arms of these Dominions' as Sir Kishen Pershad once called them) in open conflict, the bottom was knocked out from under the state structure. The connection with the All-India Muslim League, that Jinnah was able to make in 1939, indicated that Hyderabad's Muslims were also anticipating the need for strong partners in a new India in which no room would be left for the old princely states.

Hyderabad and its ruler were saved by the outbreak of the War. But this gave only temporary relief. In June 1947, a week after the British announced Partition, the Nizam declared that he would join neither India nor Pakistan. He also stressed that he was choosing independence to avoid communal riots. In October of the same year the status quo was mutually accepted by a Standstill Agreement. The HSC, a lawful organization since 1946, called for a new satyagraha demanding accession to India, but the Government of Hyderabad came to prefer a political course expressing close relations with both independent states without sacrificing its own sovereignty. The newly installed nationalist government in New Delhi nonetheless argued that Hyderabad was in fact a part of India, although by an historical anomaly it had become a semi-autonomous political unit. The only point to discuss was how and when Hyderabad would accede to the Indian Union.

In 1948 India supplemented its political pressure with an economic blockade of Hyderabad state, while political negotiations continued. In New Delhi a draft agreement was worked out, which provided for a plebiscite to determine the question of accession and promised responsible government following the establishment of a Constituent Assembly. When the Nizam refused to accept this compromise, which he saw as an imposition, in September 1948 the Indian army crossed into Hyderabad at five places and in less than a week its occupation was completed.

The number of casualties on the battlefield was small, but many people lost their lives in fierce communal fighting. In the grim atmosphere of mounting pressure preceding the invasion, the *razakars*, armed volunteers of the Ittihad, were gaining control of public life in Hyderabad. Reinforced by embittered Muslim refugees from outside the state and allegedly receiving government support, these *razakars* 'roamed the cities and eventually the villages, raping and looting, terrorizing and boasting, and dreaming wild Islamic dreams of Hyderabad-Muslim might'.[154] Even though reports of *razakar* atrocities were often exaggerated and even fabricated, as Cantwell Smith acknowledges, the plain truth was gruesome.

After the military invasion not only the *razakars* but Muslims in general had to suffer massive and brutal Hindu retaliation resulting in large-scale killings, rape, destruction and seizure of Muslim property. The only official report of investigation on these outrages has never been published, but Khalidi claims to have obtained some parts of it which he has reproduced together with other documents. That the tables were definitely turned is clear: 'After the Military Action, the Hindus generally behaved as if they were the rulers and the Muslims the slaves.'[155] About the same time, a Communist uprising in Telengana was violently suppressed. The Communists, having gained control of the Andhra Mahasabha, had actually been ruling large areas in Telengana, distributing land and cancelling debts.

After 1948 Hyderabad had to take its place in the larger India on a new constitutional basis. The sitting legislature was dissolved, the Nizam gave up his *Sarf-i-Khas*, and all jagirs were abolished.[156] In 1950 a formal agreement was concluded between the Indian government and the Nizam, which stated in its preamble '. . . that the Constitution of India adopted by the constituent assembly of India shall be the constitution for the state of Hyderabad'. The Nizam was sworn in as Governor of Hyderabad state, thus becoming a constitutional head bound to accept the advice of cabinet ministers responsible to an elected legislature. He occupied this office until November 1956, when Hyderabad was partitioned on linguistic grounds between Maharashtra,

[154] Cantwell Smith 1988: 18.
[155] Khalidi 1988: 100.
[156] Yazdani 1988: 90 ff.

Mysore and the new Telugu-speaking state of Andhra Pradesh with Hyderabad city as its capital. After that, the Nizam retired from public life. But every day the dethroned monarch used to go out in his age-old car to Chowmahal (one of his biggest palaces) and to the tomb of his mother at Joodi Masjid.[157] He died in 1967.

To this day Hyderabad remains one of the most riot-prone cities of the Indian subcontinent and the single major centre of communal trouble in Andhra Pradesh.[158] This critical condition cannot be sufficiently understood without reference to Hyderabad's last decades as a semi-independent state. From the 1930s there was considerable activity of Hindu communalist forces in Hyderabad, especially from outside. The Arya Samaj in particular thrust a communal spirit on Hyderabad by its aggressive mobilization of the Hindu majority both inside and outside the state. The Muslim dominance of the administration, for a long time undisputed, hardened in frightened intolerance when it became confronted by Hindu claims for more representative government. After Hyderabad's integration into the Indian Union, Muslims experienced a reverse social mobility.[159] Many members of the Muslim entrepreneurial and bureaucratic middle class migrated to Pakistan, while the upper and lower classes remained behind, baffled and uncertain. They are in danger of becoming a backward minority and the Ittihad has capitalized on the feeling of frustration.

[157] Yazdani 1985: 291.

[158] See for instance *India Today* 16–31 August 1984.

[159] Ahmad 1988: 173 ff.

5

Conclusion: The Princely States Compared

Communalism as a harnessing of religious differences between groups of people for secular ends could not be contained within the boundaries of the former British Indian provinces, neither before nor after 1947: it also emerged in the princely states. We have focused on the growing disparity in the process of political modernization between British India and the states, and on the long shadow that the approaching federation was casting on communal relations within these states. Let us now turn to some of the more general questions we have raised, and take a final look at the emergence of nationalism and communalism in the particular circumstances that prevailed in Travancore, Baroda and Hyderabad in the last decades of colonial rule.

Indian states generally were dominated, if not directly ruled, by communities which in the past had been able to establish their authority over the area by expansion of their patrimonial rights, breakaway from larger political structures, or invasion and straight conquest. Their dominance did not preclude the sharing of power with those who did not belong to their own community: partnerships were often deliberately sought, but the actual division of power was unmistakably clear to all those concerned. In fact, British India was just one of these conquerors' states imposing its will by force of arms, with the important difference that it retained its vital connections with a power base in distant Europe. The authority established by one group of people over others gave these states a hierarchical coherence, but was also one of their main weaknesses. As Lansdowne wrote in 1893, the condition of inferiority imposed on the underlying community, though acquiesced in by the bulk of the population, was always liable to spark off a rebellion in which religion or other cultural attributes could take a prominent part.

In the three states discussed here, Muslims were a small minority, much less than the British Indian average of 24 per cent (1931). In Travancore they numbered only about 7 per cent of the population. However, Travancore had an exceptional high percentage of Christians, some of them poor and ignorant but many well-educated and prosperous. As Travancore and its administrative services were largely under the control of caste Hindus, especially Nayars, the potential conflict was mainly between Hindus and Christians. Hyderabad, on the other hand, counted a much higher percentage of Hindus, but here state power was firmly in the hands of Muslims who numbered no more than 10.6 per cent of the population. This situation reflects the origins of the state as a political implantation by Muslim rulers from the north in a Hindu majority area. That characteristic was still reinforced by the many educated Muslims from British India who came over to Hyderabad in search of a place in the state's services. Hindus were well-represented in the professions and dominated agriculture, banking and trading, which they considered a justified (though in the long run insufficient) compensation.

The Government of Hyderabad took on an active role in the development of industry, but claimed a large part to itself and fought shy of initiatives beyond the trusted circle that it could control. In Travancore, on the other hand, the economy was to a large extent controlled by coastal firms and foreign capital, with a government more kindly disposed towards European interests than its own entrepreneurs, who were mainly Syrian Christian. The situation in Travancore and Hyderabad was thus marked by a distinct divergence between politico-administrative power and socio-economic standing. A similar divergence was lacking in Baroda where the landed elite was well represented in the bureaucracy and had the advantage of a sympathetic government, that proved compliant on the sensitive issue of land revenue and offered generous support to local enterprise. Some of Baroda's larger industries date from the last decades of the kingdom. As the ruling dynasty had come from Maharashtra as conquerors to settle in this region, the only tension before Independence that can be traced from the extant sources was between Marathi-speakers, who were over-represented in the services, and the Gujarati-speaking majority.

Modern political activity in the sense of public meetings, party organization and electioneering was slow to emerge in the states and took form only during or after the First World War. But caste associations, religious groups and their educated spokesmen gradually grew conscious of the unequal division of power, and started campaigns to abolish the most glaring aspects of the divergence existing in their society. Their campaigns were aimed at the attainment of some freedom of expression and association, and the introduction of constitutional reforms that would give the subordinate groups some say in administrative matters.

The states were generally slow to grant their people political rights. The first legislatures were a gesture of royal benevolence. The scant reforms that followed were responses to growing social tensions and the demands of a few prominent leaders inspired by developments in the British provinces. But it also worked the other way round: state political movements grew in force at times when new positions of power and influence became available. A mere announcement of political reform could spark off a wave of political unrest, as it aroused anxieties and ambitions among many communities by the prospect of their place in the state's future political set-up. In Hyderabad existing communal tensions rose to fever-pitch immediately after the appointment of an official committee to consider constitutional reform (1937). The fear of getting no fair share of power, added to the prospect of being lost in a larger Indian Union, served as a great stimulus to the organization of political associations and the formulation of political demands. Something similar happened in Baroda in 1939. When the government promulgated its scheme for a significant increase in popular influence in the legislature, it led to an upsurge of communal animosities where there were none to be traced before.

The constitutional reforms achieved in the three states showed great variation but were generally rather poor. Travancore took the lead. By the nineteenth century, a Legislative Council had been introduced (1888), somewhat later followed by a larger Assembly. In 1921 the Council had an elected majority and in 1932 it acquired the power to initiate and pass legislation. The franchise was broadened in 1936 to include 10 to 12 per cent of the population. Yet there was no Executive Council, and all power remained vested in the Dewan.

Hyderabad proved much more reluctant to grant its people a share of power. The institution of an Executive Council was eventually forced on it by the British, but the Nizam continually intervened in its proceedings or ignored its recommendations. Proposals to change the legislature from an official body to a more representative institution were shelved. Without voting rights the people of Hyderabad had no influence on its composition, and it had no influence on the government, let alone the power to legislate. Constitutional reform had to wait till 1939, but implementation of the proposals was postponed. It is difficult to disagree with contemporary witnesses who described Hyderabad as one of the most backward and feudal states in India.[1]

Baroda received a constitution at an early date (1908) and in that respect was not much behind Travancore. Its Legislative Council (*Dhara Sabha*) however, was less the result of popular pressure than the well-meaning initiative of an enlightened Maharaja who wanted to raise pubic political consciousness within his own strict limits. Legislative potential remained to a large extent unused and elections were indirect with division boards controlled by Patidars sending members to the legislative. The 1940 Act was to be the first major instalment of constitutional reform since the establishment of the legislative in 1908. There was an Executive Council and after 1940 one elected member of the legislative was appointed to that body. At that time, 8.5 per cent of the population was enfranchised and the *Dhara Sabha* received the important power to initiate and pass legislation.

It is worth emphasizing that the state political movements never declared themselves against their own princes. There was indeed criticism, especially in the case of Hyderabad, but in the three states it was absolutely clear that civil rights and more responsible forms of government were sought under the aegis of the ruling house, not overthrowing the monarchy but making the prince the head of a more democratic constitutional government.

It is not easy to give a chronology of the emergence of communal conflict in British India and the states. The situation in British India showed great diversity. Whereas some regions or cities were hotbeds of communalism, others remained virtually untouched. We may say, however, following handbook knowledge, that communalism in British India started to raise its head in the course of the nineteenth century and reached the all-India level with the introduction of separate electorates for Muslims under the Morley-Minto reforms (1906). But what about the states?

As we have seen, communal rivalries in Travancore started at an early date. At the end of the last century there was much uneasiness about the dominance of the administration by foreign Brahmins. Local Nayars managed to oust them gradually from the bastions of

[1] For instance Jawaharlal Nehru in a letter to the Viceroy, Lord Mountbatten, 9.2.1947, Mansergh X, 1981: 161.

power, but their position was in turn challenged by other aspiring groups, especially the Syrian Christians, who felt unjustly excluded. From the beginning of the twentieth century a keen fight for administrative and legislative positions ensued which resulted in a deeply entrenched communal rivalry and hostility. The main opposition was not Hindu–Muslim but Hindu–Christian, which sets Travancore clearly apart from the situation elsewhere in India. Also, in spite of all its bitterness, communalism in Travancore was not extremely violent in character[2] and primarily aimed to serve the material progress of one community in competition with the other.

Compared with Travancore the situation in Baroda was much more quiet and peaceful. Notwithstanding the disturbances in Baroda city between Gujarati and Marathi speakers in 1939, religious tensions were never acute and only after the 1940 reforms did the Muslims begin to press for separate representation. The states may have had a smaller proportion of industrial labour and fewer miles of railway than British India, but Baroda had made at least some modest progress in industrialization, primarily textiles. There was not a single communal conflict until 1939, but our scarce information indicates that textile labourers were involved in the riots in Baroda city between Marathi and Gujarati speakers.

As far as Hyderabad is concerned, till far into the twentith century this state remained free of communal trouble. After the violent conflict in Gulbarga (1924) there was a gradual increase of communal riots, but these were local and fewer than in contemporary British India. Before 1936 the reports of the Hyderabad city police stated that communal relations remained satisfactory and that the different communities lived in perfect amity and peace, although for 1936–7 it regretted that Hyderabad 'could not enjoy perfect immunity from extraneous propaganda'. Then a marked deterioration set in. For 1938 the report concluded that the traditional harmony and friendly communal relations were giving way to 'a spirit of open distrust and intolerance'. For the following year, with its satyagrahas, anti-reform agitation and violent riots, it sadly commented that 'never before within living memory were communal relations so strained'.[3]

[2] Of course, there were occasional violent outbursts, such as in Alleppey between Christians and Ezhavas versus Muslims which left five people killed (1936), see Fortnightly Report from Travancore for the second part of May 1936, R/1/1/2791. It is not always clear from these reports whether those killed were victims of communal or some other kind of violence.

[3] RAHP 1938: 2, 1940: 2 and 1941: 2. See also RAND 1941: VI.

We may conclude, also on the strength of previous chapters, that communalism emerged early in Travancore, not much later than in (parts of) British India, but became manifest in Hyderabad only in the 1930s and in Baroda even later. In my view, the main explanation for that early struggle for power and position in Travancore which took on a communal character was the level of literacy. Likewise, in British India there was an intimate connection between modern education and the spread of political consciousness. That consciousness first manifested itself among the products of new educational institutions who were eagerly looking for government jobs. In the majority of states education was poorly developed and restricted to a small elite. But Travancore enjoyed an elaborate schooling system which produced a high level of literacy. This favourable situation was made possible, among others, by missionary activities and large-scale government grants-in-aid.[4] As a result, Travancore had become a nation of newspaper readers and listeners, as Ouwerkerk wrote for the 1930s, with over a hundred newspapers and thirteen companies in printing and publishing. A lot of political activity was conducted through the press which reached a large number of people with its publication of open letters, petitions and political manifests.

Hyderabad, on the other hand, had a much lower level of literacy, the lowest in all of south India, and numbered not a single printing company in 1931. The Muslim minority was much better educated than the average population and the government of the Nizam did not allow the press much freedom of publication. Baroda was also a highly literate state, mainly because of the early introduction by the Maharaja of compulsory primary education. But there was no clear divergence between political power and socio-economic prominence in Baroda to invite people to mobilize for the redress of their grievances. I think, therefore, that not just the level of literacy in Travancore but its combination with a highly uneven opportunity structure was the main reason why communal politics in that state emerged earlier and followed a more hectic course.

An important difference between British India and the princely states lay in the general orientation of the political movement. In British India mainstream politics were dominated by the overarching themes of anti-imperialism and national freedom. Supported by a rising,

[4] Other factors in Kerala's high rate of literacy are a long commercial tradition, a more privileged position for women and—especially—pressure for education from below by caste associations and trade unions. See Franke and Chasin 1992: 47 ff.

educated middle class, the national movement aimed in different stages for an Indianization of the services, responsible government and finally a full measure of self-goverment for the whole of India in some kind of federal union. The emphasis on a common struggle of the national community against colonial domination deferred the internal distribution of power to a later date, even though the national movement was continually threatened by newly emerging groups based on caste, class or other interests.

Anti-British nationalism was not a very effective rallying cry for the movement in the states. The three states discussed here were under Indian governments unwilling to share power with fellow Indians. As these state governments were strongly coloured by particular communities, a struggle for power first of all involved an internal contest for influence in the local administration. Freedom meant first of all a removal of outside influences on the state administration and more room for participation by sons of the soil. The political movements in British India and the states may both be called national in the sense that they were primarily directed at a transfer of power to those who belonged to the state. Both movements also strove after the establishment of a government chosen by the people and responsible to that people. Although in the long run identical, for a long time they were fighting different enemies and following their separate courses. The link was established at the end of the 1930s, with elections in the British provinces, the Haripura Congress and federation imminent, but even then hesitatingly and in a limited sense. In the introduction we have asked ourselves how that link was forged. Was nationalism something imported from British India or was it a more autonomous movement?

The question is too complicated to allow for a straight answer. Many different forces were at work in the diverse conditions prevailing among the different states. First of all, we have to take account of the fact that the freedom for political manoeuvre in the states was severly restricted. There is no reason to eulogize the situation of civil rights in the British Indian provinces, but the states did have a poor record on rights of expression and association, though conditions in Travancore were better than in Hyderabad. For a free discussion of the internal situation in their states, politically interested subjects often had to take refuge in places beyond their own borders, wandering about like orphans, as one of the leaders of the AISPC once called it. Sometimes they met in the margin of the larger sessions of the INC. The place of their meetings and the support, however moral and verbal, from larger organizations in British India only strengthened the impression that these political movements were orchestrated from outside. State governments were not slow to exploit these circumstances and make accusations of external machinations. The Political Department, though in general comparing the states unfavourably to the British provinces, comforted themselves with the idea that the state subjects lived happily under royal autocracy. And in case they might feel inclined to take political protest more seriously, there was always the problem that they could not afford to offend the rulers whose support was urgently needed to get the federal scheme accepted.

Sympathizers of the states' subjects in British India insisted in speeches and publications (as through the Poona-based *The Servant of India*) that the opposition to the autocratic rulers was spontaneous and of local origin. The leaders of the AISPC, the largest association of state political movements, were however in a serious predicament. They nurtured sincere grievances and had solid reasons for criticism of their states' darbars. But from their own public statements we may infer that the local population generally remained loyal, if not submissive, to their traditional rulers. The AISPC received a poor response from the majority of the people in the states who did not share its concern for the lack of civil rights and constitutional reform. That was indeed not greatly different from the situation in British India. Yet in the course of time, the INC and other political movements had been able to build up a considerable organizational network reaching out to many parts of the countryside. State political movements were not in a position to build a similar organization and the British Indian government consistently refused the AISPC the right to speak on behalf of the people of the states. Therefore, the AISPC desperately turned to the INC for support.

The INC had a nominal presence in some states in the form of local Congress committees, but for a long time kept aloof. It was not eager to embrace state organizations, considered inefficient and prone to communal infections. Nevertheless, the INC served as a major source of inspiration to those inside the states who looked for a reform of their own government. The organization of the AISPC was shaped on the model of the INC just as the AISML—formed much later (1939)—was shaped after Jinnah's Muslim League. The movements in Hyderabad and Travancore even adopted the name Congress in spite of the INC's explicit refusal to lend its name. Especially after the INC's impressive gain at the 1937 elections it became an inspiring example worth emulating in Indian India. After the Haripura session (1938) the attitude of the INC somewhat changed. Even though the wording of the Haripura resolution on states remained restrained, there came more freedom for individual Congressmen to involve themselves in affairs of the states. Gandhi and Patel were going to make use of it.

The allegation that agitation in the states was engineered by Congress in order to capture state seats in the prospective federation, is not altogether untrue, but in its one-sidedness it ignores the sincere wish for responsible government in the states themselves. The political movements that emerged in the three states were first of all meant to satisfy local demands and not to get the Congress a majority in a federal legislative. British colonial rule was not the main enemy and although the British were inclined to protect the position of the princes as rulers, they did not reject the establishment of more responsible forms of government in the states.

Let us have a look at the individual states for a more specific answer to the question from where the political initiatives came. By political initiative we not only mean efforts to give the people some part in their own administration, but also the fierce rivalry between different communities these efforts might include.

The causes of unrest in Travancore were definitely local. They stemmed from serious discontent with the exclusion of large groups from the administration and the legislative. The political actions resulting from that discontent were not engineered from outside and started long before Congress took up any interest in the states. They were organized on state territory, without help from outside, and primarily aimed at gaining a share of local power. The form of agitation was surely influenced by Congress ideology and political techniques, but relations between the INC and TSC were not very intensive. Gandhi twice intervened in Travancore, but in both cases (the memorandum against the Dewan and the indefinite postponement of Civil Disobedience) his moderation had a dampening effect on the local movement. It did not lead to a strong support base for Congress in the state where political elements largely preferred to follow their own course.

The campaign for responsible government in Travancore was conducted mainly, though far from exclusively, by Syrian Christians. That gave the campaign a distinct communal flavour and the government, itself strongly influenced by caste Hindus, made the most of it by blaming the opposition of Christian exclusivism. Mutual recriminations may have inflated the communal content, but in any case, I see no foreign hand involved, as suggested by Copland (1988). It was an internal struggle that grew only more intense by the arbitrary rule of a shrewd and high-handed Dewan, who invited the Hindu Mahasabha to his state to consolidate the Hindu body against a perceived Christian menace. The Syrians tried to build up a Christian cause, but the poorer Christians refused to strengthen Syrian interests by lending weight with their sheer numbers, with the result that the Christians fell apart in competing sub-sects, reinforcing the communal division.

As stated earlier, the political climate in Baroda for a long time was rather moderate. Before the First World War a few extremist nationalists from British India had taken refuge in the relative safety of princely Baroda, but they remained an isolated group. Nevertheless, one of the first *praja mandals* was organized on Baroda territory during or shortly after the War. It was an internal initiative and its main objects were the redress of local grievances, the creation of internal unity and the establishment of more responsible forms of government. As Baroda's territory lay fragmented and interspersed within British Indian jurisdiction, there was a frequent exchange also of political ideas and aspirations. The Civil Disobedience of 1930–1 seems to have been conducted on both sides of the border, with the Baroda authorities not overactive in suppressing the movement on their side. Therefore, it is not suprising that the BPM was strongly influenced by INC leaders from other parts of Gujarat, like Sardar Patel and Gandhi, even before the Congress held its Haripura session. But while growing more susceptible to an all-India nationalism, Baroda remained free from outward communal infections. In 1940 its Dewan could write that the urgent order of the day was to prevent the introduction into his state of the communal animosities that had gathered around political organizations in British India.[5]

In Hyderabad the causes for political agitation were internal, just as in Travancore. But the political domination of the state by a Muslim minority seems to have been felt more sharply outside its borders than inside, at least in the beginning. Those people in Hyderabad who wanted to question the existing state of affairs in their state had to convene in British Indian territory where they received sympathy from national and communal organizations working at an all-India level.

[5] Copland 1988: 811.

Their call for a more popular form of government would give more weight to the Hindu majority and was for that reason vigorously championed by the AS and HM. These communal organizations lent their local branches vital support in terms of guidance, finance and even manpower, as local indifference made it difficult to recruit a sufficient number of satyagrahis. In December 1938 the parent bodies of AS and HM took over the local satyagraha from British India.

However, the very support received from the AS and HM gave the government an excuse to brand the demand for responsible government as a form of communalism and made the INC cautious lest it might become entangled in a communal imbroglio. Gandhi could boast that people of the HSC were acting on his advice; but his call for moderation fell on deaf ears. In face of the mobilization of the Hindu majority both inside and outside Hyderabad, the Muslim stand hardened and the demand was raised for separate electorates for Muslims, the ruling minority. The demand could not be met in public because of Hindu opposition, whereas political concessions that hurt Muslim feelings would never go far enough to satisfy the Hindus. Thus the Nizam, in the words of Lothian, was 'caught between the devil and the deep sea'.[6]

It may be clear that the seeds of communalism, like those of nationalism, were not blown one way from British India to the states. Communal forces grew in both territories, could become interconnected, and in many cases reinforced each other. The social divergences with their explosive potential were already present in the situation of Travancore and Hyderabad, and did not need to be imported. But whereas in Travancore communal rivalries emerged from within as part of local developments, in Hyderabad the communal fire was to a large extent inflamed from outside. Conditions in Baroda harboured less potential for conflict and, at least until the Second World War this state was spared the woes of communal strife. Let us have another look at the three states from a comparative perspective.

Travancore was geographically rather isolated. It lay tucked away in the south-western part of the peninsula and its communications with British India were poorly developed. The state was more *outward looking* by its relations overseas and export of raw materials. The Syrian Christians, striving after improvement of their position, could not count on support from fellow Christians in British India, but cultivated per-

[6] Lothian 1951: 186.

sonal links with prominent sympathizers in England. They petitioned the paramount power and had on several occasions questions asked in Parliament. Their links with the INC, nonetheless, remained weak and incursions from outside—for instance in the form of *jatthas*—remained insignificant.

Baroda with its intricate boundary system was better integrated in the larger world of British India and may be called a *sideward looking* state. Its political movement was more responsive to developments going on in surrounding British India and maintained personal relations with INC leaders, especially the Gujaratis among them. Hyderabad finally may be called an *inward looking* state. The Asaf Jah dynasty carefully guarded the traditions which it had received from the Mughals and was bent upon preservation of Muslim rule as the rightful successor to the Mughal vice-royalty of the Deccan. To save his state the Nizam increasingly relied on the Muslims, only to alienate the Hindus. Plagued by the incursions of communalist forces from outside, Hyderabad tried to close its borders and to exclude the HM which was invited to Travancore. Besides, the last Nizam was not mentally disposed to look at the problem of the states or India in general from a broader perspective. Whereas the Maharaja of Baroda attended two sessions of the RTC in London, the Nizam left Hyderabad only on short visits and did not have the benefit of a friendly acquaintance with other Indian rulers or public men in British India. This political insulation made Hyderabad vulnerable to outside attack.

A final conclusion to be drawn is that the states discussed here generally lacked what we have come to understand as a civil society. The term 'civil society' refers to a public sphere outside the state where people move in more or less institutionalized, autonomous organizations to administer their own affairs and engage in relations with other similarly constituted groups and with the state. Their activities may take place through the press, political parties, cultural manifestations and elections and are acknowledged by the state as a legitimate part of public life. In India without a public space to translate the political demands of officially enumerated communities into programmes for general welfare and individual benefit, more popular forms of government were under constant threat of being reduced to a mere majority rule of the minority. That distrust was only deepened by the formation of INC ministries in British India after the 1937 elections, ignoring the Muslim vote.

These apprehensions, fed by a straight application of numbers, are very clear in the statements we have quoted from Baroda and Travancore. The Dewan of Baroda was seriously afraid that responsible government would bring communal hostility to his state, and his colleague in office in Travancore resisted the introduction of responsible government as a first step to the establishment of a Christian oligarchy. Nevertheless, Travancore saw at least the beginnings of a civil society when in the 1930s members from different communal organizations proved ready to form a broad coalition to work for common political ends. In its most unequivocal form the distrust of responsible government was formulated in Hyderabad by Bahadur Yar Jung in his presidential address to the 1940 session of the Majlis-i-Ittihad-ul-Muslimin. On that occasion he denounced democracy as 'a counting of heads' and attributed Hindu fondness for that system to their wish to recapture power from the Muslims by their sheer weight of numbers. But the Western concept of democracy, he argued, could not possibly be applied to India, as majority and minority had been fixed in the terms of census figures which made the Muslim minority a constant victim. He declared that Muslims would not tolerate any system which tended in the guise of democracy to hand over power to the Hindu majority.[7]

In all these statements, democracy was seen not as an instrument for the creation of a more responsible society but as a system of government that assigns permanent power to the group largest in number. What this majoritarian argument deliberately ignored was the contradiction between the notion of a permanent majority, as one based solely on census definitions, and responsible government. From the perspective of the princely states, an independent Indian republic was perceived as another princely state writ large, with one numerically dominant community holding sway over the rest of the population. Personal rule had gone, but dynastic preferences remained, and the field for communal battles was extended, as at least in this respect the former states were able to catch up on the British provinces. India is still grappling with these problems.

[7] Full text of Bahadur Yar Jung's Presidential Address, January 1940, in L/P&S/13/1201, File 1(3).

Appendices

APPENDIX I: TRAVANCORE CONSTITUTIONAL REFORMS

	Assembly		*Council*	
	1932	*1935*	*1932*	*1935*
A. *Nominated seats*				
Officials	10	10	10	10
Non-Officials				
Ezhavas	4	0	2	1
Muslims	2	1	1	1
Latin Catholics	1	0	1	0
Others	7	13	1	3
	24	24	15	15
B. *Elected seats*				
Special constituencies (Planters, commerce and industry, landlords)	5	5	6	6
General constituenices	43	29	16	12
Reserved for:				
Ezhavas	0	8	0	2
Muslims	0	3	0	1
Latin Catholics	0	3	0	1
	48	48	22	22
Total	72	72	37	37

APPENDIX II: BARODA CONSTITUTIONAL REFORMS

LEGISLATIVE COUNCIL (*DHARA SABHA*) 1940

A. *Nominated seats*		
Officials (members Executive Council)	6	
Non-Officials[1]	17	
		23
B. *Elected seats*		
Special constituencies (landholders, commerce and industry, labour, co-operative movement)	10	
General constituencies	27	
		37
Total number of seats		60

[1] Article 11 of the Government of Baroda Act (1940) laid down that 'His Highness may nominate not more than 17 persons as nominated members of the *Dhara Sabha*, of whom not more than 3 shall be officials'.

APPENDIX III: ADMINISTRATIVE POSITIONS, 1930–1947

India Office, London

Secretary of State for India		*Secretary to Political (and Secret) Department*	
W. Wedgewood Benn	–1931		
S.J.G. Hoare	1931–5	P.J. Patrick	1931–1942
Lord Zetland	1935–40	J.P. Gibson	1942–5
L.S. Amery	1940–5	M.J. Clauson	1945–
Lord F.W. Pethick Lawrence	1945–7		

Government of India, New Delhi

Governor General or Vicerory (1937 Crown Representative)		*Secretary to Political Department (1937 Political Adviser to Crown Representative)*	
Lord Irwin	1926–31	Ch. Watson	–1933
Lord Willingdon	1931–6	B.J. Glancy	1933–40
		Fr. Wylie	1940–1
Lord Linlithgow	1936–43	H. Craik	1941–3
		Fr. Wylie	1943–5
Lord Wavell	1943–7	C. Corfield	1945–7
Lord Mountbatten	1947		

Government of Travancore, Trivandrum

Maharaja/Maharani	*Dewan*	*Resident (before 1937 Agent to GG)*
Setu Lakshmi Bai, Regent 1924–31	V.S. Subrahmanya Aiyer 1929–32	Lt. Col. H.R.N. Pritchard 1930–2
	T. Austin 1932–4	Lt. Col. D.M. Field 1932–5
	M. Habibullah 1934–6	Lt. Col. W.A.M. Garstin 1935–6
Sri Chitra Tirunal Balarama Varma 1931–49		C.P. Skrine 1936–9
	C.P. Ramaswamy Aiyer 1936–47	Lt. Col. G.P. Murphy 1939–44
		H.J. Todd 1944–

Government of Baroda, Baroda

Maharaja	*Dewan*	*Resident*
Sayajirao III 1875–1939	V.T. Krishnamachari 1927–44	Lt. Col. D.G. Wilson 1930–2
		Lt. Col. C.G. Crosthwaite 1932–3
		Lt. Col. J.L.R. Weir 1933–8
		Lt. Col. E.J.D. Colvin 1938–40
Pratapsingh 1939–48		
		Lt. Col. C.K. Daly 1940–3
	B.L. Mitter 1944–	L.W. Jardine 1943–

Government of Hyderabad, Hyderabad

Nizam	*Prime Minister*	*Resident*
Mir Osman Ali Khan Asaf Jah VII 1911–48		
	Maharaja Kishen Pershad Bahadur 1925–36	T. Humphrey Keyes 1930–3
		D.G. Mackenzie 1933–8
	Akbar Hydari 1936–41	Cl. H. Gidney 1938–42
	Syed Ahmed Khan of Chattari 1941–6	A.C. Lothian 1942–6
	Mirza Ismail 1946–	Ch. G. Herbert 1946–

Bibliography

PRIMARY SOURCES

1. Unpublished Documents

ORIENTAL AND INDIA OFFICE COLLECTIONS (OIOC) LONDON

Political Department: Crown Representative Records

The Political Department Records in the R/1 series contain the files from the Central Secretariat of the Crown Representative in India.

These records include the Fortnightly Reports (FRs) on the political situation in the Indian States which Residents and Agents submitted to the Secretary to the Political Department. The Political Department normally sent all Residency/Agency reports for that fortnight to the India Office in London and these are now also to be found in the Political and Secret Department Records (L/P&S).

The Residency Records in the R/2 series contain the files from the records kept locally by Residents and Political Agents.

Madras States Agency (including Travancore).
Baroda Residency.
Hyderabad Residency.

Political and Secret Department: Departmental Papers

The Political Internal/Indian State Files and Collections, c. 1931–50, L/P&S/13 are produced by the Political and Secret Department in London which was part of the India Office.

Collection 11 Reforms.
Collection 13 Indian States: General.
Collection 16 Baroda.
Collection 22 Hyderabad.
Collection 24 Madras States Agency (Travancore).

Private Office Papers (L/PO)

European Manuscripts (Mss. Eur.)

The Tasker Collection D 798.
The personal papers of Sir Theodore Tasker, Revenue and Police Member Nizam's Executive Council 1928–42.

The Lothian Collection F 144.
The personal papers of Sir Arthur Cunningham Lothian, Resident Jaipur (1935–7) and Hyderabad (1942–6).

The Ouwerkerk Collection F 232.
This collection contains the diaries, papers, correspondence and unpublished manuscripts of Miss Louise Ouwerkerk who served the Travancore Government as Professor of Economics and Political Science at the Maharaja's Women's College in Trivandrum (1929–39) and the University of Travancore (1937–9).

SCHOOL OF ORIENTAL AND AFRICAN STUDIES (SOAS) LONDON

London Missionary Society (LMS) Archives, incorporated into the Archives of the Council for World Mission

These archives contain the letters and reports by missionaries of the Society working in Travancore from 1806.

Travancore Correspondence Box 29–36 (1928–40).

ANDHRA PRADESH STATE ARCHIVES (APSA) HYDERABAD

Home Department

Confidential Reports

CENTRAL ARCHIVES (WEST FORT) TRIVANDRUM

Weekly Secret Bulletin

HUZUR POLITICAL OFFICE (HPO) BARODA

Political Department

Political General Correspondence
Confidential Files

STATE LEGISLATIVE LIBRARY, GOVERNMENT OF KERALA

Sri Mulam Assembly, Proceedings

2. PUBLISHED DOCUMENTS

Chamber of Princes, *The British Crown & the Indian States: an outline sketch drawn up on behalf of the standing committee of the Chamber of Princes*. London: P.S. King, 1929.

Department of Commercial Intelligence and Statistics, India, *Large Industrial Establishments in India*. Calcutta/Delhi: Government Press, Delhi: Manager of Publications, 1911–53.

Department of Commercial Intelligence and Statistics, India, *Joint Stock Companies in British India and in the Indian States of Hyderabad, Mysore, Baroda, Gwalior, Indore and Travancore*. Delhi: Manager of Publications, 1921–1943.

Census Baroda, *Census of India 1921, Vol. XVII Baroda*. Bombay: Times Press, 3 parts, 1921.

———, *Census of India 1931, Vol. XIX Baroda*. Bombay: Times of India Press, 3 parts, 1932.

———, *Census of India 1941, Vol. XVII Baroda*. Delhi: Government of India Press, 1941.

Census Hyderabad, *Census of India 1921, Vol. XXI Hyderabad State*. Hyderabad: Government Central Press, 2 parts, 1922.

———, *Census of India 1931, Vol. XXIII H.E.H. The Nizam's Dominions (Hyderabad State)*. Hyderabad: Government Central Press, 2 parts, 1933.

Census Travancore, *Census of India 1931, Vol. XXVIII Travancore*. Trivandrum: Government Press, 2 parts, 1932.

———, *Census of India 1941, Vol. XXV Travancore*. Trivandrum: Government Press, 3 parts, 1942.

Gazetteer Baroda, *Gazetteer of the Baroda State*. Vol. I with chapter on history, Vol. II: Administration. Compiled by G.H.Desai and A.B. Clarke. Bombay: The Times Press, 1923.

Gazetteer Hyderabad, *Gazetteer of India, Imperial. Provincial Series. Hyderabad State.* Calcutta: Superintendent of Government Printing, 1909.

Gazetteers, Gujarat State, *Vadodara District*, edited by S.B. Rajyagor and S. Tripathy. Ahmedabad: Government Press, 1979.

HFMK, *The History of the Freedom Movement in Kerala*, P.K.K. Menon, editor, convener of the Regional Records Survey Committee. Trivandrum: Government Press, 2 vols, 1972.

ICR, *Report on Indian Constitutional Reforms*. Calcutta: Government Printing, 1918.

ISC, *Indian States Committee 1928–29, Report of.* London: His Majesty's Stationary Office, 1929.

ISC, *Indian Statutory Commission, Report of the.* London: His Majesty's Stationary Office, 2 vols. 1930.

JPC (All Travancore Joint Political Congress), *Travancore: the Present Political Problem*, submitted to His Highness the Maharaja of Travancore. Calicut: The Empire Press, 1934.

Mansergh, Nicholas (Editor-in-Chief), *The Transfer of Power, 1942-47: Constitutional Relations between Britain and India*. London: HMSO, 12 vols, 1970–83.

Memorandum of the Indian States' People, with four supplements, correspondence with the Butler Committee and app., Bombay, 1928.

Nagam Aiya, V., *Travancore State Manual*, 3 vols. Trivandrum: Government Press, 1906.

Nizam's Government, H.H. the, *Half-Yearly List of Officers Civil, Public Works and Military Departments of His Highness the Nizam's Government, The*. Hyderabad: The Nizam's Printers, 1896.

Nizam's Government, H.E.H. the, *Classified List of Officers of the Civil Departments of H.E.H. the Nizam's Government, The*. Hyderabad: Government Central Press, 1923–.

Report of the Royal Commission on Jagir Administration and Reforms. Hyderabad, 1947.

PICR, *Proposals for Indian Constitutional Reform*. New Delhi: Government of India Press, 1933.

Ramaswamy Aiyar, Sir C.P., *Selections from the Writings and Speeches of Sachivottama Sir C.P. Ramaswami Aiyar, Dewan of Travancore*, Vols I and II, Trivandrum: Government Press, 1945.

Ramesan, N. (ed.), *The Freedom Struggle in Hyderabad*, published by the Andhra Pradesh State Committee appointed for the compilation of a History of the Freedom Movement in Andhra Pradesh, Vol. IV (*1921–1947*).

RAB, *Report on the Administration of Baroda*, Bombay/Baroda: The Times Press/Baroda State Press, 1875–1945.

RAHP, *Report on the Administration of Hyderabad City Police.* Hyderabad Deccan: Government Central Press, 1934–40.

RAND, *Report on the Administration of H.E.H. the Nizam's Dominions* (*for 1941–2*). Hyderabad: Government Central Press, 1945.

RAT, *Report on the Administration of Travancore*, Trivandrum: Government Press, 1865–1947.

RRC, *Report of the Reforms Committee 1938* [translation]. Hyderabad Deccan: Government Central Press, 1938.

Sayajirao III, Maharaja of Baroda, Speeches and Addresses of His Highness, Vol. 3 (*1927–34*). Cambridge University Press, 1934; Vol. 4 (*1934–38*), Cambridge University Press, 1938.

Sever, Adrian (ed.), *Documents and Speeches on the Indian Princely States*. Delhi: B.R. Publishing Corporation, 2 vols, 1985.

SFHS, *The Struggle for Freedom in Hyderabad State* (printed pamphlet), no place, 1938.

TEDEC, *Travancore Economic Depression Enquiry Committee, Report of*, Trivandrum: Government Press, 1931.

TEEC, *Temple Entry Enquiry Committee, Report of*. Trivandrum: Government Press, 1935.

TERC, *Travancore Education Reforms Committee, Report of*. Trivandrum: Government Press, 1933.

TPPP, *Travancore: The Present Political Problem*, by the Executive Committee, the All-Travancore Joint Political Congress, submitted to His Highness the Maharaja of Travancore. Calicut: The Empire Press, 1934.

TPSRC, *Travancore Public Service Recruitment Committee Report, The 1933*. Trivandrum: Government Press, 1934.

Travancore State Congress, the Working Committee of, *Travancore To-day, Her Struggle for Freedom*. Cochin: The Union Press, 1938.

Velu Pillai, T.K., *Travancore State Manual*, 3 vols. Trivandrum: Government Press, 1940.

SECONDARY SOURCES

Abhyankar, G.R. and Manishanker S. Trivedi, *The Indian States' People's Conference: Report of the Bombay Session, 17th, 18th December 1927*. Bombay, 1928.

Ahmad, Akbar S., 'Muslim Society in South India: the case of Hyderabad'. *Journal Institute of the Muslim Minority Affairs*, 1985 VI, reprinted in Khalidi: 173–88, 1988.

Ahmed, Feroz, Ethnicity, Class and State in Pakistan, *Economic and Political Weekly* XXXI (47): 3050–4, 1996.

Ahmed, Imtiaz, Political Economy of Communalism in Contemporary India. *Economic and Political Weekly*: XIX (22–3) 903–6, 1984.

Alavi, Hamza and John Harris (eds.), *Sociology of 'Developing Societies': South Asia*. Houndmills: Macmillan, 1989.

Anderson, Benedict, *Imagined Communities: reflections on the origin and spread of nationalism*. London: Verso, 1991.

Ashton, S.R., *British Policy towards the Indian States 1905–39*, London: Curzon Press, 1982.

Baak, Paul E., Out of the Shadow, into the Spotlights. The 'Indigenous' Aspects of Plantation Development: the case of the emergence of Syrian Christian planters in princely Travancore in the first half of the twentieth century. *Itinerario*, XVII (2): 74–97, 1993.

———, 'Plantation Production and Political Power: plantation development in southwest India in a long-term historical perspective, c.1743–1963'. Ph.D. thesis, University of Amsterdam, 1995.

Bagchi, A.K., *Private Investment in India: 1900–39*. London: Cambridge University Press, 1972.

Baker, Christopher John, *The Politics of South India 1920–37*. Cambridge: Cambridge University Press, 1976.

Banu, Zebab, *Politics of Communalism: a politico-historical analysis of communal riots in post-Independence India with special reference to the Gujarat and Rajasthan riots*. London: Sangam Books, 1989.

Barth, Fredrik, 'Introduction', in Fredrik Barth (ed.), *Ethnic Groups and Boundaries: the social organization of cultural difference*. London: George Allen & Unwin, 1969.

Barton, Sir W., *The Princes of India*. London: Nisbet & Co., 1934.

Bawa, Vasant Kumar, *The Nizam between Mughals and British: Hyderabad under Salar Jang I*. New Delhi: S. Chand (new edition 1996), 1986.

———, 'Partizan Views on Nizam's Hyderabad'. *Economic and Political Weekly* XXV (40): 2249–51, 1990.

———, *The Last Nizam: the life & times of Mir Osman Ali Khan*. New Delhi: Viking Penguin Books, 1992.

———, 'Constitutional and Administrative Structure', in K.S.S. Seshan (ed.), *Hyderabad—400: Saga of a City*. Hyderabad: Association of British Council Scholars, pp. 17–37, 1993.

Bayly, Susan, *Saints, Goddesses and Kings: Muslims and Christians in South Indian Society, 1700–1900*. Cambridge: Cambridge University Press, 1989.

Brass, Paul, *Ethnicity and Nationalism: theory and comparison*, New Delhi: Sage, 1991.

Breman, Jan, 'Anti-Muslim Pogrom in Surat'. *Economic and Political Weekly*, XXVIII (16): 737–43, 1993.

Burke, S.M. and Salim Al-Din Quraishi, *The British Raj in India: an historical review*. Karachi: Oxford University Press, 1975.

Butler, Sir Harcourt, *India Insistent*. London: Heinemann, 1931.

Cantwell Smith, Wilfred, 'Hyderabad: Muslim Tragedy'. *The Middle East Journal* IV, 1950; reprinted in Khalidi 1988: 1–26.

Chakrabarty, Dipesh, 'Modernity and Ethnicity in India'. *South Asia*, XVII (Special Issue): 143–55, 1994.

Chand, Tara, *History of the Freedom Movement in India*, Vol. III. New Delhi: Government of India, 1972.

Chandra, Bipan, *Nationalism and Colonialism in Modern India*. New Delhi: Orient Longman Ltd., 1981.

———, *Communalism in Modern India*. New Delhi: Vikas Publishing House, 1984.

———, *India's Struggle for Independence 1857–1947*. New Delhi: Viking, 1988.

Chandra, Sudhir, 'Of Communal Consciousness and Communal Violence: impressions from post-riot Surat'. *Economic and Political Weekly*, XXVIII (36): 1883–8, 1993.

Chavda, V.K. n.d. (1966) *Gaekwads and the British: a study of their problems (1875–1920)*. Delhi: University Publishers.

Chiriyankandath, J.L., 'Social Change and the Development of "Modern" Politics in Travancore: from the late nineteenth century to 1938', unpubl. Ph.D. thesis, University of London, 1985.

———, ' "Democracy" under the Raj: elections and separate representation in British India'. *The Journal of Commonwealth & Comparative Politics*, XXX (1): 39–63, 1992.

Cohen, A.P., *The Symbolic Construction of Community*. London: Routledge., 1989.

Copland, Ian, 'Sayaji Rao Gaekwar and Sedition: the dilemmas of an Indian

Prince', in P. Robb and D. Taylor (eds.), *Rule, Protest, Identity: aspects of modern south Asia*. London: Curzon Press, pp. 28–48, 1978.

———, *The British Raj and the Indian Princes: paramountcy in Western India 1857–1930*. Bombay: Orient Longman, 1982.

———, 'Congress Paternalism: the "High Command" and the Struggle for Freedom in Princely India, c.1920–1940'. *South Asia*, VIII (1 & 2): 121–41, 1985.

———,' "Communalism" in Princely India: the Case of Hyderabad, 1930–40'. *Modern Asian Studies*, XXII (4): 783–814, 1988.

———, 'The Integration of the Princely States: a "bloodless revolution"?' *South Asia*, XVIII (special issue): 131–51, 1995.

———, *The Princes of India in the Endgame of Empire 1917–47*. Cambridge: Cambridge University Press, 1997.

———, 'The Political Geography of Religious Conflict: towards an explanation of the rarity of communal riots in the Indian princely states'. Paper submitted to European Conference on Modern South Asian Studies, Prague (also published in *The International Journal of Punjab Studies*), 1998.

Daniel, D., *Struggle for Responsible Government in Travancore 1938–47*. Madurai: Raj Publ., 1985.

Datt, Indra, *Baroda: a Study, Constitutional and Political*. Lucknow: Saraswati Press, 1936.

Desai, Govindbhai H., *Report on Compulsory Primary Education in Baroda State*. Baroda: Department of Education, 1926.

———, *Forty Years in Baroda: being reminiscences of forty years' service in the Baroda State*. Baroda: Pustakalaya Sahayak Sahakari Mandal Ltd., 1929.

Engineer, Ashgar Ali, 'Ethnic Conflict in South Asia'. *Economic and Political Weekly*, XXXII (33, 34): 2108–9, 1997.

Erdman, Howard L., *Political Attitudes of Indian Industry: a case study of the Baroda business elite*. London: Athlone Press, 1971.

Ex-official of Hyderabad (Ali Yavar Jung), *Hyderabad in Retrospect* (reprinted from articles published in *The Times of India*), Bombay and Calcutta: Bennett, Coleman & Co., 1949.

Forster, E.M., *The Hill of Devi and Other Indian Writings*. London: Edward Arnold, 1983.

Franke, Richard W. and Barbara H. Chasin, *Kerala: development through radical reform*. New Delhi: Promilla & Co. Publishers, 1992.

Gaekwad, Fatesinghrao P., *Sayajirao of Baroda: the Prince and the Man*. Bombay: Popular Prakashan, 1989.

Galanter, Marc, *Competing Inequalities: law and the backward classes in India*. Berkeley: University of California Press, 1984.

Gandhi, M.K., *Indian States' Problem.* Ahmedabad: Navajivan Press, 1941.

Handa, R.L., *History of Freedom Struggle in Princely States*. Delhi: Central News Agency, 1968.

Hardgrave, Robert L., *Essays in the Political Sociology of South India*. New Delhi: Usha Publications, 1979.

Hardiman, David, 'The Structure of a "Progressive" State', in Robin Jeffrey (ed.), *People Princes and Paramount Power: society and politics in the Indian princely states*. Delhi: Oxford University Press, pp. 107–35, 1978.

Hasan, Syed Abid, *Whither Hyderabad? (A brief survey of some of the outstanding problems of the Premier Indian State)*. Madras, 1935.

Hasan, Zoya Khaliq, 'Communalism and Communal Violence in India', in Ashgar Ali Engineer (ed.), *Communal Riots in Post-Independence India*. Delhi: Sangam Publications, pp. 68–88, 1984.

Houben, V.J.H., 'Native States in India and Indonesia: the nineteenth century'. *Itinerario*, XI (1): 107–35, 1987.

Hurd II, John, 'The Economic Consequences of Indirect Rule in India'. *The Indian Economic and Social History Review*, XII (1): 169–81, 1975a.

———, 'The Influence of British Policy on Industrial Development in Princely States of India, 1890–1933'. *The Indian Economic and Social History Review*, XII (4): 410–24, 1975b.

International Aryan League, *Nizam Defence Examined and Exposed* (A Rejoinder to the Pamphlet 'The Arya Samaj in Hyderabad'). Delhi, 1939.

Isaac, T.M. Thomas and P.K. Michael Tharakan, 'An Inquiry into the Historical Roots of Industrial Backwardness of Kerala: a study of the Travancore region', Trivandrum: Centre for Development Studies, Working Paper No. 215, 1986.

Iyengar, S. Kesava, *Economic Investigations in the Hyderabad State, 1929–30*. Hyderabad, 1931.

Iyer, P.G. Sahasranama (ed.), *Selections from the Writings and Speeches of Sachivattoma Sir C.P. Ramaswami Aiyar, Dewan of Travancore*, 2 vols. Trivandrum: Government Press, 1945.

Jeffrey, Robin, *The Decline of Nayar Dominance: society and politics in Travancore, 1847–1908*. New Delhi: Vikas, 1976.

———, 'A Sanctified Label: "Congress" in Travancore Politics, 1938–48', in D.A. Low (ed.), *Congress and the Raj: facets of the Indian struggle 1917–47*. London: Arnold-Heinemann, pp. 435–72, 1977.

———, *People, Princes and Paramount Power: society and politics in the Indian princely states*. Delhi: Oxford University Press, 1978.

———, 'Religious Symbolisation of the Transition from Caste to Class: the Temple Entry Movement in Travancore 1860–1940'. *Social Compass*, XXVIII (2-3): 269–91, 1981.

Kaviraj, Sudipta, 'The Modern State in India', in Martin Doornbos and Sudipta Kaviraj (eds.), *Dynamics of State Formation: India and Europe compared*. New Delhi: Sage, pp. 225–51, 1997.

Khalidi, Omar (ed.), *Hyderabad: After the Fall*. Wichita, Kansas: Hyderabad Historical Society, 1988.

Khodwe, Achyut (ed.), *The People's Movement in Hyderabad*. Poona, 1947.

Kloos, Peter, 'The End of the State', in M.A., van Bakel and J.G. Oosten (eds), *The Dynamics of the Early State Paradigm*. Utrecht: ISOR, pp. 117–31, 1995.

———, The Dialectics of Globalization and Localization, paper presented at the workshop on "Global Culture and Local Indentities", organized by the Department of Cultural Anthropology/Sociology of Development, Free University, Amsterdam, 1996.

Kooiman, Dick, 'Plantations in Southern Asia: indigenous plants and foreign implantations'. *South Asia*, XV (1): 53–79, 1992.

———, 'Political Rivalry among Religious Communities: a case study of communal reservations in India.' *Economic and Political Weekly*, XXVIII (7): 287–95, 1993.

———, *Communities and Electorates: a comparative discussion of communalism in colonial India*. Amsterdam: VU University Press, Comparative Asian Studies 16, 1995.

———, 'Who is to Benefit from Missionary Education? Travancore in the 1930s', in Robert A. Bickers and Rosemary Seton (eds.), *Missionary Encounters: sources and issues*. Richmond: Curzon Press, pp. 153–74, 1996.

———, 'The Strength of Numbers: Enumerating Communities in India's Princely States'. *South Asia*, New Series XX (1): 81–99, 1997.

Koshy, M.J., *Constitutionalism in Travancore and Cochin*. Trivandrum: Kerala Historical Society, 1992.

Kumar, Suresh, *Political Evolution in Kerala: Travancore 1859–1938*. New Delhi: Phoenix Publishing House.

Kusuman, K.K., *The Abstention Movement*. Trivandrum. Kerala Historical Society, 1976.

Lannoy, Mark de, *The Kulasekhara Perumals of Travancore: history and state formation in Travancore from 1671 to 1758*. Leiden: Research School CNWS, 1997.

Leonard, Karen, 'The Hyderabad Political System and its Participants'. *Journal of Asian Studies* XXX (3): 569–82, 1971.

———, 'Hyderabad: the Mulki - Non-Mulki Conflict', in Robin Jeffrey (ed.), pp. 65–106, 1978a.

———. '*Social History of an Indian Caste: the Kayasthas of Hyderabad*. Berkeley: University of California Press, 1978b.

Lobo, Lancy and Paul D'Souza, 'Images of Violence: Surat riots II'. *Economic and Political Weekly*, XXVII (5): 152–5, 1993.

Lothian, Sir Arthur Cunningham, *Kingdoms of Yesterday*. London: John Murray, 1951.

Mahadevan, Raman, 'Industrial Entrepreneurship in Princeley Travancore: 1930-47', in S. Bhattacharya (ed.), *The South Indian Economy: agrarian change, industrial structure & state policy, c. 1914–47*. New Delhi: Oxford University Press, pp. 159–207, 1991.

Mammen, P.M., *Communism vs. Communalism: a study of the socio-religious communities and political parties in Kerala 1892–1970*. Calcutta: Minerva Ass, 1981.

Manohar, N. Austin John, 'The History of South India United Church 1908–1947' unpublished Ph.D. thesis, University of Kerala, Thiruvananthapuram, 1992.

Manor, James, *Political Change in an Indian State: Mysore 1917–55*. Columbia: South Asia Books, 1978.

Mansergh, P.N.S., 'Some Reflections on the Transfer of Power in Plural Societies', in C.H. Philips & Mary Doreen Wainwright (eds.), *The Partition of India: policies and perspectives 1935–47*. London: George Allen and Unwin Ltd., 1970.

Mathew, George, *Communal Road to a Secular Kerala*. New Delhi: Concept Publ., 1989.

Matthen, C.P., *I Have Borne Much*. Madras: Ampthill (1951), 1943.

Mayaram, Shail, *Resisting Regimes: myth, memory and the shaping of a Muslim identity.* Delhi: Oxford University Press, 1997.

Menon, V.P., *Integration of the Indian States*. Hyderabad: Orient Longman Limited (1st edn. 1956), 1995.

Naidu, Ratna, *Old Cities, New Predicaments: A study of Hyderabad*. New Delhi: Sage, 1990.

Nayar, N.S., *History of Travancore Legislature*. Trivandrum: Kerala Historical Society, 1984.

Oommen, John, 'Politics of Communalism in Kerala'. *Economic and Political Weekly*, XXX (11): 544–8, 1995.

Ouwerkerk, Louise, *No Elephants for the Maharaja: social and political change in the princely state of Travancore (1921–1947)*. Edited with an introduction by Dick Kooiman. New Delhi: Manohar, 1994.

Pandya, Thakorlal Ranchhodlal, *A Study of Education in Baroda*. Bombay: Maneckjee Nowrojee, 1915.

Pandey, Gyanendra, *The Construction of Communalism in Colonial North India*. Delhi: Oxford University Press, 1992.

Pendse, S.S., *The New Regime*. Baroda: Atmaram Printing Press, 1940.

Pernau-Reifeld, Margrit, *Verfassung und Politische Kultur im Wandel: der Indische Fürstenstaat Hyderabad 1911–48*. Stuttgart: Franz Steiner Verlag, 1992 (also published in English by Manohar, New Delhi, 2000).

Phadnis, Urmila, *Towards the Integration of Indian States, 1919–47*. Bombay: Asia Publishing House, 1968.

Radhakrishnan, P., 'Communal Representation in Tamil Nadu, 1850-1916: the Pre-Non-Brahmin Movement Phase'. *Economic and Political Weekly*, XXVIII (31): 1585–97, 1993.

Raghunadha Rao, P., *History of Modern Andhra Pradesh*. New Delhi: Sterling Publishers, 1988.

Rajendran, D., *Ezhava Community and Kerala Politics*. Trivandrum: Kerala Academy of Political Science, 1974.

Ramusack, Barbara, *The Princes of India in the Twilight of Empire: dissolution of a patron-client system 1914–39*. Columbus: Ohio State University Press, 1978.

Rangaswami, V., *The Story of Integration: a new interpretation in the context of the democratic movements in the Princely States of Mysore, Travancore and Cochin 1900–47*. New Delhi: Manohar, 1981.

Ray, Bharati, *Hyderabad and British Paramountcy: 1858–83*. Delhi: Oxford University Press, 1988.

Raza Ali Khan, *Hyderabad 400 Years (1591–1991)*, Hyderabad: Zenith Services, 1990.

Razvi, S.M. Jawad, *Political Awakening in Hyderabad: role of youth and students (1938–56)*. Hyderabad: Visalandhra Publishing House, 1985.

Reddy, V. Ramakrishna, *Economic History of Hyderabad State (Warangal Suba: 1911–50)*. Delhi: Gian Publishing House, 1987.

Richter, William L., 'Traditional Rulers in Post-Traditional Societies: the Princes of India and Pakistan', in Robin Jeffrey (ed.), People, *Princes and Paramount Power: society and politics in the Indian pricely states*. Delhi: Oxford University Press, pp. 329–55, 1978.

Richter, William L.and Barbara Ramusack, 'The Chamber and the Consultation: Changing Forms of Princely Association in India'. *Journal of Asian Studies* XXXIV (3): 755–76, 1975.

Robinson, Francis, *Separation among Indian Muslims: the politics of the United Provinces' Muslims, 1860–1923*. London: Cambridge University Press, 1974.

Rudolph, Lloyd I. & Susanne Hoeber Rudolph, *In Pursuit of Lakhsmi: the political economy of the Indian state*. Chicago & London: The University of Chicago Press, 1987.

———, 'Confessional Politics, Secularism and Centrism in India', in James Warner Björkman (ed.), *Fundamentalism, Revivalists and Violence in South Asia*. New Delhi: Manohar, 1988.

Rushbrook Williams, L.F., *The Cultural Significance of the Indian States*. Proceedings of the British Academy, Vol. XVI. London: Humphrey Milford Amen House, 1930.

Rutten, Mario, *Capitalist Entrepreneurs and Economic Diversification: social profile of large farmers and rural industrialists in central Gujarat, India*. Ph.D. thesis, University of Amsterdam, 1991.

Sarkar, Sumit, *Modern India 1885–1947*. Delhi: Macmillan, 1983.

Sen, S.R., 'Communal Riots: Anticipation, Containment and Prevention'. *Economic and Political Weekly*, XXVIII (15): 627–32, 1993.

Sergeant, Philip W., *The Ruler of Baroda: an account of the life and work of the Maharaja Gaekwar*. London: John Murray, 1928.

Shah, Ghanshyam, *Caste Association and Political Process in Gujarat: a study of Gujarat Kshatriya Sabha*. Bombay: Popular Prakashan, 1975.

———, 'Identity, Communal Consciousness and Politics'. *Economic and Political Weekly*, XXIX (19): 1133–40, 1994.

Shah, M.H., *Baroda by Decades: 1871–1941*. (no place, no publisher), 1942.

Simmons, C.P. and B.R.Satyanarayana, 'The Economic Consequences of Indirect Rule in India: A Re-appraisal'. *The Indian Economic and Social History Review* XVI (2): 185–207.

Spear, Percival, *A History of India*. Harmondsworth: Penguin Books, Vol. II, 1978.

Stavrianos, L.S., *Global Rift: the third world comes of age*. New York: William Morrow and Co., 1981.

Streefkerk, Hein, *Industrial Transition in Rural India: artisans, traders and tribals in south Gujarat*. Bombay: Popular Prakashan, 1985.

———, 'Gujarati Entrepreneurship: Historical Continuity against Changing Perspectives'. *Economic and Political Weekly*, XXXII (8): M2-M10.

Subbarao, C.V., 'Role of the State in Industrialization: the case of Hyderabad', in S. Bhattacharya (ed.), *The South Indian Economy: agrarian change, industrial structure & state policy, c. 1914–47*. New Delhi: Oxford University Press, pp. 208–42, 1991.

Tharakan, P.K. Michael, 'Socio-economic Factors in Educational Development: case of nineteenth century Travancore'. *Economic and Political Weekly*, XIX (45): 1913–28 and XIX (46): 1959–67, 1984.

Tharakan, Michael and K. George Tharian, 'Penetration of Capital into a Traditional Economy: the case of tea plantations in Kerala', 1880–1950, in *Studies in History*, N.S. II (2), 1986.

Thompson, E., *The Making of the Indian Princes*. Oxford: Oxford University Press, 1944.

Thurston, E., *Castes and Tribes of Southern India*, Vol. 5. Madras: Government Press, 1909.

Tirtha, Swami Ramananda, *Memoirs of Hyderabad Freedom Struggle*. Bombay: Popular Prakashan, 1967.

Tripathi, Dwijendra, 'Business and the Princely States: the case of Baroda', in Idem (ed.), *State and Business in India: a Historical Perspective*. New Delhi: Manohar, 1987.

———, *Historical Roots of Industrial Entrepreneurship in India and Japan: a comparative interpretation*. New Delhi: Manohar, 1997.

Tripathi, Dwijendra and Makrand Mehta, *Business Houses in Western India: a study in entrepreneurial response, 1850–1956*. Delhi: Manohar, 1990.

Upadhyay, K.S., 'Industrial Development in Hyderabad District 1860–1948', in *History of Hyderabad District 1879–1950*, Vol. I. Hyderabad: Bharatiya Itihasa Sankalana Samiti.

Varughese, K.V., 'Growth of Communal Parties and Vote-banks: a challenge to secular democracy'. *Religion and Society* XXXIV (1): 20–31, 1987.

Veer, Peter van der, *Religious Nationalism: Hindus and Muslims in India*. Berkeley: University of California Press, 1994.

Vidal, Denis, *Violence and Truth: a Rajasthani kingdom confronts colonial authority*. Delhi: Oxford University Press, 1997.

Wood, John R., 'British versus Princely Legacies and the Political Integration of Gujarat'. *Journal of Asian Studies*, XLIV (1): 65–99, 1984.

Wright Jr., Theodore Paul, 'Revival of the Majlis Ittihad-ul-Muslimin of Hyderabad', in *The Muslim World* 53: 234–43, 1963; reprinted in Khalidi 1988: 132–42.

Wylie, Sir Francis, 'Federal Negotiations in India 1935–9, and After', in C.H. Philips and Mary Doreen Wainwright (eds.), *The Partition of India: policies and perspectives 1935–47*. London: George Allen and Unwin Ltd., 1970.

Yazdani, Zubaida, *Hyderabad during the Residency of Henry Russell 1811–1820*. Oxford: Oxford University Press, 1976.

———, *The Seventh Nizam: The Fallen Empire, 1853–1948*. Cambridge, 1985; partly reprinted in Khalidi 1988: 90–5.

Index